"David Bosworth is a first-rate cultural critic who brings to vivid life the full range of issues confronting us at the present moment. To read him on what has lately happened in American society is to become suddenly alert to the interpenetration of political, economic and cultural forces and to the fact that the most important questions we face are not primarily political in nature, however they may seem in a media-saturated age. Though Bosworth operates comfortably within the discourse of the academic left, he is by no means the prisoner of an ideological constituency. In fact he writes with extraordinary grace and lucidity and calls to mind the work of earlier practitioners like Christopher Lasch, Jacques Ellul and David Riesman, each of them notable for their cogency and for combining a devotion to understanding the past with a passion for confronting the present."

—ROBERT BOYERS (EDITOR, *SALMAGUNDI*)

"I've been reading David Bosworth's insightful work for many years, and always find my dearly held positions on poetry and the culture we inhabit altered and deepened in important ways. He is a brilliant contrarian, the kind of thinker who identifies and cuts through what passes for the true, and provides us with the language for what we only half-knew prior to reading him. His new book does this, and more. Like all great moral thinking, it's a warning and a beacon. It's Bosworth at his best."

—STEPHEN DUNN (PULITZER PRIZE-WINNING POET)

"As a reader, editor, and publisher of David Bosworth's essays for more than two decades of my tenure with *The Georgia Review*, I have been ever more impressed by his commitment to providing qualities that are vital yet increasingly missing from writings about crucial political and cultural matters: a long sense of history; a respect for facts; an evenhanded approach to analyzing those facts; a readiness to speculate intelligently (and often entertainingly); and a lucid—I am tempted to say poetic—writing style. Bosworth is, to my mind, a secular Emerson for our time."

—STEPHEN COREY (EDITOR, *THE GEORGIA REVIEW*)

THE DEMISE OF VIRTUE IN
VIRTUAL AMERICA

The Demise of Virtue in
Virtual America

The Moral Origins of the Great Recession

David Bosworth

Front Porch Republic *Books*

Front Porch Republic
An Imprint of Wipf and Stock Publishers
199 W. 8th Ave., Suite 3
Eugene, OR 97401

www.wipfandstock.com

ISBN 13: 978-1-62564-812-9

Cataloging-in-Publication data:

Bosworth, David.

The demise of virtue in virtual America: the moral origins of the great recession / David Bosworth.

p.; 23 cm—Includes bibliographical references and index.

ISBN 13: 978-1-62564-812-9

1. Virtual reality—Social aspects—United States. 2. National characteristics, American. 3. Technology—Social aspects—United States. 4. United States—Moral conditions. 5. Recessions—United States. 6. Global Financial Crisis, 2008–2009. I. Title.

E169.1 B79 2014

Manufactured in the USA.

In memory of Russell H. Bosworth
who showed us those treasures
that neither moth nor rust can corrupt

. . . Mammon led them on—
Mammon, the least erected spirit that fell
From Heaven . . .

—John Milton, *Paradise Lost*

Contents

Tables

Acknowledgments

GENEROUS GRANTS FROM THE University of Washington's Royalty Research Fund and the John Templeton Foundation funded some of the research presented here. Also, portions of this book first appeared, in an altered form, as essays in the following publications: *The Georgia Review, Salmagundi, The Ohio Review,* and *The Public Interest.* My thanks to those organizations for their support and to the editors for providing a public forum for testing the narrative and analysis that follow.

Entrance:
Virtual America's Convention Hall

Demise—1) the conveyance of an estate; 2) transfer of the
sovereignty to a successor; 3) a: death, b: cessation of existence
or activity, c: a loss of position or status.

—*Merriam-Webster's Collegiate Dictionary*

IN 2008, THE U.S. stock markets lost almost seven trillion dollars of share-holders' value, and in the aftermath the very experts who had recently boast-ed that we had scientifically solved the instability inherent in our economic system's boom-bust cycle were suddenly sounding more like English Ph.D. students as they turned away from their arcane mathematical formulas to cite the history of a single word. Ambushed by a financial meltdown they had failed to predict, these reluctant etymologists were rediscovering that the word *credit* evolved from the Latin *credo*, meaning *I believe*. They were reminding themselves, even while informing a stunned American public, that the whole enterprise—their supposedly self-correcting marketplace, this highly rationalized perpetual motion machine of unending material prosperity—actually floated on faith, on belief. And as the numbers then proved, that faith had been radically misplaced.

The dive in stock values then may have been devastatingly quick, but the evolution of the bad faith driving their collapse is a much longer story, and the one this book aspires to tell. It is the story of a profound transforma-tion in the national character, in our actual and not just ceremonial *credo*, and how an American ethos initially geared toward prudence, pragmatism, and plain speaking came to generate instead the greatest con game in hu-man history. It is not simply the tale of an economic crash but of a failure of the moral imagination in the broadest sense, one whose impact could be spied in the barbarism at Abu Ghraib, the cynicism of pop culture, the co-opting of art, the corruption of science, the decline of both family ties and local communal authority, and in the enfeeblement of commonsense thinking that helped license them all.

To accurately assess a series of changes this widespread requires forgoing the usual parochial blame-game, with its scornful scapegoating of this or that corrupt official. The problem hasn't been just a few "bad apples," nor even a mismanaged orchard on the left or the right, but the long-term revision of a cultural environment whose "moral field" we all share and for whose current ill health we are collectively, if not equally, responsible. To make sense of that decline, we need to consider instead a broader set of ruling ideas, managerial decisions, and architectural designs that, taken together, have slowly revised the underlying logic of everyday experience and so, too (if often cryptically), our conventional beliefs about the good, the true, and the beautiful.

Already I trespass into controversial territory on two fronts. In the land of the free, where rebellion has been historically esteemed and is now routinely marketized through the many iterations of MTV, few would choose to define themselves as *conventional* thinkers. So it is that movie stars grown rich on the most fatuously formulaic of cinematic plots tout their hobbyhorse causes with the moral fervor of Samuel Adams, even as right-wing sons of multimillionaires storm the Bastille of the inheritance tax, using the fervent rhetoric of liberation. I have sat through meetings where the most slickly ambitious of academic administrators have proclaimed themselves subversive and seemed to believe it. Even those who profess to hate the sixties tend to borrow its ruling temper, the moral grandeur (and personal exemption) of romantic rebellion. Like the relaxed jeans we now wear, the role of rebel has been stretched to fit a wide range of self-promoting careerists, from Lady Gaga to Ayn Rand acolyte Paul Ryan.

In an age characterized by the adman's omnipresent ironies, such pseudo-rebellion has become a standard stance: an unacknowledged plank in the platform enforced inside our new convention hall. Although it is not my intention to deny the uniqueness of individuals or the diversity of the many subsets of our postmillennial society, I will insist in the chapters to come that an ever-expanding ruling philosophy has been drawing all our many vivid differences in the same overall direction, and that, as a consequence, it is not only still possible but increasingly necessary to describe the American experience in the first person plural, the collective *we*.

The second of my controversial assertions is the insistence on linking, in these claims about our conventional thinking, the good with the true. In a nation that touts objective expertise and cedes to its technocratic elite enormous political and cultural authority, overt discussions of moral premises are seen as embarrassingly archaic. Like spells against witchcraft, complaints about "character" are thought to belong to a bygone era. Instead, our new credo presumes that soon, very soon, our bad behavior will be scientifically solved, our dysfunctions debugged by our pharmaceutical labs and by the better angels of our beltway think tanks' latest apps.

I don't dispute that our culture war debates have been debased and, yes, embarrassing. But the poor quality of our discussions about the virtues we prefer in no way discounts the importance of the subject and is, in fact, a symptom of the very demise under study here. As etymology reminds us, all evaluations are expressions of value, and an objective expertise that refuses to acknowledge its own (and necessarily subjective) ethical premises is all the more likely to lead us astray. Methodically blind to its own motives, such a science is especially susceptible to a self-deceiving disingenuousness.

In an attempt to suggest both its temper and its tactics, I have been calling this self-deceiving science of ours Evangelical Mammonism. Like most manifestations of modernity, the roots of its practice reach back to the philosophical turn toward rational materialism in the seventeenth and eighteenth centuries. Insomuch as they led to the scientific and industrial revolutions, the core ideas of this philosophical approach have been highly influential, but social history and tradition have also mattered. When practically applied, any new philosophy will assume something of the tenor of the cultural place and time of its adoption, resulting in very different species of social governance. In the East, rational materialism eventually assumed the form of a "scientific socialism" (aka communism), which, despite its purported ideals, generated many of the moral catastrophes of the last century. Earlier in the West, this philosophy, however, took on a very different form, one in which the collateral cruelties of a highly productive but narrowly focused economic system—let's call it "scientific capitalism"—were gradually ameliorated by the institution of various kinds of democratic reform.

In America, that often tenuous equilibrium between economic interests and democratic practices has now been broken, and one sign of the ineptitude of our cultural wars has been a refusal to recognize this growing imbalance as a primary source of the ethical changes driving our debates. For as was made manifest by the astonishing scale of fraud and folly that generated the housing bubble, the critical ethical issue of our era has *not* been the erosion of the separation between church and state (whichever side one thinks is the true transgressor) but the gradual conversion of both populist Christianity and democratic governance to the ways, means, and ruling ideals of Evangelical Mammonism.

Some notes on terminology, then. By Evangelical Mammonism I mean the now toxic version of scientific capitalism that has been progressively usurping the traditional authority of church and state, even while shirking the ethical responsibilities that normally attend them. Like most forms of rational materialism, this version is utopian in cast, evangelically touting the "good news" of one or more final solutions to the human predicament: not just the elimination of the boom-bust cycle, but also the happy "end of history,"[1] the erasure of pain or even death, and (in the worried words of T. S. Eliot), the creation of "systems so perfect that no one will need to be good."[2] Given that the path pursued to achieve this good news focuses so fiercely on material improvements and acquisitions, it is aptly classified as a latter-day form of Mammonism, and like all Mammonites, its adherents tend to cleave, self-consciously or not, to the crude moral premise that *more must equal better.* As our promiscuous use of the summary cliché "the bottom line" now proves, most forms of evaluation these days are becoming a subspecies of financial accounting. Under the sway of Evangelical Mammonism, all higher meanings, sacred or secular, are made to submit to the measures of money.

This preface's title, *Entrance: Virtual America's Convention Hall,* metaphorically suggests how our conversion to this decadent credo has been taking place. Due to the penetration of electronic communications over the last hundred years and to the privatization of civic spaces during the last sixty, we now routinely convene inside a *virtual* America in both senses of that word: we are increasingly enclosed within a deceptive physical and digital sphere whose supposed allegiance to traditional values routinely conceals their active subversion. The *demise* of virtue inside this new Virtual America refers, then, to two of the definitions of the word cited earlier—not just "a loss of position or status" but also the "transfer of sovereignty to a successor." That transfer is best understood as a radical shift in the balance of power between everyday moral influences as the nation's two foundational ethical traditions, the republican and the Judeo-Christian, are both yoked to serve the now conventional beliefs of Evangelical Mammonism.

A few brief examples of this submission will have to suffice for now. Politically, the conservative's often honorable resistance to the intrusion of the state into local affairs has increasingly fronted for corporate interests whose own impact on local life is even more destructive to the very customs that conscientious conservatives have traditionally revered. On the civic front, the deep penetration of marketplace values can be traced in all those liberal universities and newer philanthropies that now focus so fiercely on polishing their "brand." And any possible spiritual resistance to our age's unrepentant materialism has been greatly weakened by the popularity of a so-called prosperity theology that is little more than Mammonism in pious disguise.

The period covered in the analysis to come begins in the 1950s, when these trends—already present in American life but largely deferred by an economic depression and a world war—were given the chance to accelerate, and it stretches through those two national fiascos of the postmillennial era, the invasion of Iraq and the Great Recession that began in 2008. Venue by venue, this survey of Virtual America's construction and character will reveal how the economic virtues narrowly associated with production and consumption—ruthless efficiency in the workplace and seductive salesmanship in the marketplace—have come to suffuse both our public institutions and private lives, co-opting alike the themes of our narratives, the planks of our parties, the practice of medicine, the profession of art, and the most intimate aspects of our personal lives, including our beliefs about God, marriage, and childcare.

This extended critique of current American beliefs and practices is not intended to inspire a literal return to some fabled era, whether the staid fifties or the turbulent sixties, as they are idealized by opposing factions of our culture wars. I want to be very clear on this: there is no ethical Eden in our collective past whose practices we might now resurrect through reflexive imitation. Such a nostalgic agenda merely recasts the fantasies of utopian thinking in reactionary terms. Nations will always to some degree, and periodically to disastrous degrees, fail to meet their own ethical standards. The difference this time is that those standards themselves—our default conceptions of the good and the true, as repeatedly endorsed inside Virtual America's conventional hall—have been skewed in ways that have effectively disarmed the usual sources of revival and reform.

Although the ideas outlined here are finally mine, along with any blame for their failure to convince, they were inspired by and borrow from other works, especially the cultural criticism of Wendell Berry and Christopher Lasch. Both a writer and teacher of literature, I am by nature a generalist, and so, when addressing certain technical subjects, I have relied heavily on specialists in the field, for whose scholarly labor I am deeply grateful. Some influences, however, have penetrated so deeply that their impact transgresses the boundaries of any single chapter. In ways I never anticipated, the story I have told here was prefigured by Herman Melville's later fiction. American to the core, this literary prophet foresaw very early on the demise that I have charted here. The various species of duplicity that he first satirized in the 1850s are as current as Bernie Madoff's fifty billion dollar Ponzi scheme and as familiar as the jargon that justified our latest misadventure on foreign shores. If this book does nothing more than call renewed attention to Melville's vision, it will have served a vital civic function.

That abbreviated list will have to do for now, along with the admission that it only begins to sketch an accurate chart of influence and, with it, the genealogy of my gratitude. Most of my discoveries here—most all human discoveries—are, in essence, *re*coveries. We bravely disembark on yet another New World's empty shore only to find, if we look hard enough, the footprints of previous explorers. Swimming against the current of the times, our mad rush to copyright everything, I find that fact profoundly comforting. The great storyteller of the New Testament had it right. The truth does set us free—not *from* others but back into their company.

It is precisely our exclusion from that good company, especially from the collective conversation of the dead, that the walls of Virtual America have been built to enforce. When we step inside *its* convention hall, we enter a realm whose constant commandments to produce and consume also induce our two most common conditions of complaint: the stress that comes from working too hard, wanting too much, and the slump of an almost unappeasable loneliness. The special character of that loneliness defines the most revealing irony of our time: how perpetually inside now we nevertheless feel, in some fundamental and soul-suffocating way, *left out*.

If you know that feeling—the echo of its emptiness, the seal of its despair, that wordless "hurt" which (in the words of Emily Dickinson) leaves "no scar / But internal difference / Where the meanings are"[3]—then you will quickly understand why I say: I no longer want to live in such a place. And when I ask you now to enter with me on a tour of Virtual America's complicated maze, I do so with the promise that I am seeking a truly collective escape. I want the way out that will lead us back into the grave and graceful acts of a democratic community.

1

The Aging of Aquarius

"I would prefer not to."

—Herman Melville
"Bartleby, the Scrivener: A Story of Wall Street"

THE SUBJECT, THEN, IS the demise of American virtue. The primary period under study is from the early 1950s through the Great Recession—that is, during the "aging of Aquarius." And I will begin with two overviews, one narrative and the other analytical: the first a personal history that aims to allegorize key indices of collective change and the second a preliminary mapping of Virtual America's now conventional domains.

I. Mutiny of the Scrivener

"Pain is itself an evil, and indeed without exception, the only evil."[1]

—Jeremy Bentham

Some years ago, as I watched a news feature in which a woman sang a song of praise, Joni Mitchell-style, not to her lover or her God but to her medically prescribed, "mood-enhancing" drug, Prozac, I suddenly understood why Woody Allen's films had rarely achieved box office success. The usual explanation—that his serial portrait of the post-Freudian self was too urban, too ethnic—still made sense but masked for me a more telling truth, which was the tale of a temper out of tune with its time. A comedian whose shtick was "anhedonia," who projected a persona allergic to pleasure, was less and less likely to tickle the psyche of a populace dosed with mood-enhancers. Nor was he apt to bring down the house in a nation housed in those myriad "stately pleasure-domes" (malls, casinos, stadiums) that our Khans of consumption had everywhere decreed. Woody's act, I grasped that night, wasn't "where we're at" now. His has been a mostly modernist laugh at our highly enclosed postmodern life.

Once alerted to the trend, I found this emphasis on boosting the communal mood increasingly intrusive and so hard to deny. Whether I scanned the *Wall Street Journal*, where I quickly learned that the entertainment industry was the virtual engine of the new economy, or sent my kids to public school, where every day was a "celebration" designed to protect the fragile bud of their self-esteem, I was made to confront the new imperative. How did we get here, I wondered? How could we plumb our nation's passage from the Puritan's theology of coercive earnestness to the Mouseketeer's strategy of mandatory fun?

Thesis: the ideal state of mind towards which America has been striving since the fifties—when the first popular mood-enhancers, Equanil and Miltown, hit the scene—is not the comic's anhedonia but the junkie's analgesia. Pain has replaced sex at the top of our list of forbidden sensations, the faintest twinge of which we would girdle or repress. And given that, as Anne Sexton once said, pain tends to engrave a deeper memory,[2] this emotional analgesia has naturally engendered a cultural amnesia. We've been dumbing down through numbing out. To borrow from Milan Kundera's title, ours truly has been an era of "laughter and forgetting."

Rest assured that I'm not merely fretting here, op-ed style, about falling test scores or the lagging skills of the U.S. work force. That our kids don't know their math facts is, frankly, far less worrisome to me than their almost total ignorance of our culture's signal stories. The risk is just as real when our myths turn to mush as when our flesh can't feel. The disneyfied mind, like the anesthetized body, loses its way without a constant measure of the world's many hard edges, including those perennially painful consequences that our oldest stories plot to reveal. Life here is wondrous but also dangerous. So says not just *Paradise Lost* but "The Three Little Pigs," and all our chances for an exodus from our own era's peculiar bondage begin with this one, hard, and irreducible fact of existential math: *to live is to hurt*, in both the active and passive senses of that verb.

The Seder of safety demands that we savor the bitter herb.

Long ago, I thought these things through in another guise. A fiction writer who had learned his craft alone, I was mostly ignorant then of standard workshop nomenclature; and when, very suddenly, with babies in tow and bills to pay and a new literary prize hanging from my lapel like a Sunday school pin, I made the grand leap from basement sweeper to college teacher, I had no colleagues from whom I might seek practical advice. Due the day before yesterday, my syllabus required a terminology, and so I set about to improvise. One of the terms of my improvisation, a term I still favor, was "the irritant."

The irritant was not the conflict of the story but rather the struck flint or rubbing stick that set the conflict's fuel ablaze. As such, it could be purposeful and dramatic (the snatching of Helen) or random and pathetic (the thorn infecting the fabled lion's paw). It could range from the flagrantly exotic (Sir Gawain's ghostly Green Knight) to the apparently mundane. (A jar of mayonnaise, say, left outside one humid August night, its contents quickly spoiling to the yellow of a bruise on a middle-aged thigh. In the morning, over the irritant's remains, a couple begin exchanging blame for their two-dollar loss. Voices rise in Massapequa's morning light, their anger spiraling from irritation to rage as the topic turns from housekeeping roles to money woes, exposing finally the real worm boring at the core of their married life: suspicions of infidelity. Meanwhile, their four-year-old child—a boy named Merritt, after the parkway where his erstwhile hipster parents met hitching a ride—hoists himself into their side-loading drier. There, curling into a ball, he closes the door to shut out their cries.)

The irritant proved a useful teaching tool and, as a bonus, implied a broader metaphor for how beauty is made out of the grit and grind of our everyday world. Consider, one might say, an oyster's irritant, the constant pain when rubbed by sand it is helpless to move. Consider how the very record of its suffering, and of the roughness of the world, is both preserved and cultivated by the roundness of a pearl.

I intend poetry here, not parody. I mean these classroom things I say. Life does stroke, prick, poke, scrape our beings into thoughtfulness. Incidents, grains of beached time, lodge themselves inside our minds, provoking tides of mediating consciousness. Slowly we refine the rough incident into a round anecdote; and then, with practice, rounded anecdote into a polished story—maybe even a parable. And we all do this: meaning-making through storytelling is not just the privilege of professionals but our common gift and constant need. Nor is it merely entertainment. These stories we shape both correct and direct the steps we take in our everyday lives. The world *hurts* us into heeding it, and we *hurt* the world in turn. We learn our place, we leave our mark. To move purposefully in time is to marry—both obey and revise—the site we inhabit. Otherwise we waste away like Echo, restating a world we are helpless to change. Or we starve like Echo's poster-boy Narcissus, cutting off the world to sight our face.

Although ancient myths such as theirs now tend to be dismissed as superstitious or ethnocentric, the haunting demise of Echo and Narcissus echoes back all too exactly in our postmodern times. For they died, this perfectly mismatched couple, from the affliction we know best, from a dis-ease that all our laugh tracks, Muzak, and iPod play lists can never quite mask, much less arrest. They died, that is, from loneliness. They failed, as I believe our whole culture has been failing, because the world (the *real* world) was too little with them, and they with it.

Echo, locked in, couldn't speak for herself, couldn't hurt the world into heeding her passion. Narcissus, locking out, couldn't see beyond himself, couldn't heed the world's hurting because he lacked compassion. Punished by the gods for abusing love, *their* shells were tightly closed, their souls were shut in: the careless woman forbidden to give, the heartless man unable to accept the bounty of life's irritants, and so too its saving luster—pain's potential gem. And without genuine exchange, action and reaction, the trading off of pain, their bodies wasted away to mere echo and reflection—ellipses on the page . . . No body: nobody: no story to tell. The absence of pain is the stilling of change, is the banishment of hope. Better, though not easier, to be raging in Massapequa than sentenced to that hell.

Living's Town: A Suburban Allegory

All my life, I realize now, I have felt that same itch of the incomplete. Too little with the world. Too enclosed within some shell to fashion those stories we are born to live and tell. Even as a child inside the mild and milky precincts of Ike's suburbia, where we sucked on flavor-straws filled with fun and flattery (how bright, how flush, how *right* we children were, spokesmen all agreed); even then, before sex, drugs, and Vietnam, although I wanted to and tried, I couldn't quite believe.

It wasn't just the Gospel of Good Cheer that seemed so fake but the very texture of the physical place: subdivided, fenced in, plastic-wrapped, fluorescent-lit; vitamin-, nitrogen-, super octane-fed. Somewhere (Asia maybe?) people must have breathed the real air, ankle-deep in the paddy of rank and primal things. But we seemed to live instead inside a diorama where the grass was painted green and the foliage was made from shredded cellophane, our smiles the smiles that children tend to paint, crooked cups of dazed cheer on heads without bodies. Life seemed as packaged then as those shows on Parents' Night where kids were placed on stage in rows arranged by height, reciting there the measures of the goodly and the godly.

Remember those nights? The town's self-confirming pleasure, its almost catechistical delight at seeing "Youth" assembled? It wasn't our singing or acting, usually inept, that mattered then so much as the fetching aspiration, Youth willing to affirm the weary wisdoms of the age. It was our willingness to merge, however awkwardly, into a single social creature, one whose collective voice could then be cued by the miming lips and crisply metrical baton of the fervent Miss Brightly, the district's music teacher. And allegiance was pledged. And the band played on.

Obedient, I played my part (second row, to the left) but even then I felt a fraud: part Echo, rotely reciting those instructions we received; part Narcissus, unable to see through the glazed image of myself to that which lay beyond. I would hear schoolmates earnestly parroting the phrases of teachers, parents, of other schoolmates. And, although I would parrot them, too, repeating the same wish lists of possessions and approved but now laughably irrelevant political truths (remember the missile gap? or Quemoy and Matsu?), what I lacked then was the candor of conviction. "Really?" I wanted to say so much of the time, to adults and kids alike. *Really?*

For we seemed, most days, at least four steps removed: living in a drawing of a drawing of someone's cartoon of the world as it was. In some fundamental and faintly frightening way, we didn't have a clue . . . we didn't "get it." But *it* was there, all right—all about us, every day—and had a way of bursting through like a pencil punching holes in our dioramas' shells, leaving blistered gaps in our model of the world. For me, that *it* first struck just one block over, one block up.

A neighbor, *my* neighbor—new, yes, but a neighbor nonetheless. A boy about my age and yet bereft now in my memory of even a name. This boy who lived just one block over, one block up, did a very foolish thing. He ignored the warning of every anxious modern mother, every cautious father. True to his species and his sex, a budding lover of tools and prober of holes, he picked up a screw driver one fine day and stuck its metal blade into a slot meant to hold instead an appliance's plug. Abracadabra, contact was made, and joined there to the magic that lit our Christmas lights, this boy-about-my-age rapidly rode the current of Progress—which was, we'd all been told, "our most important product"—over the threshold and out of this life.

An ambulance came to take him away from the basement where they found him to the street where we would play. Already he was covered, his smallish body draped, a featureless shape beneath a stretcher's sterile sheet. White. Blank. Never really known, he left without a trace, his erasure complete—for us at least, there would be no funeral or wake to make the moment real, to engrave a deeper memory of his image or his name. (I feel that I *ought* to remember his name.) The house remained shuttered and the family, now appalled by our "safe" suburban setting, would quickly move away.

That very evening, though, in every house on nearby streets, over family dinners or interrupting the canned laughter on network TV, a warning was repeated by panicky parents, the tenor of their love turned tyrannically forbidding: *never-never-never-NEVER.* The *it* word itself, though, mostly went unsaid, as if, like tribal priests, our parents believed that to mention the word was to beckon its fate.

⊕

I can see it there, I now believe: see the self-esteem age in the cradle of the fifties, with its desperate normalcy and urge toward self-deceit. I can start to sketch, from its impingement on my block, that will-to-avoidance soon rendered concrete by domed stadiums, enclosed malls, surround-sound systems, and wall-to-wall screens. Even the town's name contains an obvious allegorical key. For it was called Livingston—which is to say, Living's Town—and Living's Town, I now believe, was shaped to fit the era's secret central theme. Yes, the evolution of such a place is deeply rooted and complex, but if you wish to quickly grasp the suburbanization of American life, forget for now the history of technology, the lessons of sociology, the economic theories of the left and the right. Understand instead that our pull toward perfection was also driven by a fear as old as Adam. Understand that Living's Town was raised, its scenery subdivided in just such a way, so that we, its inhabitants, its children especially, would never have to see an unembalmed corpse.

A good intention, of course—the best, one wants to say. To wish your children safe. To try to make the magic circle of immunity an actual *inhabitable* place. As many a parent knows, the urge to protect can be as fierce a drive as sex and even more exhausting, inspiring wall after wall, fence within fence, a blaze of hazard signs, warning labels, and double yellow lines.

Good intentions go awry, though. We can't fence out that which lurks within, nor forbid the laws that made us. People die—children, too. Even in Living's Town. Despite the baffle and the maze of our subdivided place, the fact of *it* slipped through even as its sights, scents, and sounds were increasingly excluded. In a realm where the musk of living bodies was masked by chemists' smells and babies fed on formulas drawn from no one's breasts, Death arrived as a "datum," all the more disturbing for having been extracted from its grounding in the flesh—sense-less, and thus senseless. No body: nobody: no story to tell. No locus for the pain, and so no center for the pearl. No setting to measure those edges that make the unknowable real.

Or almost no setting. For although the grand cover-up was well under way, our total enclosure was not yet complete. Vestiges of older economies still remained, lovely, scrubby patches of unassimilated space—an overgrown field recalling rural days; a muck-hemmed pond or a strip of real woodland, whose footways were spongy from leaves never raked. Such a place had managed to survive just behind the houses across the street from mine. And despite all the parks and schools that planners would provide, this narrow island of undeveloped space and unsupervised time was, for me, the truest education that Living's Town supplied.

There, densely clustered trees—tilting maples, scarred oaks—battled for sunlight, starving the scrub growth and screening our eyes. There, ribboned by a footpath our feet had beaten wide, the woods sloped down a hillside and toward a lusher lowland called by us the Vines: a temperate-zone jungle where we swung and climbed, and where dying trees were draped with thickly leaved and latticed creepers, forming tents about their trunks where crawling kids could hide . . . how wonderful to hide! The narrowest stream, unpicturesque and only seasonally fed, drained nearby. At any moment, at any spot, a revelation might arise. To kick some leaves might bare the skull of a squirrel, or a bone-flecked pellet spit up by an owl. To glance behind a log might reveal some orange fur and lusterless eyes, the meaning of whose stillness you couldn't deny. For you had found *it* again (or *it* had found you). That hole in the box. That place toward which your neighbor's pet cat had crawled off to die.

At the same time, from behind the gray veil of pond scum or piles of plain rock, came the opposite surprise: life, life erupting. Chipmunks dashing. A locust hatching. Once, a six-foot snake weaving through weeds glazed by the sun. In that nearby stream—which, on first glance, seemed so empty—we'd find finger-length crayfish, aggressively pinching. Down by the Vines, we'd pick "poison" berries and grapes so sour that our tongues stung for hours, their gritty small seeds stuck in our teeth.

Summers, we could play there till supper, our minds enclosed in the shell of our fantasies, the usual boy-games of raiding and rescue. Sometimes, though, we would pause, our inventiveness exhausted; and with our bodies slumped, our voices stilled, with the shell of our fantasies finally unhinged, the presence of the place would slowly seep in: a lyricless music, a slow basal chord. It was large, this music, and it was long—so long that even our longing was lost in its rhythm. We'd sense then a dimming, by degree, of all ambition; an erasure, through immersion, of all subdivisions: no magic circles to be entered, not a fig leaf to be found. This was the grounding the ground itself grew from. And to touch it, to be touched by it, however briefly as we sat on a log with our sneakers planted in the soil's soft rot, beckoned a feeling, wordless and healing, of deep rootedness in the world as it was.

Yet, within those same pauses, we might have heard, too, the engines of progress encroaching our play. Bulldozers, backhoes, truck- after truck-load of gravel and curbstones, the smoke of hot tar smudging the air. To come of age in that time and that place was to witness a vanishing, one whose completion defines a largely unnoted historical divide: the permanent erasure for whole generations of undeveloped space, unsupervised time.

By the year I left junior high, the woods, the Vines, the footpath were gone. The fields I knew had been turned into lawns. Native trees were giving way to ornamental shrubs in fertilized beds. Actual settings had been rendered into "texts," signs labeled with the likes of Deer Run Lane or The Princeton Estates. Going, too, were the small, affordable homes with lowball loans, the stable neighborhoods and long-lived marriages: the whole ecosystem of good intentions, its habits and its habitats, its fanciful narratives "on behalf of all children," going awry.

Mobile was the word, and even now the sixties seem a fast-forward blur of renouncements and departures, residence and precedent likewise deserted, entanglements averted, presidents shot. (Goodbye, Camelot.) Going, neighbors; going, friends; and soon, too, I was gone—to college and beyond. My brother, my sister, then my parents moved on—new homes, new jobs, our nuclear family spread to four states. Only my in-laws remained in town, and even they had switched homes, moving up and over to a newer subdivision, on whose wide and wending streets, I was jogging one day near the end of the seventies when the full force of those vanishings finally struck.

I stopped abruptly in the middle of the street. It was a midsummer day like so many of my childhood—bright and hot, perfect for play—yet empty of movement, eerily tame: the wind barely stirred the leaf-dense trees, and the only sound to be heard was the hum of compressors cooling the air for rooms unseen. No high-pitched shrieks. No scraping of chalk on the crackless walks. No blur of looped rope rhythmically spanking the neighborhood's streets.

It had come to this, the vanishing complete: that on a perfect summer day, in childhood's planned estate, not a child could be found—much less "Youth assembled"—not a single boy or girl during the whole of my five mile jog. The seventies had come and the children, too, had gone. Where had the children of Living's Town gone?

Party in Transit

Years later, I was standing at a bar in Sea-Tac Airport, just prior to boarding a midnight flight. By then I had fathered two sons and published two books, and much else had changed in the charting of my life, including the coast of my residence. To visit my original and still mobile family had come to require this longest of journeys across the lower forty-eight: from top left, in what is now frequently called America's "most livable" city, to the bottom right of the Sunshine State.

The trip itself was a happy occasion. For although I disliked much of the culture of southern Florida—its shabby buildings and shallow social roots, its scary segregation of communities by age—I was as tempted as anyone then by the almost silky softness of its tropical sands. More importantly, the sequence of related emergencies that had kept my soul in a vise for a number of years had loosened just a bit. My students' stories were all read, my grades were in. And now, having dragged my bags, heavy with books and sporting gear, to the bar nearest the gate of my departure, I was ready at last for a little peaceful celebration—a good book and a good beer—to mark the real start of this rare vacation.

Something was wrong, though, something not quite right. After ordering a beer, I had the edgy sense that even this small plan had somehow gone awry, and as I surveyed the space behind me for a quiet, empty table, I slowly realized why. For although there were many tables empty, none were quiet that night. None were quiet because every fifteen feet or so, in each corner of the room, a large video screen was radiating sounds and imagery in a relentless cross-fire of atmospheric entertainment. I scanned left, then right. But wherever my gaze was fixed, save at my feet, my field of vision was eclipsed by one of those screens while the borders of my thoughts were constantly infringed by a single soundtrack buzzing in, with an eerie omnipresence, from every side at once. I paused, momentarily dumbfounded. In the parlance of old cowboy shows, they'd "got me surrounded": the literary man ambushed by a band of surround-sound speakers and wall-to-wall TVs.

"Excuse me, but can one of those screens be turned off?"

The bartender, change in hand, greeted the question as if I had just asked her to remove, barehanded, a view-obscuring wall. I refused to move, though. I kept her in sight. What to do, what to do? Pull a plug out? Demand a refund and, wheeling about, take my business some place else? . . . Where, though?

I glanced down at the bags surrounding my feet. My palms were sweaty, my shoulders still ached. Worse, given Sea-Tac's design then, to find another bar meant leaving this wing and so having to pass through security again: more ringing bells and racing hearts, more suspicious stares from the luggage police.

Beaten, I took a seat. In two awkward trips, I brought my bags, beer, and change to a table, where, attempting to settle, I became part of a scene that had fewer customers than video screens. Writers are stubborn, though, and even here I wouldn't quit on my planned celebration. I unzipped my bag, retrieved a book. Sipping from my beer, I started to read a three hundred year-old George Herbert poem . . . and so arrived, unaware, at the little irritation out of which all these pages, this unanticipated book, would eventually be formed.

I had a friend in college—let's call him Bart—in whom earnestness, sociability, and the urge to get ahead were merged in equal parts, and who decided, therefore, to pursue the Law. As a result, language turned puffy in Bart's apprentice mouth. Meals became *repasts*, a toilet the *commode*. The most mundane of frat boy topics—the best NBA franchise, the ideal breast size—he'd gravely drape in a verbal wig and gown. Nevertheless, as I sat in the bar I was astonished to find that an old phrase of Bart's, as puffy as ever yet eerily apt, floated back to mind: *the juxtaposition of the incongruous.*

There could be few juxtapositions more incongruous than the spiritually intense, verbally complex George Herbert and the vacuous sphere of banal entertainment in which I was presently trying to read him. At first, though, it wasn't the special irony of the selection that rubbed me the wrong way—the problem was wider and blunter than that. I simply couldn't read. The video's soundtrack kept breaking in, derailing comprehension again and again.

And this wasn't, mind you, some body-blasting wall of bass and drum. I hadn't wandered into some den of MTV, with its prepackaged (and highly profitable) "affronts to common decency." No, the content—bland music, smooth voice-overs—was even less interesting than that robotically "rebellious" capitalist fare. Neither so rude nor so loud, less commanding than distracting, the volume had been set at a level meant to skim, with a dietician's fervor, all the curds and cream from consciousness, the shapely mind denied all richness, complexity, all density of thought. I could "read" but not read: a sports column, yes; some tabloid piece; a headline, a horoscope; more advice to the lovelorn, with numbered tips, on the ins and outs of orgasmic bliss. But it wasn't possible to reason, calculate, ponder, or compose.

Forbidden to read, I put down the poem. Beaten again, I did what was expected (that is, as the airport's environment coercively directed): I looked up. Irritated, I watched and listened with full attention to the presentation still impinging from every side at once. On each screen, a creamy mountain scene with slender folks skiing quickly gave way to some information piece—on vitamins, I think. This, in turn, quickly faded into an interview with someone semi-famous (a quiz show habitué? a failed athlete turned spokesman-for-the-game?): the sort of public figure one knows one ought to know but never quite recalls. And so on, and so on. No topic serious, no segment allowed to last more than a minute, no relation between the pieces, and so no rhyme or reason to the constant transitions: the whole show a kind of illustration of Bart's "juxtaposition of the incongruous"—the incongruous rendered innocuous, though, by the shallowness of the topics, and by a mood-soothing music thickly applied, like a mud bath to the hide of the postmodern soul.

I tried to resist, but the compass of my senses felt oddly deranged. It didn't matter if I swiveled in my chair: my perspective couldn't change. In this simulated world that had captured my attention, each direction seemed the same, exactly the same: front mirrored back, left mirrored right; and given the nonsense sequence of innocuous segments, *now* also blurred with *then*, too little to distinguish time from time. There was nothing to engage in any meaningful way, but with the volume too loud to allow an escape, I was still forced to abide in this virtual place—out of real space and out of real time, or rather out of an awareness of real space and time. I was still forced to be *there*—a there which, although nowhere really, was a nowhere impinging from everywhere at once.

Where was I? What was it—this place of continual "dissolves" and perpetual distraction, of monotonous mood coercively applied? Some new form of Muzak, engaging the eye as well as the ear? A kind of dentist's waiting room, but outfitted with screens, its sound turned up to the exact pitch and hum that would block out the neurotransmitters of fear? As in the old elevator music's mind-numbing medleys, this video imagery, while constantly changing, seemed essentially the same, processed like cheese into a textureless range of emotion and reason. Not only fear was being blocked, but wonder, exasperation, exultation, and sadness, in all their subtle mixtures and heady evocations, a whole palette of possible responses lost.

Some line had been crossed—when? how? by whom? and for what?—in the right to regulation: between public and private, between exterior and interior forms of behavior. Something had launched a high-tech invasion of the self's secret spaces, its most sovereign occasions. New if implicit bans had been added to those normally posted. Here, not only *NO SMOKING, NO TIPPING*, but *NO INTRICATE FEELING, NO VEXATIOUS THOUGHT*. Or, as we might choose to phrase it in the ever polite Pacific Northwest: *THANK YOU FOR NOT THINKING*.

Soon, of course, the soft sands, the hot sun—the real party I wanted—would be mine, and I would return to Seattle both relaxed and revived.

But something had entered that night when, hoping to celebrate, my own shell had opened up; something small but hard had lodged in my mind, like a shard in a shoe I couldn't take off. And although it seemed at first an irritant of the banal sort (more mayo jar than Helen's fateful snatching), the longer I thought about it, the more like a snatching it seemed to be. A hijacking of the queen—by *whom*? and for *what*?—that most royal queen called consciousness.

Over and over in the months to come, I recalled that bar and the strange space it carved. Over and over, my memory would insist on its own obsessive security check, its fluoroscoping eye repeatedly searching the scene of the crime until, at last, a new form was traced, a danger spied . . . until the subliminal voices of commonsense caution seemed to emerge, answering the question I had posed long before. *Listen*, those voices seemed to say: *you really need listen*. For this is the place that, willingly or not, we all have entered. *This* is where the children of Living's Town have gone.

Just Saying No

Can we open the shell? Can we break the magic spell of these pseudo-places and touch again our native ground? It used to be that when the circus came to town, the challenge was to sneak our way into the tent; now that its virtual big top encloses our town, the new and ever more urgent task is to search its rim for a safe way out. Where might that be, though? They stream Lady Gaga in *Nepal* now. A decade ago, I read a poll of Beijing students who, when asked to select the greatest people of the age, chose the following two: Chou En-lai and Michael Jordan. Now, one presumes, they're singing songs to Prozac and saying: "Chou En - *who*?" Here's a puzzle to ponder as our masts begin to shudder in the new global order's turbulent air: how can we disembark from the voyage of our times when its vehicle is virtually everywhere?

This is the age of airways, though, not sea lanes. And when I try to select an apropos scene—one that might capture our era's special mix of spiritual banality and material rapture, one that might pose the key dilemma we now face—I return to Sea-Tac airport. I recall especially those moments after take off when your fear first fades and, hung like a hammock between security and dread, your mood becomes as buoyant as the body of the jet. You bend down, glimpse out and, just that quickly, you are gone. You feel the whole of your mind intensify as it funnels through your window to giddily expand in the space beyond. This is it: that sphere of pain and play where, once upon a time, for reasons unclear and without ever asking, we as a species were licensed to range. Translucent tufts of cloud, say, sailing above the ocean's shadowed blue. Or the serrated violence of a mountain ridge rising, its cliff-faces scored in astonishing hues.

You can see the human settlement, too: our patchwork fields, our network of roads, houses hung on hills, ports clinging like barnacles to coastal folds. What you see most clearly from the thermal you ride is where Living's Town fits within the whole: how the pittance of our genius can only faintly glint, as if a penny tossed for luck into a canyon's gaping bowl. And perhaps the plane tips, banking to turn. And you catch your breath then as the arc of the horizon seems to be drawn like a cello's curved bow, long and slow, across some resonant chamber inside.

Suddenly, though, a voice intrudes, a perkily officious spokesperson for the crew. And you *have* to listen. Even tuning out, face toward the window, you can't exclude her chipper message: how they're presenting today a "major motion picture," *Wood Nymphs in Winter*, starring Marcie as Echo, Brendan as Narcissus. "A romantic comedy," she says, "with the pace of a thriller." The sales pitch concludes. Minutes pass. But as you try to slip back to the space beyond, you're captured again by that intercom voice which, even as it asks, always seems to insist. And this time it has an all too relevant, personal request. (One you knew to expect, so why react with this sudden chill?) Could those in window seats please pull down their shades, so that the passengers who paid might better view their film?

Such a trifle, it would seem—to comply with the needs of the nameless crowd. And no one else seems to mind. All about you now, you can hear the sound of the shades going down, you can sense the communal light growing dimmer. You shift in your seat, you loosen its belt. As the darkness thickens, you're made aware again of the cabin's curving walls, the tight tube they form—were they always this small? You're about to bend again toward your window's soothing light when, from the corner of your eye, you spot a flight attendant fast approaching.

Glancing her way, you can't help but see on a neighbor's small screen a portion of the movie's opening scene. There, a pining Marcie repeats the lines from a thousand prior flicks. There, a preening Brendan leans in to admire himself again on the moon of her passion's total eclipse. Even without the sound, you know the script. Just the briefest glimpse and you know what you will get if you pay to tune in: Echo with spin, the candied climax of unconditional bliss where girl gets boy and both get rich. Yes, this is the sort of "myth"—American-born, virtually fashioned—where everyone will live happily ever after (*ever after, ever after . . .*) Where, against all odds, a glistening Sisyphus plants his flag on Everest's top, and a certain small child, "wise beyond his years," emerges from a drier to dry the jar of his parents' tears. Abracadabra, all across the nation, dead boys arise—light as Lazarus, with milk-sweet smiles—to play again in childhood's basement.

"Sir?" the flight attendant says. Like the lettuce they serve, the smile she gives is wilting at the edges: she is "sad," that's the message, and her sadness now is meant to chasten. She bends, she blinks; obsequious with concern, she tilts toward your face. Nevertheless, you refuse to act; you want at least to make her ask. And so: she does.

"For the sake of your fellow passengers, Sir, would you mind pulling your window shade down?"

Anxiously now you shift in your seat. You didn't ask for this, you think—you didn't want the attention. And it doesn't help now that, somewhere behind you during this pause, you can hear a fellow rebel giving up the cause. It's unnerving somehow, the soft scraping of his shade, the further dimming of our cave, as yet one more outside view is lost.

Listen—you really need to listen. For this is where we are, you and I; this is the challenge our age has staged, a choice we can't refuse. Between engagement and entertainment. Between the old Nature, where beauty's veined with pain, and the new-and-improved Nature 2.0. This is where we are and, Solomon or not, each of us must judge. To which of these places should we sing our songs of praise? In which realm should we house, day-in, day-out, the royal queen of consciousness? . . .

Press *1* if you want the old; press *2* for the new. This is a highly advanced form of parable—wisdom in its interactive mode. Thanks to the boys in the lab, truth itself can be custom-made now; and soon, with a virtual catalogue from which to choose, each story will work out "as you like it" (*as you like it, as you like it* . . .). Every day, in every way, more autonomy here for you and me.

The temptation is old; the warnings against it, too. Far better writers than I—from Hawthorne to Melville, Wendell Berry to Christopher Lasch—have left behind their cautions. It is after them that I simply ask: where would we be if even our wildest materialist wishes came to pass? This, I believe, is how they would answer.

We can set up house on virgin Mars, or even beyond; we can fuse energy from the sea or, sucking data from the stars, definitively prove the Big Bang right or wrong; we can mass produce the golden goose, or that sporting shoe that tooled mercurial Michael's magical jump, so that all of God's children can eat the cake of kings and, heels sprouting wings, surge to power-dunk; every home from Singapore to Nome can be Wi-Fi connected so that the global mind is firing all its synapses at once—and still it wouldn't be enough to tip the scales of human fate. Beneath the cover-up of progress, certain facts refuse to budge, the elemental holds its sway. The worm's still in the apple. The kid's still in the drier. And the heart still wants the planet on its plate.

My heart, too, as those authors I admire repeatedly admonish. Which is why, after them, I keep trying to remember that autonomy is less a quantity of choices than a quality of intention, a way of *seeing through*. Less a menu of accessible fantasies than a mapping of one's will to the landscape of reality—an obedience to the true. Now, rather than rewriting the world "as I like it," I keep trying, after them, to school my stubborn heart in how to like the world. "The fact," G. K. Chesterton wrote—not the wish or the hope but the fact—"that [we] must somehow find a way of loving the world without trusting it."[3] Now *there's* a hard number, a knotty problem posed by our existential math, for to be a lover of the world, we have to risk its rougher edges, probe its darkest holes. To be the world's lover, we have to open up our shells—even knowing, as we do, that the current which cleanses can also kill.

So it is that, in schooling my heart's likes, I keep trying to say: no immunity, please. No extraterrestrial Edens for me. I want access, not exits. I want what Narcissus never gave and so, in turn, could not receive: intimacy, not expertise.

Irritation, negotiation, interaction: exchange. Dialogue, not monologue. Marriage, not reportage with its mindless echoing of cultural clichés: "inside sources have reported" . . . "experts said today." All those glib consultants from Jargonese & Jade: what do they really *mean*? All those insinuating lyrics and enclosing screens, the unscrolling of their "myths" . . . (They're *dying* up there, Marcie and Brendan, the souls behind the masks: they're dying up there from loneliness.) Again and again a voice intrudes, more perkily officious spokespersons for our crew: "for the sake of your fellow passengers, sir . . ."

You'll know by now which button I would choose—or rather, honoring the difference between intentions and actions, which I want to choose. How strange that, at the very stage of my life when I most desire to obey, I feel compelled to rebel, to resist or escape the order of the age. I think of Melville these days: how hard *he* found it to love the world, to balance truth with hope; how angry he was with our nation's cultivation of a phony innocence and with our addiction, evident even then, to mood-enhancing happy endings. I think of Bartleby, too, from "Bartleby, the Scrivener." I recall that pearl which Melville managed to make out of his own rage at our nation's blurring of greed with grace—that perfectly pitched parable of wry refusal.

Set on Wall Street, too. In the epicenter of American can-do, of get-up-and-go, this comic incarnation of "just say no."

It is after Bartleby that *I* say, then: no more copy, thank you. No more utopian systems, video sugar plums or I.P.O. visions shall be mnemonically scriven inside my head. Someone else can spell-check the Ten Steps to Success, or cock-a-doodle-doo the latest laws of salesmanship. There are other laws—hymns, fables, koans, psalms—that I would rather engrave inside my head as guide and pilot to my actions. That the wages of work are not merely money. That love's not a spoonful you can suck clean like honey. That while our smiles may be winning, our gadgets neat, the only bottom line that finally matters is the one which waits beneath our feet. I might be wrong, but according to those laws, the real Invisible Hand couldn't care less what the Market does.

All easy enough to profess, I admit. Words *are* cheap if you publish only not to perish on ambition's tenure ladder. In the world as run by Jargonese & Jade, we find it hard *not* to blather. In the new Nature, mood-enhanced, it is fantasy that abhors a vacuum. The crap, the unmitigated shit that's filled my head—all those sports star fantasies, Nobel-speech pufferies; all the hours, the days I've managed to kill. (And that's a phrase, "killing time," that doesn't seem so bad until you learn, too late, that time is all we have.) Believe me, there's not a day during which my finger doesn't itch to push button #2. I mean, how great it would have been if the boy *had* arisen from his basement floor. How sweet, oh how sweet it would be if most-livable cities could guarantee a more livable life . . .

Against the pull of such delusions, I cling to the news left by my betters. They're the ones who remind me that our fondness for spin can only make us dizzy. They're the ones who insist that there can be no letters more dead than those we pen in the offices of what-might-have-been.

Time is all we have. It matters what we choose—Echo in her cave, Narcissus by his pool. Pull down the shade? For my own sake, and maybe, just maybe for the sake of my fellow passengers: I would prefer not to.

II. Inside Story: A Preliminary Mapping of Virtual America

> *Hamm: Nature has forgotten us.*
> *Clov: There's no more nature.*
> *Hamm: No more nature! You exaggerate.*
> *Clov: In the vicinity.*[4]
>
> —Samuel Beckett, *Endgame*

Having made my intentions clear in the most personal terms, I am now obliged to provide a preliminary mapping of this artificial place that "I would prefer not to" inhabit. To that end, two anecdotes can quickly sketch something of the source and the substance, the psychological origins and moral consequences, of our aggressive investment in a Nature 2.0 largely designed for and by Evangelical Mammonism.

The first is the tale of a toddler who fell so in love with his favorite storybook that he opened its cover and tried to step inside. Anyone who has loved a book (or a movie or a TV show) understands that desire to make the imaginative literal, to convert the womb of a well-wrought fantasy into the wrap of a real life, and this fetching urge to escape inside is reenacted in ways only a degree less literal throughout our lives. We see it in the teen who watches *The Dark Knight* fifteen times, in the fundamentalist mind wrapped in the scriptural bandages of the biblical message, and in the public intellectual whose ideas have been permanently bronzed with the coinages of Marx or Friedman, Darwin or Derrida. Still, it is the image of the boy footing the pages of his storybook that best captures for me both the lasting allure and the ultimate limits of this desire to abide in a world of our mind's own making.

The second anecdote is far more astringent, the very opposite of cute. It occurred when, crossing my sons' school yard on a sunny autumn day, I was run into by a boy no older than first grade. The impact was nothing really, a little bump that caused us both more surprise than pain. Yet when I glanced down, ready to appreciate fondly "the child at play," I was stunned into silence by a look in his eyes that made vividly real every statistic I had read about the American family's brute demise. The cold fixity of his rage and the glaze of his undiscriminating hate belonged on a battlefield not a playground, and I knew then, in an instant and with a chill, that this little boy beneath me might eventually kill. I saw then that, given half a chance (a handy pistol, say), he might have mowed me down right there for merely being in his way, and that he would have snuffed my life out then—as the light of his had been snuffed out—without a hitch of hesitation or beggar's dram of pity. Already, before the age of eight. Right there, in the place where *my* kids played, in America's so-called most livable city.

I asked myself where a boy like that, so many boys like that, had come from. What I discovered—a discovery that shapes both the form and the content of the pages that follow—is that such a disturbing question cannot be framed in isolation. To probe it sets in motion a whole web of related questions. The erosion of responsible parenting, the rapid dissolution of the tacit agreement as to what one generation owes in commitment and caring to the next, resembles multiple other dissolving agreements: between stakeholders and shareholders over corporate policies, artists and audiences over aesthetic conventions, and teachers and citizens over an acceptable curriculum. Physician and patient, editor and author: the list goes on and on, and should touch anyone who has had the sense in his personal or professional life that the "rules of the game" have mysteriously changed—that they've gone subtly (or not so subtly) wrong.

I have been calling this rapid collapse of consensus "the killing of the covenants." I chose the phrase carefully. For while no society stands still and some quotient of change is not only tolerable but morally necessary (witness the postwar pivot against racial prejudice), the speed and aggression of the transformation under way don't resemble a reform so much as an extinction. Ironically, many of the features of this extinction resemble the rapid demise of tribal societies when invaded by the West, and as with those societies, the "killing" that matters most has less to do with formal laws or political agendas than with the most intimate beliefs of ordinary citizens.

These beliefs are the habits of mind, the tacit agreements about morals, manners, and purpose, that bind any society together. Because they define which behaviors are worthy, these agreements calibrate not only our capacity for public civility but also our most intimate conceptions of private self-worth; and because they give rhythm and shape to our everyday lives, they are as much our homes as the houses that hold us—more so, in that they move with us wherever we go. To lose them is to feel in a very real way, then, both worthless and homeless. To sense them dying all around us (and within us) without understanding why makes us anxious, angry, even terrified.

More than any fear of violence or economic envy, this double loss of inner compass and communal purpose generated the peculiar desperation that lurked just below the surface of our apparent prosperity prior to becoming mired in the Great Recession. It was the thirst that drove our constant feckless search for the prize of self-esteem in the platitudes of quackery, and was the hunger that funded our perpetual quest for Reality™, as if gangsta garb could turn the clueless adolescent into a formidable man with a credible history, or a pricey jeep's four-wheel drive could find and grip those elusive off-roads to authenticity and so stop our slide into decadence. We "celebrated" everything, we were wed to our jobs and shopped till we dropped, yet how much of our busyness then was just an alibi to cover this fundamental bafflement? Better to keep moving (morphing and surfing, producing and consuming) when behind every pause lurked the gaping maw of meaninglessness—that black hole in the soul that no scientist can solve, nor cornucopia of point-and-click products finally fill.

I call these crucial habits of mind covenants to emphasize first their mutuality: how they direct what we expect both from ourselves and others wherever we meet, whether in a classroom or a board room, or in the back seat of a car when on a first date. I chose the word, too, because of its age and place in the evolution of American democracy (dating back to the Pilgrims), wishing to stress the long continuity of aspiration that goes into the making of any society. Finally, I chose covenant specifically because of its religious connotations. When discussing a culture both blessed and blinded by the separation of church and state, I thought it especially important to emphasize that there *is* a link between ordinary behavior and ultimate beliefs. If our manners and morals have changed, then so have our metaphysics. If we are behaving differently as artist-father-physician-wife, then we are likely acting out of a new, if still dimly defined, set of beliefs about the nature and purpose of human life.

Why, during an era of relative peace and almost unthinkable plenty, did we initiate this unnerving change? Isn't such a crisis of belief normally the fate of the defeated nation, and didn't America win both World Wars, the Cold War, the first Gulf War, the economic war with Japan, Inc.? Who or what then was bent on killing the old covenants? And what scheme has been gradually taking their place?

Oddly, the answer lies in a completion of the plot line supplied by that cute little boy, for in ways unimaginable just fifty years ago, we have actually succeeded where the toddler failed, stepping every day into a world increasingly built from our own ideas. After the fall of the Berlin Wall, headlines focused on the opening of the East, with all its hope for freedom and danger of anarchy. At the same time, though, in the victorious West, many other walls were being built. Millions of democracy's citizens were entering enclosed malls, domed stadiums, walled-in communities and amusement parks, and bars like the one at Sea-Tac airport; they were wrapping their minds in the surround-sound space of Walkmans and home video systems, and were losing themselves in the virtual realms of the Internet.

More and more, everyday life was becoming an *inside* experience, and the real story of the age was, and still is, being told by the nature of *these* walls—the social space they shape, the behavior they aim to induce or disallow. The real story of the age is, in short, enclosure. This process of enclosure has been going on in the West since the Industrial Revolution, but it was much accelerated with the invention and proliferation of the mass media. To grasp why, we need only accept one simple but central concept of this book—namely, that information *is* architecture. This idea that information itself can constitute a kind of domesticated place is precisely what we mean by the phrase "virtual reality." It is also what the toddler intuitively understood, why he believed that he could physically enter his book.

Once we accept that information can construct a kind of place, it is easier to grasp the profundity of the change enacted by the postwar information explosion. Starting in the mid-fifties, TV could project a single show into nearly every American home at once. Add the Internet, cable, radio, and cinema to the daily bombardment of billboards and logos—our every view stamped, our every pause filled with some sort of message; add them all, place them inside the opaque walls of our domes, malls, and gated communities, and what we get is the new sprawling, multidimensional enclosure that has become our homeland. Yes, the nation's geological coordinates are basically the same as they were in 1946, but our social and, too, sensory coordinates have radically changed. We are living now in a dramatically different place: all humanly built or composed, whole days spent inside the artificial landscapes and mindscapes of Virtual America. Today, the womb of human thought *has* become the wrap of real life, and the problem we now face is the opposite of the toddler's—not how to get inside this alternative world but how to get out.

Why would we want to leave this comfort zone, with its gorgeous goods and multiple entertainments? First, and most obviously now, its vision of material prosperity has proven to be an unstable one. Worse, it is in many ways an insidious place to be, dangerous to ourselves as free-thinking individuals and to the civic soul of our democracy. It is insidious because the simple central truth stated above is also reversible: not only is information a kind of architecture; architecture is information. Like all human artifacts, Virtual America has been built from ideas, a set of beliefs about what is good and true, and ideas can be powerful shapers of daily behavior. This proves especially true when the scale is flipped, the idea projected into an entire and enclosing environment, for when that occurs, rather than our "having" an idea, the idea "has" us. In that case, by predesigning all that we sense, a set of linked beliefs can change our most intimate behaviors without our conscious knowledge, and so without our full consent. Without a law being passed or a leader overthrown, it can kill the old covenants of daily governance, transferring their sovereignty to itself.

We have arrived at an answer to our original question, then, and one that may startle many Americans. We have undergone such an unnerving change in our national character because we are now living in one of the most ideologically invasive social spaces ever constructed. We are being converted because the new enclosure of this Virtual America is so intensely, relentlessly, and ubiquitously indoctrinating. That the temper of its indoctrination is more seductive than coercive helps conceal from us the extraordinary power of its persuasiveness. That the climate of its enclosure seems so complex (full of noisiness, busyness, surface diversity) effectively masks the simplicity of the ideas that shape its spaces, drive its systems.

How do we find these simple ideas whose sovereignty has been supplanting our older beliefs? "Follow the money," that was Deep Throat's advice, to which I would add this closely related imperative: unmask the meaning. Before we enter any of these brave new worlds that have been reconfiguring America, theoretically to improve it, whether Disney World, *Second Life,* or Minnesota's city-sized Mall of America, we should ask ourselves: what is this place finally *for*? My promise is this: if we answer that question honestly, the confusion of our times quickly clarifies. Clearly, these spaces have not been built primarily for parenting or philosophizing, for preserving the past or serving God; nor have they been designed to enhance those traits, such as plain speaking and self-restraint, that gave birth to our democracy—otherwise, we would be behaving far differently than we are. No, following the money, we can see that Virtual America has been largely built by incorporated commerce and for its own ends. Although decorated by the arts and delivered by science, the conventional virtues pitched inside its convention hall have been designed primarily to generate profits.

This simplicity of motives has driven the history of the nation's new enclosure. What we have seen during the aging of Aquarius is the conversion of nearly every corner of our living space into a new niche for the marketplace, every activity into a leasable service with accessories for sale. Locales that were once partially economic are now totally economic. Organizations that once served other ideals now adopt the ways and means of the corporate world, torquing their efforts toward Mammonite ends.

Under this evangelizing regime, the civic center of the town square has been replaced by the corporately owned enclosed mall—with grave implications for democratic practices, as we shall see next chapter—and the Olympics have been reduced to a global trade fair, the athlete's allegiance to his or her nation effectively transferred to a corporate sponsor. So it is, too, that the public university, one of the great achievements of our democracy, has been reduced at times to a parody of the marketplace, complete with a gold rush for patents, the egregious padding of administrative salaries, free agent bidding wars for star professors, and the reinvention of the curriculum as a catalogue of fashions.

Everywhere we look, the trend has been the same. In travel, the sites we choose to tour have shifted from historic monuments to marketing centers like Nike Town or the Disney Store. In journalism, "all the news that's fit to print" increasingly becomes commercial news as stealth ads and infomercials blur coverage with sales. Civic services like garbage collection, prison management, and military provisioning have been privatized, which means, of course, commercialized. School buses now bear burger ads, and the charitable "volunteer" at your door is likely just another salesman working on commission, taking 30 percent of every donation toward saving the whales. The Beatles may have believed that "money can't buy you love," but a host of wildly popular TV game shows, laughingly branded as "reality television," preach otherwise.

Ever more specialized professional advice is now brokered via consulting fees, even as traditional American traits like self-reliance are repackaged as "self-help" and "self-esteem" to support a booming industry of books, DVDs, therapies. And as we shall see in chapter 4, health care has also been co-opted by commerce, the Hippocratic oath "creatively destroyed" and subtly rebranded by the ethos of the Invisible Hand. Closer to home, nearly every object of feckless fun—the sports card, comic book, doll, or bottle cap—has become a collectible with its own specialized market modeled after the commodity exchange. Monetary speculation replaces manual play as kids refuse to unwrap their sports cards, hoping to keep their value up, and since the seventies, our shoes, shirts, and pants have become corporate billboards, so that every day we compliantly suit up as team-players in the consumer economy.

But the most telling sign of this commercial invasion, and proof of its power as indoctrination, can be found in the index of our innermost thoughts. Like our crowded closets, our storehouse of memories is overstocked with the logos and emblems of advertising. Where poems, parables, and patriotic songs once whispered in our ear to steer us through our lives, we now hear the aphorisms of shoe companies and the hymns of cola copywriters who would "like to teach the world to sing in perfect harmony." More and more, *they* are ones who instruct us as to what is "the real thing."[5]

Aiming to change the default motivations that drive behavior, Mammonite marketing has been co-opting our everyday emotional affiliations. As Proust demonstrated, certain scents can powerfully evoke cherished past events, triggering an instant homecoming for the ambushed heart, and for a quick-and-dirty tracking of how such sensory memories have been hijacked for commercial ends, we can turn to a poll conducted by the Smell and Taste Treatment and Research Foundation. This survey found that odors associated with food proved to evoke fond memories in people of all generations, but other categories differed greatly depending on the respondent's age. Below is a summary of "where we were," decade by decade, not as the eye scanned or the ear sounded but as the nose knew.

TABLE 1: What the Nose Knows: America's Remembrance of Things Past

Birth decade	Most Nostalgic Non-Food Odors
1920s	flowers, grass, roses, pine, soap, manure
1930s	flowers, hay, sea air, pine, baby powder, burning leaves
1940s	baby powder, Mom's perfume, cut grass, flowers, sea air, roses, tweed
1950s	baby powder, Mom's perfume, Dad's cologne, crayon, pine, Play Doh
1960s	baby powder, Mom's perfume, chlorine, window cleaner, Dad's cologne, detergent, paste, Play Doh.[6]

Certain trends are obvious here and, from an historical perspective, exceptionally rapid. Note how for the generation born in the twenties all the fondest odors are still natural, with the single exception of soap. Such a memory map bespeaks a life largely free of artificial scents, along with the marketing that boosts their sales, and a character still familiar with (and unoffended by) the odors of the farm. It suggests, above all, a childhood still spent outdoors. With each ensuing decade, however, we find a further intrusion of artificial scents to mask natural odors (baby powder in the thirties, followed by perfume in the forties and cologne in the fifties) and a multiplication of memory associations that demark an indoor upbringing (crayons, Play Doh, window cleaner). The most dramatic shift occurs between the forties and fifties, the cradle years of the early Aquarians, by which time the original ratio has been completely reversed with only one natural scent (pine) remaining on the list. By the sixties, the shell of our enclosure is complete: all the non-food odors that most evoke a nostalgic response are humanly made and corporately sold.

In our memory banks, the sensory map of agrarian America has been replaced by that of Virtual America. As Beckett's Clov observes in this section's epigraph, "nature" is no longer "in the vicinity," and although that natural world may not have "forgotten us," we have forgotten it. Commerce instead now animates and constellates our remembrance of things past. We have, in effect, bonded with our products.

Not all of this is bad, of course—as Katrina and Sandy reminded us, nature can be vicious. Nor should we discount the astonishing material achievements of the age. One reason we face the problems we do today is that scientific capitalism has attended so well to more perennial ones. That divorce, desertion, and careerism now separate many parents from the company of their children is a lamentable fact made possible, in part, by an extraordinary leap in life expectancy. In another century, many of us wouldn't have been alive to make that choice. That most of the causes of that separation are also rooted in scientific capitalism—that, for example, the diaspora of families and the derangement of communities that so disrupt childcare are a direct result of this economy's imperatives, or that the ethos of parental desertion is but another form of the profit motive, a progressive privatizing of the heart's domain—is an irony that captures both the complexity of, and our complicity with, these worrisome changes.

Although its tone was too arrogant, the Vietnam era chant that we were all part of "the war machine" did suggest a hard truth about our subservient place inside this same political economy. Despite a mythos of heroic individuality still stoked by Hollywood action movies and the flagrant flattery of ad campaigns, Americans are now far less self-sufficient than we were in centuries past. Specialization of task, a key discovery of early capitalism, unleashed a surge in productivity that has, over time, made us far wealthier than our ancestors but also far more dependent on the larger economy: more vulnerable to its shifts, more subservient to its commands, more complicit with its acts. As we were rudely reminded in 2008, we have all become part of Evangelical Mammonism's intricate (and now global) "money machine."

As the restocking of our memories with corporate jingles vividly suggests, our complicity with this money machine involves more than just the practices demanded by our nine-to-five jobs. We not only obey its commands in the workplace; we often tacitly accept them in the privacy of our homes. They inform our common sense and calibrate our passions; they direct and misdirect our everyday lives. No plan to recover a more gracious and meaningful American place has a chance without acknowledging this parallel entrapment. The outer walls that confound us now have also become our inner blinders. The same enclosure, we need to know if we wish to escape it, abides in our own minds—yours and mine. I raise these points here to moderate the tone of the critique to come. What we face now, I want to keep reminding myself, are truly communal problems, and ones so deeply rooted in the structural design of everyday life that they prefigure not just the policies of our leaders on both the left and the right but also their personalities.

That said, if we ever hope leave this self-deluding place, we first have to mind how it was made. Evangelical Mammonism does have a history. Virtual America wasn't built in a day, and, in the chapters to come, I will trace its construction in key domains, revealing in the process how our gradual submission to the fiats and fantasies of a utopian materialism eventually led to both the fiasco in Iraq and the Great Recession.

2

In The Mall of Virtual America's Mind

"Don't Fence Me In" [1]

—hit tune written by Cole Porter and sung by Roy Rogers

THE RAPID ENCLOSURE OF the postwar generations within Virtual America's commercially controlled architecture and information, and our subsequent emotional bonding with the many products that filled those spaces, had multiple long-term effects on communal behavior. By the 1980s, the covenants of our convention hall had gravitated toward idealizing strictly commercial motivations, one visible sign of which was the elevation of even a vulgarian magnate like Donald Trump to near heroic status. (Trump's aggressive investment in legalized gambling during the same period provided an all too accurate preview of the newly "conservative" political economy's actual moral compass.)

The new sense map of daily experience—whose roads were lined with commercial signs, rooms perfumed with commercial scents, airwaves busy with commercial messages—also helped to draft a new political orientation, one that would closely serve the values endorsed by that enclosure's moral field. For those Aquarian high-achievers who had managed to star on the stage of counterculture radicalism, the new necessary path to power and status produced some amazing turnarounds. In one of the more memorable of these born-again moments, ex-activist and Chicago Seven defendant Jerry Rubin—Yippie turning Yuppie, picketing-the-pigs revised to pocketing-the-profits—suddenly discovered on his road to Damascus that the pursuit of money was, after all, a revolutionary activity. But the most passionate equation of the motives and methods of commercial success with the moral high ground of political liberation occurred on the Republican right, which, long allied with commercial interests, had the weight of history on its side.

Just as the New Left in the sixties, thumbing its nose at the stodgy earnestness of orthodox Marxism, associated sensuality and playfulness with political righteousness (in the hip slang of the day a high quality batch of drugs was often called "righteous"), the New Right in the eighties now causally linked conspicuous luxury and unchecked acquisitiveness to civic virtue. According to their utopian view, the profit motive was not only consistent with, but generative of, the public good. (That these internal revolutions on the left and the right actually shared an antipathy to agrarian America's traditional virtues such as thrift, modesty, and self-restraint—a key theme in my ongoing argument—was scarcely noted at the time.) Richly funded by corporate-sponsored think tanks, exploiting the allure of the new high-tech economy with its multiple opportunities to strike it rich, and borrowing from the theories of the Chicago school of economics, a new "movement conservatism" arose and was soon spewing out a confident stream of policy critiques and initiatives. The primary goal of all this fervor was privatization: not just the deregulation of industry but also the widespread transfer of both moral and political authority from elected government to corporate commerce. Ronald Reagan's election initiated the movement's ideological triumph, which was then pragmatically sealed in 1994 when Newt Gingrich engineered a Republican return to power in the House of Representatives.

As a resident of the Northwest, whose shortage of spotted owls was being offset by a surge in twenty-something millionaires, I had an apt ledge for observing the political triumph of this movement's evangelizing Mammonism. Back in the summer of '95, while more Northwest salmon fisheries were being closed and consumers world-wide were avidly awaiting the release of Windows 95 as if it were the next blockbuster film, I recall spying a news photo of Gingrich on a working holiday, lounging around a pool with two key allies. The new Speaker was at the height of his popularity then, and though details were scant, one could easily imagine how the trio were planning to sell their agenda by following the script of their presidential mentor, the former actor, whose official campaign photo had depicted him in a Western shirt and white cowboy hat. Here were three pale, pool-side, political John Hustons, planning a remake of the nation's favorite film. In this version, though, the global economy was now the new frontier, big government the corrupt sheriff, and the entrepreneur the new lonesome cowboy who would ride into town to save the day.

As proof of the broader shift in conventional thinking, their nominal opponent then, Bill Clinton, didn't significantly disagree with this revised script, at least as it applied to the redemptive virtues of entrepreneurship.

The fantasy that market forces, no longer "fenced in," would revive the heroic frontier of American freedom floated as easily on President Clinton's promises to "grow" the economy as it did on Speaker Gingrich's prophecies of little ghetto children giving up their guns for handheld computers. Not only did the forces driving the commercialization of public spaces have access to political power; the habit of idealizing the civic virtues of Mammonism was by then deeply ingrained in the nation's conscience. In conventional thinking, the instruments of moneymaking, seductively linked to the cowboy mythos evoked in Cole Porter's song, were now presumed to be inherently righteous.

Such optimism played well here in Puget Sound where software money was filling the waterways with sails and where Mammon's evangelists drifted through town, floating on the thermals of corporate think-tank money, to speechify about the new "healing capitalism." From a certain angle of vision—east of Lake Washington where Microsoft reigned—the heroic rescue proposed by the old Western myth could pass for a social reality here. In the same decade that agencies were meeting to slash timber harvests and salmon hauls, Bill Gates was named the richest man in the world, Boeing successfully sold its latest plane, grunge rock topped the charts, Nordstrom's became a national model for retail sales, and the Port of Seattle expanded its Pacific Rim trade. In few places was the radical switch from a local economy of natural resources to a global economy of software, travel, entertainment, and trade more evident or compelling.

Even the most utopian of claims by the New Right—that capitalist prosperity would necessarily engender democratic virtue—seemed plausible here in '95. In a region afloat with new money as yet unattached to an established social class, it was easy to miss this economy's radical inequality of wages and its export of sweatshops to outposts in Asia; easy to dismiss the insider schemes of Wall Street investors as the few bad apples in an otherwise pest-free and bountiful orchard. The old class-bound critique of capitalism's danger to our political freedom had been finessed. If the consumer was being well-served, then so, too, must be the citizen. The new digital technologies, and not some radical ideology, would bring "power to the people." How could democracy possibly be at risk in a social sphere where the streets were clean, millionaires wore jeans, and the customer was always made to feel right?

In fact, the wreckage of 2008 was already implicit in the conventional values of 1995, but the commercial enclosure of everyday life had rendered the American mind insensible to detrimental changes in its own environment. The danger was analogous in some ways to the decline in the local salmon populations that was occurring at the same time, for although no one knows the exact ratio of causes, the demise of certain spawning runs here has clearly arisen in large part from our many distortions of the natural environment. With its dams and logging and housing construction, our everyday economy has radically reconfigured physical space and so, too, changed the range of possible behaviors within that space, trapping and at times directly killing the salmon, even while providing the trash that allows gulls and crows to thrive. More broadly, humankind's domination of the planet—our relentless "fencing in" of its open spaces—has revised Darwin's survival of the fittest in just such a way. What each living thing must "fit" is, increasingly, our own extensive rearrangement of the natural world.

Although rarely recognized, this imperative to adapt is just as true for our own learned behaviors as it is for the instinctual repertoire of the gull or the owl. Cultural species no less than biological ones must fit or die. Democracy, too, has its necessary habitats, and the question now arises whether our own species of political freedom, first designed to thrive within a set of thinly populated and preindustrial colonies, can survive inside this rapidly privatizing environment. For that reason, this chapter will take a close look at the moral field enforced by the places we now routinely inhabit, starting with the physical space of the enclosed mall—that site which, from the mid-fifties on, replaced the civic square as the central meeting place for the American public—and concluding with the virtual space of the electronic media.

I. In the Mind of the Mall:
The Corporate Co-opting of Civic Space

We are governed, very infallibly, by the "sham hero"—whose name is Quack, whose work and governance is Plausibility, and also is Falsity and Fatuity. . . . And Quack and Dupe, as we must ever keep in mind, are upper-side and under of the selfsame substance; convertible personages: turn up your dupe into the proper fostering element, and he himself can become a quack; there is in him the due prurient insincerity, open voracity for profit, and closed sense for truth, whereof quacks too, in all their kinds are made.

—Thomas Carlyle, *Past and Present*, 1842[2]

With the collapse of the Soviet empire, we witnessed the end of a great competition between varieties of social order, a latter-day version of Athens versus Sparta. But the broad assumption then that the demise of communism had secured a safe passage for political freedom—much less signaled the happily-ever-after "end of history" that Francis Fukuyama proclaimed in 1989[3]—was far less certain than it seemed to some, even discounting the later rise of Islamic terrorism. I see freedom in the past hundred years as having been forced to navigate its way through the ever-narrowing straits between a Scylla of coercion and a Charybdis of seduction. As types of governance, coercive social orders constrict freedom through physical force, brandishing pain; seductive ones confuse freedom through psychological guile, promising pleasure. The former draw up draconian rules, dictating what its people must do (the fiat of the fascist, the endless regulations of the apparatchik). The latter create an atmosphere of ceaseless need and narcissistic fantasy where all are induced to "prefer" the same objects and actions (the addiction of consumption, the conformity of fashion).

Reality proves far more ambiguous and changeable than any such either-or division could ever fully address, of course, and that is why, short of extinction, there can be no ever-after "end" to the history of human governance, happy or otherwise. As styles of social control, coercion and seduction are perennial, adaptable, and frequently intermixed—they are potentials ever present in the complex nature all of us possess. Aiming to clarify through simple abstraction, the following table, *Coercive versus Seductive Social Control*, avoids such ambiguities by dividing and opposing two separate sets of cultural characteristics. Even this exercise in generalization, however, cannot escape the specific embodiments of history. As the two lists will quickly reveal, I have used the old Soviet system and postmodern America as my primary models for, respectively, the coercive and the seductive social orders. So it is that when, under the category of "philosophical orientation," I note that the coercive social order treats religion as its enemy, such an observation holds true for the twentieth century's totalitarian regimes, which were uniquely secular in their orientation. In the deeper past, coercion has gladly donned religious robes and, given the global rise of fundamentalist politics, it may yet do so more broadly again.

But right now, in the developed world of the West, seduction still prevails as freedom's greater threat. Seduction proves the greater threat because progress and prosperity, as Evangelical Mammonism has come to define them, increasingly require it. Not only is the seducer's strategy of control through dupery the logical resort of a consumer economy obsessed with boosting sales; it is also more compatible with cyber technology's easy evocation of virtual realities. Why plot a putsch when one can process a Potemkin village in the safety of one's study with the stroking of some keys? Why plunder a country (and risk being killed) when one can "make a killing" by manipulating numbers and diverting liquid money into one's cybernetic

TABLE 2: Coercive versus Seductive Forms of Social Control

	Coercive	Seductive
Center of Power:	one-party or -person polity	corporate-run consumer economy
Expansive Ambition:	global empire	global market / monopoly
Order of Leadership:	autocratic highly visible / fixed (dictator / general)	plutocratic invisible / mobile (corporate board)
Philosophy:	RATIONAL materialism (commerce serving state) (science serving party line) religion as enemy	rational MATERIALISM (state serving commerce) (science serving bottom line) religion as commodity
Ultimate Value:	power (most whips)	money (most toys)
Social Status:	proximity to power (Soviet May Day picture)	conspicuous consumption (Life-styles of the Rich and Famous)
Cultural Character:	repressive masculine patriotic puritanical earnest	expressive feminine self-centered sensual ironic / hip
Propaganda Tool:	ideology (party line) state hero	fantasy (pop culture) media star
Modes of Control:	command / conquer conscription physical threat party loyalty fiat censorship the Big Lie	tempt / co-opt addiction financial debt brand loyalty fashion saturation the Big Top (omnidirectional quackery)
Representative: art form: story line: polemic: architecture: profession: psychosis: model world:	 collage ministry's agitprop 3 hour speech Berlin Wall apparatchik paranoia Skinner box	 montage Hollywood's as-you-like-it 30 second ad Mall of America salesman / adman narcissism Circe's Isle

till? Such was the tacit calculation, legitimized by a highly disingenuous libertarian philosophy, that transformed our nation's housing market into a gargantuan Ponzi scheme.

As a means of social control, seduction is hardly new, of course. It was a characteristic ploy of the preagrarian trickster, Satan's tactic with Eve, and is still the preferred method of carnies and con men of every stripe. Such figures, however, have typically occupied the social margins, and as Thomas Carlyle grasped very early on, marketplace capitalism was unique in the way it actively institutionalized the "fostering element" of seduction's duplicities, routinely dividing society not just into opposing classes of owners and workers but also into reversible casts of "Quacks and Dupes." But it was only with the rise of the Information Age, through its combination of invasive communications, adept simulation, and physically enclosed cultural spaces, that seduction could be applied in such an integrated way as to create an entire environment with its own pervasive moral climate: an ecosphere of quackery.

This graduation in seduction's scale from niche to whole environment is of revolutionary significance, and the dramatic enlargement of its effects can best be measured by considering the subject of optical illusions. Most of us have seen those carefully crafted pen-and-ink drawings that can suggest, with but the slightest mental shift, either a vase or a human face, either a young woman's profile or lantern-jawed hag. Our ambivalence in these instances is both amusing and instructive. The initial confusion that we feel is harmless, for our lives don't depend on a definitive recognition (as they might, say, when trying to identify in wartime the silhouette of an approaching plane.) But an educational point is made, too. We don't simply see: visual perception is a mental process dependent on specific kinds of cues, and those cues can be manipulated in ways that fool us.

Clearly, such manipulations can be beneficial and constitute, in fact, the standard bag of tricks for every visual artist; they also can be misused by the quack or the spy to sell his separate lies. In either of those baneful instances, we presume that the individual illusion can be eventually judged (if sometimes too late) by turning to some larger context for orientation. But what if the horizon itself is an illusion? What if the pen-and-ink game is expanded into the realm of three-dimensional space, the perimeter as well as the point manipulated to fool the process of perception? What if an entire room, a kind of Skinner box of optical illusions, was self-consciously constructed and we, pigeon-like, were trapped inside it?

Anyone who has entered a fun house—where, for example, through a careful revision of visual cues, a skewing of lines and a scaling of furniture, *up* is actually made to seem *down*—knows the peculiar power of such fakery. Disoriented, we lose our way, freeze in place. Our ability to act at all—in this case, to simply move through space—proves deeply dependent on those mindless readings our senses supply. No matter how much we tell ourselves that the room's apparent *up* is its actual *down*, the body instinctively attends—trusts, if you will—the inaccurate sensory cues. They are more persuasive, bearing more weight in the self's moment-to-moment deliberations, than the factually accurate but abstract thought.

Marshall McLuhan was quick to grasp the profound implications of this humbling truth—why it is that even the most literate people can be controlled by manipulating the surrounding and largely subliminal field of sensory cues. "Everyone," he wrote, "experiences far more than he understands. Yet it is experience, rather than understanding, that influences behavior."[4]

Health food fanatics are fond of theorizing that "we are what we eat," but as political and economic beings, it is far truer to say that we tend to embody what we see and hear daily. Command our two most commanding senses, self-consciously structure the sights and sounds that surround us daily, and you will influence our conventional behavior. You don't have to preach a philosophy or stridently list a set of rules; you needn't hector that up is down, as was done by Orwell's regime in *1984*, if you can design the substrate of perceptual cues. Control the layout of our rooms, compose their medley of sights, scents, and sounds—those sensory mappings that direct us just beneath the level of our attention—and we will tend to move where you want us to and reliably "choose" what you have preselected.

In the economy of seduction, the analogue of the elaboration from the single optical illusion into an entire room of illusion is the commercial evolution of the marketplace into the enclosed mall, stadium, or entertainment center. The idea of clustering businesses is an ancient one, as old at least the farmer's market, and has a sound economic basis at its heart: an efficiency of commercial exchange that can also enrich social exchange, benefiting shopper and merchant alike. Yet each new stage in the postmodern intensification of this clustering has had a profound effect on the nature and nurture of civic life. First the zoning of businesses into separate districts; then the transplantation of those districts into outlying areas; then, beginning in mid-fifties, the rapid enclosure of those suburban malls; and finally the expansion of those enclosed shopping zones into the scope of small communities—each step has been one of increasing isolation and control. Each new phase has granted the nation's merchantry a more complete command of our sensory cues, and so, too, a better chance to package a new if ersatz "reality" (a *virtual* America) more favorable to their goals.

As should be obvious yet strangely is not, such a place, however posh, is the ideal ideological environment, one in which each stimulus can be designed to elicit a desired response. That those privatizing cowboys who clamor for the unfenced spaces of deregulation are also the sponsors of these most intensely regulated social places is an irony with serious implications for the ecological survival of democratic behavior.

The New "Old Marketplace"

Convenient examples of both the old and the new commercial environments coexist in close proximity within Seattle's city limits. Pike Place Market, poised high above the waterfront in the city's downtown, self-consciously aspires to recreate both the activity and atmosphere of the old farmer's market, urban-style. As an architectural space, the Market has two distinguishing traits, its desire for historical authenticity and its openness to the surrounding setting: it is a place whose surfaces are both scuffed and porous. Rescued from razing and redevelopment in the early seventies, the central building remains a rabbit warren of small and untonified rooms connected by warped and sloping plank floors—floors which, unlike those in L.A.'s CityWalk, are actually and not just virtually old. Yet even downstairs, within the building's darker bowels where the card traders, magic shops, and vintage clothing stores are housed, one can catch occasional glimpses of Seattle's stunning natural setting through dusty windows or stairways with views of Puget Sound. And while the back affords its vistas of geography, the top floor fronts on the heart of the city, an open gateway to its varied sociology. There, the produce market, with its many separate stalls, is only partially enclosed, allowing easy access to Seattle's street life, including its runaways and winos panhandling for bottles, and its upscale condo owners shopping for flowers.

Economically, too, the Market is infused by its natural and social environment. Most of the goods are locally grown or made, the businesses that sell them are locally owned and mostly small-scale, with a notable absence of familiar franchises and national chains. Here, in some rough approximation of Jeffersonian democracy, the economy consists of small shopkeepers, family farmers, craftsmen, and artists—each of whom, as a voting member, has some say in managing the Market's operations.

With its diversity of goods, diversity of views, and (to a degree, anyway) diversity of social classes, it is hardly surprising that the Market invites a diversity of allowable behaviors. Unlike a mall, there are no implicit dress codes, restrictions on language or permissible postures; you are allowed to be conspicuous, even ridiculous, if you so desire. Unrestrained in those ways, the Market becomes a noisy place, with something of a carnival atmosphere and shifting centers of activity; a cappella singers, street violinists, and balloon-sculpting clowns compete for attention with the theatrical hawking of produce sellers and fishmongers, each of whose performances invites participation from the passing crowd. Business is business, and even the artist takes plastic, but like the markets of old, commercial exchange is woven through with social exchange—with the possibility, that is, of actual conversation. Purchasing becomes, potentially at least, both personal and improvisational. We interact with someone who may have made the product in question, allowing for a richer exchange of information and the possibility of negotiation over price, quantity, and packaging.

What I wish to stress here is how much this potential for diverse, democratic, and spontaneous behavior depends on the openness of the Market's borders. More a membrane than a wall, its circumference allows the influx and outflow of both people and information—a wider range for our sensory substrate. As with an artistic form, the place does have a shape, and not just any behavior is allowable, but the limits imposed are loosely drawn and invite variation: more chances for real choice for those shopping which then help to determine the changing nature of the Market itself.

In the Market, as in life, though, to choose well requires that we know exactly where we are. To make an apt selection, we need a context that provides us with a rich and accurate measurement—otherwise, we might confuse up with down, the friendly plane with the approaching foe. This is precisely what the open borders of Pike Place Market tacitly supply: a sensory grid for demarcation of various kinds. With local goods and local merchants, within a building unafraid both to show its own age and to allow us views of other places, we are constantly aware of where we are—physically, historically, socially. The authenticity of the Market itself depends, of course, on this overt expression of its own location in space and time. The experience of shopping there seems unique and unrepeatable precisely because it is so suffused with its actual (and unrepeatable) locale: the city of Seattle, the region of Puget Sound. We not only know that we are in Seattle rather than, say, Boston— which, with a separate history and distinct geography, would have different architecture, a different ethnic mix, and a different array of local products—we also know that we are shopping rather than panhandling, singing, sailing, or mountain climbing, activities whose possibilities are also visible from the Market's aisles.

We can measure and grade, then, not just the particular product or place but also the activity we are engaged in. We are made aware of shopping's own place in the broader scheme of reality: how the Market is but one small part of the city's active social life, and how the city itself is but one small part of the natural creation surrounding it. One could argue, of course, that very few of the Market's shoppers are self-consciously aware of this complexity of perspectives and so aren't actively making those measurements necessary for choosing well. But as McLuhan observed, a lack of self-consciousness on the part of its inhabitants does not undermine a physical environment's moral influence—more likely, enhances it. Architecture preconfigures behavior. When we enter a place, our paths are shaped more by the immediate grounds of our experience than by the passing figures of conscious understanding. It is what we see and hear moment by moment, more than what we think abstractly, that structures the agenda of likely action.

I mustn't romanticize Pike Place Market, however, casting it as some island of innocence, or even an island of purely preserved commercial history. Although it has remained literally "in place" both geographically and architecturally, the Market, too, has had to adapt in order to survive economically. Precisely because it is interactive—that is, open to the world and so influenced by the nature of the people who frequent it—its current identity has necessarily been changed by the values of Virtual America. Just as the original financing that saved the Market had to come from both the small donations of local citizens (Jeffersonian democracy) and the megabucks of outside investors (the plutocracy of speculative money), the success of the Market today arises from the way it manages to preserve the traditional, preindustrial economy of craftsmanship, producership, and animal husbandry, even while serving the postindustrial economy of salesmanship, spectatorship, and the commodification of experience.

The nature of this compromise is revealing and hardly unique to Seattle's streets. Everywhere today, the past is preserved only to market it as a consumable experience. That one key feature of the authentic lies precisely in its refusal to label itself in any such way; that the claim to authenticity, like a boast about one's modesty, is always to some degree self-negating—these are observations which, while often noted, hold little or no practical sway. Preserve the past and someone soon will market it: mass-manufacture its imagery, buy the rights to broadcast its wisdoms, schedule its location as the latest stop on a package tour of local history.

So it is with the Market whose very authenticity has transformed it inevitably into a tourist attraction, a must-see stop and photo op for the vacationer. The old market was merely a place to do business; the new "old market" is also a place to watch others do business, and to partake in the "educational" experience of bargaining and purchasing as the locals once did. History becomes shopping, as shopping becomes touring, the seat of old commerce replacing the art museum, civic building, or nation-forming battle site as the favorite attraction of the out-of-towner.

And it isn't simply that our view of the Market is changed by this self-consciously proclaimed "authenticity"; the very flux and flow of its social exchange, its actual identity as living place, has to be affected by the shift in population that any surge of tourism inevitably brings. Now one might think that an influx of out-of-towners would increase the diversity of the Market and so enrich its social life—and in some ways it does. But the cost of travel homogenizes the crowd economically, skewing it towards the upper classes; and when the purpose of shopping shifts from everyday need to souvenir, the pressure for products also shifts from practical items to predictable kitsch.

Theoretically at least, this, too, should not be the case. According to Evangelical Mammonism, each purchase is supposed to reflect the individuated taste of the citizen-consumer making it, the sum of all purchases enacting a plebiscite on what is valued, and so expressing, through the goods and services selected daily, the choral voice of community character. But in practice, as we well know, the tourist doesn't tend to purchase according to his own taste—that is, as an intelligence shaped by his own special history, by his own unique and unrepeatable home base. Rather, he buys as he sleeps and eats—in a chain motel, on franchise food; he buys, that is, *as* a tourist, obedient to tourism's own rules, its generic sensibility of prepackaged experience. He is attracted to those products (coffee cups, sweatshirts) which, although flagrantly stamped with the logos of place, bear little of its character, or to products whose themes (rain, forests, and salmon in Seattle's case) he already assumed to be representative. Such purchases do not dynamically create the character of a place so much as mechanically reflect the image of that place, as it has been projected by the many agents of salesmanship, the flaks of "authenticity." Rather than a city discovered or a free choice expressed, a cliché is confirmed, a behavioral schedule reflexively met.

Those very qualities that make the Market authentic, then, are threatened by the tourism they inevitably invite and whose business is required if the Market is to thrive economically. Its diversity, democracy, and spontaneity, its locality in a unique and unrepeatable place, beckon ironically the placelessness of tourism, with all its homogeneity and implicit, if polite, compliance to rules. *(Back on the bus by 10:05, please!)* The ethos of the porous market is made to serve its virtual antithesis, the tourist package—though here the thing packaged is less the item purchased than the consciousness of the compliant consumer.

Virtual Public Square, Actual Corporate Lobby

Pike Place Market may suffer from its own variety of postmodern self-consciousness, idealizing commerce and commodifying history, but it does provide a far livelier environment than the enclosed malls that have proliferated throughout the country since the mid-fifties. To see this, one only has to drive five miles or so up Interstate 5 and enter Northgate Shopping Center. That I require far fewer words to depict for you this mall's basic layout and atmosphere is proof in itself of the central point I wish to make. Whether or not you have ever visited the Northwest or shopped in Seattle, you will have in mind a reasonably accurate image of Northgate's spaces, just as you know what any McDonald's, GAP, or Motel 6 in any state of the union is basically like.

This standardization of architectural space, whereby commercial environments are designed according to the abstract specs of systems and sales analysis, reflects that collaborative compression of science and capitalism which is the reigning ethos of Western life—rational materialism in its most practical and profitable guise. In the invention, proliferation, and elaboration of the enclosed mall, we can see more clearly than anywhere else how business has come to appropriate not only the products but the methods of experimental science. For although he, too, wishes to make discoveries, the commercial investor, like the scientific investigator, values predictability over spontaneity. He avidly aspires to the scientist's standard of verifiable proof—repeatable results—but with repetitious profits replacing repetitious truths as the explicit goal. To achieve that result, he borrows as well from the rigorous regimens of the scientific method: its enclosure and isolation, its reduction of variables, its use of abstract measures, its relentless insistence on external control. The result is a highly specialized and self-contained sales environment, one whose sphere of activity, as sealed as an aquarium, should perform in precisely the same way whether it is placed in Seattle, Chicago, Miami, or L.A. In the applied science of salesmanship, the mall merchant's profits—like the chemist's proven truths, like the aquarist's originally tropical fish—should know no civic or geographic bounds.

It is not surprising, then, that the very quality that most characterizes Pike Place Market (its expression of, and openness to, a unique and unrepeatable setting) has been intentionally expunged from its neighbor to the north. Oh, there are two totem poles at Northgate's northern entrance, but they are merely momentary escutcheons of local history, logos of "authenticity" that dissolve from mind almost instantly as one engages the more pressing problem of finding a space to park. Once inside—and such malls are exclusively indoor experiences—the erasure of regional signs is nearly complete. In every dimension, whether the economic, the sociological, or the sensory, we are surrounded not by Seattle (the historical place), nor by the Northwest (the geographical place) but by marketing's own ahistorical, transregional, transportable place—a realm designed to ease the task of Carlyle's Quack.

Like most malls, Northgate is anchored by large department stores (Nordstrom's, Macy's, J.C. Penney) that are the sales outlets of multimillion dollar national and international corporations, and all of the smaller shops arrayed between (Old Navy, the GAP, Victoria's Secret) are also some form of franchise or national chain. Obviously, then, most of the products are not locally made; the profits they earn are distributed far beyond the city and the state; and the work force consists not of craftsmen but salesmen, the frontline troops in our culture of seduction's perpetual campaign.

The identity of the products sold is dislocated, too, each commodity carefully removed from the defining facts of its generative progress through time and space. Because all deliveries are made through a tunnel beneath the mall's single building, one never actually witnesses their arrival and unwrapping, and this last act of concealment completes the segregation of selling from making that began in earnest in the Industrial Age. Now the whole complex process of product creation—including not only harvesting and crafting but packaging and transportation, requiring many sorts of skills by people of various social classes—has been hidden from view, and the product, with its own actual history concealed, seems to have arrived almost magically. It appears to exist only here, only now, within the virtual reality of the mall's sales display, and so more easily assumes the seductive identity evoked by that display: the faux history supplied by the salesman's patter and the atmospheric dupery of ad campaigns. These days jeans are sold as sexy and glamorous, athletic shoes as high-tech wonders, but neither of these images could easily survive if the bleak reality of their manufacture—by poorly paid women in Asian sweatshops reminiscent of Dickens's doleful London—were made visible at the point of sale

But, of course, we don't see the seamstresses at Northgate's mall, nor the truck drivers, nor the delivery personnel; we don't hear their comments, engage their stories, and so can't measure ourselves, our social standing and our wealth, in relation to theirs. The isolation of products and concealment of their history also conceal the human reality of the producer economy and help to enforce a de facto segregation—of Third World from First, blue collar from white collar, makers from sellers and, to the extent that race still determines the pocketbook, black and brown from middle-class white. By design, then, the outer sphere of the enclosed mall is only partially porous; its borders are passable but their weave is tight. Like the fashionable nightclub whose bouncers overtly choose by type which would-be partiers they allow inside, the mall predefines, if more covertly and abstractly, whom it would invite.

And once we are inside, this reduction of variety extends far beyond designations of class and into the realm of allowable acts: behavior itself is deliberately restricted to a narrower band. Northgate, and malls like it, do beckon the privileged, but they beckon them into a sphere of severely (if discreetly) regulated activity. That we become less free when entering an enclosed mall; that we actually have fewer available choices there, even leaving behind certain supposedly inalienable rights, forced to check them like bags at the door—these are not generally acknowledged facts. They are not acknowledged because they are not directly sensed, and they are not sensed because the substrate of sensory cues has been carefully designed to suggest something else. In the enclosed mall, the living body of democracy has been cleverly supplanted by a look-alike mannequin, one dreamt by Mammon's evangelizing salesmen and dressed by his agents of behavioral control.

Our malls *are* plentiful, of course. To recent immigrants, or the escapees from the East's utopian economies, accustomed to privation, long queues, and the bleak domain of empty shelves, the American mall can seem wonderfully diverse: a blaze of many-colored clothes in every size and fashion, appliances for necessities they had yet to imagine, multiple luxuries in extraordinary wrappings. Yet this flagrant variety is misleading in a way. Like the paperback bestseller bound in multiple colors, a sameness lurks beneath the surface display. Like all scientifically designed experimental domains, a radical reduction of variables calibrates the mall's actual aims. Its apparent diversities are, instead, something more like accessories—which is to say, they multiply options for but a single activity, excluding in the process most other activities. How can I consume: let me count the ways.

Not only are there fewer kinds of things to do in situ; there are fewer things one is allowed to do de jure. Again, however, this doesn't appear to be the case, for the sensory cues have been carefully designed to simulate the opposite. With its broad and bright spaces, its planters and fountains and occasional park benches, the enclosed mall's arcade seems to suggest the open streets of the city. It seems to present an upgraded version of Seattle's Pioneer Square—one airbrushed of flaws by the science of progress, and so litterless, weatherproof, and panhandler free.

This apparent likeness, however, is less actual than virtual. We are, after all, not outside but inside. While the walks and streets and lantern-lit park in Pioneer Square are public property, Northgate's arcade is privately owned. Rather than confusing up with down, then, as the fun house might, the mall's ecosphere of quackery confuses inside with outside—and so, associatively, private with public. And these confusions are deliberate. They are crafted in pursuit of seduction's usual goal: to make us feel free even as we submit to the seducer's own schedules of behavioral control.

The political guarantees that we expect in public spaces do not apply within the mall's rigorously controlled commercial domain. What we have entered, in effect, is a corporate lobby, and as in any such lobby, we are constrained to behave in only those ways the corporation will allow. Although a few states have affirmed a limited right to free speech within shopping centers, even there the implementation has been left to the corporation. Elsewhere, malls ban all forms of what they call "non-commercial expressive activity"—a prohibition that can include wearing a T-shirt with a political message. In general, when shopping in today's enclosed mall, the citizens of the world's first modern democracy cannot leaflet, speechify, picket, panhandle, pass out balloons, or play a guitar without the explicit permission of the management.[5]

This unpleasantly ironic political truth was exemplified by an incident at Disney World, which, as a self-contained amusement park, is a close first cousin to the enclosed mall, alike in its pursuit of a scientifically controlled sales environment. When a visitor there dared to bear a picket sign protesting the cost of a hamburger (oh, the radicalism!), she was quickly whisked away by security. Out of sight, out of mind; there then gone, with but a wave of Tinker Bell's censoring wand. With the stakes so small, such an incident seems more a parody of oppression than a real political event. Yet the woman's mild statement and the sudden appearance of a heretofore invisible security force together accentuate how blandly obedient our behavior tends to become inside these spaces—how we seem to "get it," narrowing the range of what we do or say without ever being explicitly told.

Unlike coercive governments, which tend to favor shows of force, the mall's seductive simulation requires that its machinery of control remain concealed. In fact, surveillance is everywhere—such is the nature, after all, of science's domain, its experiments requiring constant observation. Minnesota's enormous Mall of America has well over a hundred surveillance cameras, all feeding their images to a constantly manned security center. How they might be put to use was discovered by a *Harper's* reporter when his official guide chastised him for being seen on camera conversing with a janitor. In *this* civic square, talking to the help (like protesting burger prices) is out of bounds, and journalists will be watched to see that they don't.[6]

The social control built into the mall's design depends especially on this sensory inequality, best symbolized by a one-way mirror's lack of reciprocity. Once inside, we are constantly being watched and objectively measured by people and machinery we cannot, in turn, watch or measure. Computers, hidden cameras, plainclothes police trace our credit and track our movements. Highly paid consultants study our behavior on slow-motion videos in an earnest search for the perfect layout for product display, even as experts in sensory research supply those subliminal medleys of sound and scent that have been scientifically shown to maximize sales.

That most of this observation-for-manipulation is done without our permission would disturb us mightily if it were, say, the FBI that was filming our movements in Harvard Square. But this is different. What is being protected here isn't the authority of a repressive regime but the integrity of a seductive atmosphere, the efficiency of a profit machine. Besides, we are not outside but inside. Despite appearances, we are not in a public sphere which, ruled by a democratic government, has been designed to value free exchange and spontaneous behavior; we are in a private sphere that is ruled by a commercial management and that values instead financial exchange and predictable behavior. We are less citizens of a community than subjects in a laboratory, submitting to controls seductively arranged to maximize sales.

Like laughing along with a laugh track or walking in line on a prepackaged tour, this submission to seduction seems benign. We scarcely notice the homogenization of people and behavior that these commercial domains both invite and require. How easy (if unexciting) it is to swim in the aquarium of their micromanaged serenity: the lack of crime; the freedom from bad weather; the removal of annoying clocks and stressful sirens; the litterless glide from store to store, free of the open palms and misspelled signs of the drunk, the deranged, the guilt-inducing poor. We don't really want to search out the mildly retarded employees who, hidden away in the Mall of America's concrete basement, sort our trash for less than minimum wage.[7] And what losses we do acknowledge can seem justified by the material plenty that the mall readily supplies.

One could argue, too, that this trade-off—of rights for goods, of civic and sensory diversity for commercial accessories, of freedom *to* experience for freedom *from* certain unattractive experiences—is merely temporary and, in the legal sense at least, always voluntary. We freely choose to visit these posh yet subtly restrictive domains, and if we violate their special rules, those speech and dress codes designed to boost sales, our worst punishment is to be expelled. Yes, the protester is made to relinquish her sign, but she isn't sent packing to a Vietnamese-style "re-education camp," nor even forced to buy one of Disney World's exorbitant burgers.

Yet what "temporary" and "freely choose" mean bears a closer scrutiny in a nation increasingly configured by Virtual America's sophisticated duperies. Are we really freely choosing to surrender certain of our rights when the environment we enter so deftly simulates their perpetuation? We may *understand* (to use McLuhan's terms again) that we have entered a private sphere, but what can that understanding mean, what weight can it carry practically, when our moment-to-moment sensory *experience* strongly suggests the opposite? Even if we could translate such abstract knowledge into the sort of belief that actually affects embodied choice, where could we choose to shop instead? How easy is it for us now to follow that blithely voiced, libertarian advice and "vote with our feet" economically?

Free choice presumes real and readily accessible alternatives. But as Wal-Mart replaces the neighborhood clothier and Home Depot the local hardware store; as franchise strip malls proliferate and mega malls merge with amusement parks and gambling casinos; as mail order, the home shopping channel, and tele- and cybermarketing compete with them all for our shopping dollars, transforming retail sales from a social engagement into a disembodied data exchange—it becomes increasingly difficult to find, much less frequent, truly local and democratic markets.

Worse, the places where we work are themselves becoming less local and more global, less attendant to community needs and more obedient to the protocols of external control and efficiency: outsourcing, downsizing, mandatory overtime, employee surveillance. And when we aren't working or shopping, we may frequent one of our new entertainment centers—a domed stadium, casino, educational theme park, or video arcade—more sealed spheres within which the fiats of fun tacitly exclude the right to free expression. In such a linkage of closed spaces, "temporary" becomes customary as, domed-in and dammed-up, we lose our democracy's most indigenous places. Like the free-running salmon, freedom itself becomes endangered: a species of behavior bereft of the habitats required to sustain it.

II. In the Mall of the Mind:
The Commodification of Consciousness

Nature today is the social absolute, or better still (for we are not concerned with politics here) the Gregarious.[8]

—Roland Barthes

Even if we could rigorously avoid the enclosed mall and all its architectural cousins, we would have difficulty escaping the subliminal influence of its acquisitive values, for the moral field that prevails there transgresses the mere bounds of physical space: the ethos of the mall can haunt our minds even if we don't haunt the mall. That uneasy truth was brought home to me by another child-centered anecdote. Some friends were leaving a restaurant in the mid-seventies when, already buoyed by the warm glow of good companionship, Szechuan spicing, and a couple of beers, they were greeted by a spectacular sunset: day effusing into night, crimson-fringed clouds streaking across a cobalt evening sky. That rare conjunction of inner well-being and outer beauty held them still for an awe-filled moment until the silence was broken by a little girl who, exiting the restaurant behind them, blurted out: "Look, Mom—just like on TV!"

One of our primary ways of gauging the world is through comparison. We are constantly measuring each new event against a store of past experiences to find those likenesses that can reframe the alien within the terms of the familiar. For that little girl, the virtual reality of television programming had become the common grounding of her experience, the once natural sunset now the figurative oddity which she could only explain by reference to TV. That this flip in grounding is broadly representative of the postwar period can be supported statistically. From 1950 to 1960, the percentage of American households that owned a TV surged from 9 to 87 percent,[9] and by the early seventies, the average citizen's weekly TV viewing rose to twenty-six hours, even as radio listening equaled some twenty-one.[10] Presuming a forty hour work week and eight hours of sleep per night, that means many Americans were spending up to 65 percent of their free time inside the virtual worlds of the electronic media. With the arrival of the Internet, the ratio between the various media has changed but not the overall time devoted to them or the degree to which those communications are saturated with commercial solicitation. As of 2010, the average time per day spent by U.S. adults on all media was eleven hours, with nonstreamed TV still the dominant mode.[11]

In that little girl's response, then, I see living proof of the historical arrival of Roland Barthes' "social absolute." Her story, along with the statistics that support it, confirm the findings collected last chapter in the chart *What the Nose Knows*. Together, they point to the practical demise of "outside": that is, to the ongoing replacement of unenclosed space and unsupervised time by the ambient and invasive productions of the Gregarious. The erection and projection of this social absolute is a foundational attribute of both Virtual America and the international economy it aspires to hew after its own image: McLuhan's global village privatized and monetized into an exitless mall. The institution of this artificial place on such a scale has been made possible by the inherent qualities of the electronic media—their speed, pervasiveness, and psychological persuasiveness. Yet the constellation of values that defines this social absolute, it is crucial to note, was not technologically predetermined: the medium did not define its current supervening message

That is why—unlike Barthes, who was writing about Pop Art—I *am* concerned with politics here. There are, after all, other financial forms the electronic Gregarious might have taken—as, for example, a public utility or a private but ad-free subscription service. But with the ceding of the media to consumer advertising, beginning with radio (a political decision that was, by no means, a foregone conclusion), *our* social absolute began to assume a specific ethical character: a hyper materialism whose triumph required the tacit demise of many of the old American virtues. Unlike the mass-market books and movies it supplanted, radio and TV programming was being "brought to us by" the consumer corporation's marketing division. What their game shows, sit-coms, and dramas were finally *for*—to answer that critical question I posed in chapter 1—was the pitching of their sponsors' products, and that same economic model's primary intention has been rapidly applied to each of our new electronic media.

Despite the utopian claims of early enthusiasts and the genuine achievements of the open source movement, our digital revolution has followed the same pattern. Each new instrument—email, the search engine, the social networking site—has been converted to serve the needs of advertising. As the civic square was replaced by the enclosed mall, the new civic meeting place online is now being cluttered with pop-up billboards, banner ads, and inbox spam. And just as we do when entering a mall, we now tacitly surrender the rights of privacy in these digital locales; our online searches and messages are routinely recorded, analyzed, and then packaged as data to be sold to the nation's advertisers. No third party was reading our personal letters or recording on our phone calls, but in the upgraded age of gmail and Facebook, our personal communications (like our televisual entertainments) are being "brought to us" not only *by* but also *for* the consumer corporation. The task at hand now is to consider why this commodification of nearly all our civic and private meeting places has occurred.

↬

To begin, let's admit that Mammon's current evangelists have a valid historical point, if one that their linear thinking erroneously extends to the "end of history": in the cradle of modernity, economic materialism was, in fact, a crucial ally of religious and political liberty. Through selective grants of ownership, the possession of private property did provide the grounds for freedom from feudal control, each freeman's farm or craftsman's shop circumscribing a protected space within which a single family might begin to shape its own destiny. Ownership not only offered a chance for wealth and status; over time, it also provided the protection of law and the possibility of precious, selective political rights. Indeed, as they evolved in the West, Mammon and emancipation were so intimately intertwined that the license to do business and the right to vote were eventually encoded within a single word: "franchise."

During capitalism's long middle phase, however, while democracy was established and extending its base, and while the aristocracy of blood was slowly giving way to the oligarchy of money, ownership became less a means to independence than an end in itself. As political rights were guaranteed and religious values faded, possessions themselves began to seem right—not the just means to, but the core meaning of, the burgher's good life. This commodification of Western values began in earnest in the nineteenth century when it was described, decried, or celebrated by a variety of thinkers ranging from Mill to Melville, from Carlyle and Marx to Whitman and Dickens, but the process intensified greatly after World War II when capitalism, shifting technologies and targets for conquest, extended its domain to the service economy. As we were once trained to desire and so acquire "hardware" products (furniture, cars, appliances), we were eventually induced to desire and acquire "software" experiences (exotic meals, extended therapies, entertainment of all types, astonishingly diversified professional advice). Mammon had furnished the home, had cluttered every corner and living room shelf, and in desperate need of *Lebensraum*, he turned to the mind, the very seat of acquisitive desire. The brain had shape, size, and weight, but the mind was an apparently dimensionless space and so, too, a market incapable of satiation. Into it, merchants might pitch innumerable units of packaged experience, a whole new line of infoproducts designed for the mind.

In the mania of its expansionism, economic materialism had "dematerialized." Whereas a hardware product had to be designed to fall apart and took up space even when thrown away, a software service erased itself—the meal gone, the movie over. Inherently consumable, it lent itself more readily to that addictive process through which the unnecessary was made necessary and thus exploitable for repetitious profit.

One can't overestimate the importance of this shift in marketing domains from artifact to information, for it enacted a truly epochal change. Under the extended regime of this new economy, all things were reconceived as commodities: personalities were sold by publicists, reputations leased for sponsorships, wombs rented out as rooms once were. Under this regime, controlling as it did the electronic media, all domains of American life were suffused with the messages and motives of marketing until the inner sanctum of the mind itself became a closet crowded with the logos and logic of consumer commerce. Fully saturated (a mental state closely akin to, but subtly distinct from, indoctrinated), we began to conform reflexively to that logic, losing in the process that negative capacity, so crucial to freedom's actual practice, to "just say no"—the clarity and courage, in Bartleby's words again, to "prefer not to."

So it was that an economy that once provided us the grounds to free ourselves from feudal oppression and churchly dogma began to assert itself dogmatically through its new control over both civic space and public communications, creating a social absolute more purely keyed to the needs and beliefs of its Evangelical Mammonism.

These interrelated findings about "the mind of the mall" and "the mall of the mind" cast the utopian claims of the privatization movement in a very dubious light. Yet Newt Gingrich and crew did get one thing right back in 1995. Our democracy's future does now rest on a vigilant quest for deregulation—but only if we understand where, by whom, how often, and in what guise, our lives are being regulated. Yes, like the immigrants who still risk all to reach our shores, we should believe in the sweet-voiced dream of Cole Porter's song—but only if we grasp how our latest version of that heroic script has the danger all wrong. In Virtual America, it is not government's sheriff but commerce's cowboy that has, increasingly, "got us surrounded." Every day, in multiple ways, he is the one who is fencing us in.

3

In the Shrine of Virtual America's Soul

If you can write a nation's stories, you needn't worry about who is making its laws.[1]

—George Gerbner

IN AN AMERICA THAT officially endorses science and whose formal validation of truthful doctrine is usually swaddled in the reassurance that "studies have been done," one also commonly hears the dismissive phrase "it's just a myth." But that is the prejudice of the rational-materialist mind speaking, a mind whose means for knowing the world, however acute and useful, cannot fully measure, much less produce, mythological truths. We remain a storytelling species. And because the stories we habitually tell ourselves about ourselves become crucial mental tools in the maintenance of both stable communities and coherent personalities, the supposedly trivial pursuits of our entertainment industry, when taken as a whole, are hardly trivial in effect. The demise of virtue—that is, the "transfer of (moral) sovereignty" under study here—could not have occurred without a parallel transformation in our most popular narratives, especially in those broadly presumed to be "good for the kids." That same little girl who had become accustomed to TV's version of a sunset's material reality was also absorbing as normative that medium's version of moral reality, the ethos conveyed by its stories, games, and ads.

When evaluating the influence of popular narratives on America's children, one name predominates: the Walt Disney Company. The maturation of the postwar generations has been inseparable from the tutelage of this entertainment empire, whose unvarying sensibility was shaped by its founder in the 1930s. One historian has gone so far as to call "Disneyism . . . the

world's cleverest and most successful new religion,"[2] and because successful new religions do both reflect and enforce changes in the covenants that
direct everyday behavior, the bulk of this chapter will take a close look at
Disney's radical revisions of the traditional fairy tale and amusement park.

A common danger of any close reading, however, is that the very act
of magnifying the subject at hand can obscure the social context that in-
forms it. And so I will begin by taking a broader look at the sorts of editorial
changes that Americans have been imposing on children's stories "for the
good of the kids."

Disney's Tale: UnGrimming the Judeo-Christian Conscience

"Put on a happy face."[3]

When, in chapter 1, I insisted that pain was an indispensable feature of the
human experience, the excessive numbing of which can sometimes prove
morally as well as physically dangerous, I supported my argument by citing
both *Paradise Lost* and "The Three Little Pigs." Here was a truth so universal,
I implied, that it calibrated the plain folk wisdom of the child's fairy tale no
less than the baroque sensibility of the theological epic. What I failed to
specify then, however, was *which* version of that fairy tale I was referring to,
for among the many signs of our national commitment to a wish-fulfilling
analgesia has been an earnest rescripting of the children's classics. This
collective intention to, as it were, *un*Grimm the traditional fairy tale was
analyzed by child psychologist Bruno Bettelheim in his 1975 study, *The Uses
of Enchantment.*

> . . . the prevalent parental belief is that a child must be diverted
> from what troubles him most: his formless, nameless anxieties,
> and his chaotic, angry and even violent fantasies. Many parents
> believe that only conscious reality or pleasant and wish-fulfill-
> ing images should be presented to the child—that he should be
> exposed only to the sunny side of things. But such one-sided
> fare nourishes the mind only in a one-sided way, and real life is
> not all sunny.[4]

Bettelheim then provides a more detailed critique of the revisionism
driven by these parental beliefs. He sees two primary intentions at work
here, each detrimental to the therapeutic power of the time-tested narrative: *rationalization* (a reduction of complex symbols that are rich with
emotional resonance to abstract morals) and *prettification* (an overemphasis
on the sunny side of things.)

The desire to rationalize is a natural expression of our scientific world-view, its overweening need to convert mythical thinking into the logical terms it prefers. The urge to prettify emerges either out of a utopian denial of the darker side of human nature or, contrarily, out of a fearful recognition of it, which then spurs overprotective parents to insulate their children from the nasty news for as long as possible. On the surface, the second motive might seem more justifiable, but as Bettelheim points out, children already feel the impress of that nastiness; they *have* a human nature and so experience rage, terror, aggression, oversized desires, and self-centered appetites no less than adults. The original tales were designed to both admit and restrain those impulses—to domesticate them through the ritual rehearsal of the narrative—and in ways specifically appropriate to the various stages of a child's development. Lighten the nature of the stories, and that chance for domestication is weakened or lost.

This drive to unGrimm the classic fairy tale can be found on all sides of our culture wars. Although the standard assessment of the politics of censorship would distinguish the right's squeamishness about sexuality from the left's aversion to violence, in actual practice such a distinction is rather blurry in the field of children's literature. The supposedly conservative Disney often softens the violence as well as removes the emblems of carnal desire in its animated versions of the traditional tales, while some feminist revisions prove to be as prudish about sex as the kiddy lit sanitized by the Christian right.

In the first printed version of "The Three Little Pigs," collected in J. O. Halliwell-Phillipps' *The Nursery Rhymes of England* (1842), there are severe consequences for irresponsible behavior. Having foolishly built their houses from insubstantial materials, the first two little pigs are summarily eaten by the voracious wolf who, famously, huffs and puffs and blows their houses down.[5] But by 1892, in a collection called *Green Fairy Book*, the prettification process has already begun. In this longer and more prosaic revision by the English folklorist Andrew Lang, the wolf has been replaced by a fox. The change is more than merely decorative, for Lang's villain is a sophisticated predator, one who has learned the virtues of delayed gratification, capital accumulation, and communal sharing. Rather than instantly devour the two imprudent pigs, the fox carries each of them back to his den, saving them for a feast that he is planning for his friends once the third has been captured. In this version, the villain is still outsmarted and slain by that last little pig, but unlike the original, the hero doesn't eat his adversary. Instead, he frees his captured siblings who, we are assured, have learned their lesson, and all three now get to live "happily ever afterwards" in the bastion of the brick house.[6]

A hundred years later, the prettification is complete. In Golden Books' nonviolent revision not only do all the siblings survive, the reckless along with the prudent, so does the wolf himself. A pale version of the earliest ravenous predator and a slacker compared to Lang's industrious fox, this huffer-and-puffer literally falls asleep on the job, at which point, rather than being boiled alive and eaten by the pigs, he is merely imprisoned. Abracadabra, the 'd' word has been fully expunged from the mythic vocabulary. No capital punishment can be permitted in *this* fairy tale kingdom where the grimmer symbols of psychic reality must conform instead to make-nice sentiments.[7]

As silly as such changes might seem, they do succeed in sapping the psychic impact of the original tale. If all the pigs are allowed to survive and the villain is shown falling asleep on the job, the stakes of the story are trivialized. And if the victorious pig doesn't finally eat as well as slay the wolf who has tried so hard to devour him, then the symbolic power of his final triumph is greatly diminished. For, as Bettelheim notes, the voracious wolves in these tales are not just emblems of external danger; they are also projections of the raw appetites that all children have and must learn to control.

In "The Three Little Pigs," the physical story about protecting oneself from a perilous world is also a psychological drama about self-discipline's mastery over unchecked desire. Without any overt moralizing, the symbolic structure of the plot has externalized the inner battle between two varieties of appetite: between the raging hunger of the wolf (which, destroying all but the sturdiest of boundaries in the form of the brick house, would devour instantly and completely anything edible) and the appetite of the third little pig, who, through careful planning, manages to satisfy his hunger three separate times without being caught by his adversary. Illuminating the crucial distinction between prettification and domestication, the plot is constantly acknowledging the reality of appetite, the necessity of eating, even as it aims to discipline that most fundamental of human desires. In this sense, the original conclusion achieves the perfect symbolic register, a happy ending rooted in a plausible passage into a new maturity. Not only is the third pig, and he alone, fully victorious over the wolf (prudent desire defeating voracious desire); he is victorious *through* eating. The value of appetite is endorsed, even as its most primitive incarnation is slain and consumed.

Children don't understand this on a conscious level, of course. They can't explicate the moral of the story nor articulate the nature of the profoundly pleasurable reassurance they feel when hearing it. But through a bee sting or a dog bite or a close encounter with an unhappy playmate, all children recognize that the world can be a perilous place. And because they can't escape their emotions and desires, because they do have a human nature, they are also painfully aware that they themselves are not always sunny on the inside. The prettified tale falsifies the profound psychological realism of the original's symbolic terrain. Unable to identify as closely with these new-and-improved characters, children lose the chance to take the transformative narrative journey with them. Literally too good to be true, these revisions are not actually good for our kids.

My concerns here, of course, apply only to those children whose guardians are actively intervening in their lives, and too many kids in Virtual America, cable-fed or streamed adult entertainment on a nonstop basis, have no supervision over the narratives they absorb on a daily basis. But for those who do, the linked habits of rationalization and prettification prove to be an equal-opportunity danger. The political allegiance may vary from camp to camp, but when the nation's kids gather around the evening fire for the supervised tale these days, the sunny side is usually up.

Still, no one has proselytized for the sunny side more thoroughly or effectively than Walt Disney, whose influence on the national character commenced nearly two decades before the first Aquarians were born. In 1928, just a year prior to the market's crash, Disney released the wildly popular animated cartoon *Steamboat Willie* and never looked back. Translating one of the oldest storytelling forms (the fable, whose origins go back to preliterate animism) into the most potent narrative medium of the day (the moving picture newly enriched by sound), the company had created in Willie a comic hero who resonated powerfully with the common man. Quickly renamed Mickey, this plucky mouse who whistled his way past adversity, this meekest of mammals made mightily immune by his ever buoyant mood, supplied a reassuring model of triumphant survival—not just for the kids, who are always the smallest and weakest members of society, but also for the adults of that era, whose sense of self-reliance was being overwhelmed then by a newly emerging mass society of teeming cities, huge corporations, and electronic media on a national scale, and, too, for a workforce greatly shaken by the Great Depression.[8]

Having struck box-office gold, Disney never strayed far from the soul and substance of his original formula as it evolved in those early years: the "imagineering" that conveyed populist fantasies through the very latest technologies, in story lines that promised a feel-good experience for the mouse-in-all-of-us. As a pioneer in the new information economy, Disney was offering an assembly of simulated experiences as uniform, repeatable, and predictable in their own way as Henry Ford's mass-manufactured automobiles, but although this product, too, promised its customers reliable transportation from here to there, the film's destination was a temperamental one: a guaranteed ride, in difficult times, to "the sunny side of things."

Through a process of identification native to all narrative art and previously enacted through the totemic rituals and myths of the preliterate tribe, the audience would bond with this virtual mouse who was the new totemic creature for our post-literate age. To watch the show was to join the clan, now called a "club." It was to borrow the psychic power of the totemic creature by donning not just Mickey's ears (which were sold in abundance as a spin-off product starting in the 1950s) but also, and far more importantly, Mickey's smile—the outer emblem of his very American-style insouciance. Time after time, the Disney brand would supply the same empowerment first encoded in Mickey's character: the existential impotence of the mouse magically cured by the psychological tonic of irrepressible hope.

This "mind cure" was often achieved through the process of unGrimming someone else's story. Such is the case with the company's second full-length animated film, arguably most revealing of Disney's many products. Glauco Cambon has called the 1883 children's novel *The Adventures of Pinocchio* by Carlo Collodi[9] one of the three most influential works in Italian literary history.[10] Yet most Americans have no familiarity with the original, relying instead on Disney's animated adaptation, which has been repeatedly shown for over seventy years. In an animated film, a simulation of bodily motion is achieved through carefully drawn discrepancies in the physical positions of a cartoon figure within consecutive frames. Likewise, if we look at Collodi's original story and then at the pattern of discrepancies present in Disney's adaptation, we can see the *moral* configuration of the conventional American imagination in cartooned motion, rapidly fleeing, as if Road Runner from Wile E. Coyote, the traditional cautions of the Judeo-Christian conscience.

First sung in 1940, subsequently used in promos and intros as a kind of company anthem, and now saturated deeply into the mindscape of four consecutive generations of American kids, Jiminy Cricket's promise in Disney's *Pinocchio* that "when you wish upon a star / makes no difference who you are" expresses the promissory premise of Disney's moral vision, its seductive blurring of American egalitarianism with infantile narcissism—a democracy of rights with an imperium of desires. Believe, just believe in this fantasyland and, with a wave of its wand, the many impediments of reality's land are instantly gone. Abracadabra, wishes become facts, irrespective of both the limits of one's identity and the resistance of one's locality. No need,

59

then, to "know thyself" or to survey the surrounding circumstances. No need either to account for others' star-cast wishes when "if your heart is in your dream / no request is too extreme." In the pat guarantee of that true rhyme's closure, as borne on the sweetly soporific swing of Leigh Harline's melody, we can hear a newly evolving twofold credo for the American child: a superstitious belief in the Magic Moment (that our dreams *can* come true "out of the blue") and a disingenuous faith in the Fable of Innocence (that the fulfillment of those dreams, no matter how extreme, will be ethical as well.)[11]

In Collodi's novel, a series of fantastic episodes allegorically traces that coming-of-age which, ideally, transforms each of us from a juvenile puppet-ry, pulled hither and yon by our immediate desires, into a mature adulthood which, self-disciplined by love, accounts for others. That plot's basic shape does remain evident in the film, but this version was being made in Hol-lywood, the ideological capital of a new consumer economy whose ultimate mission was to "close the sale," and whose success so often depended on the conjuring of seductive semblances to conceal moral essences. Such was the spirit of Disney's adaptation where the appearance of the old parable of maturation was co-opted to serve the economy's ethos of avid entitlement.

At its subtlest level, this co-opting was temperamental, Disney's imagi-neers using the soundtrack and backdrop to create the upbeat mood of a song-and-dance show. But as was the case with the unGrimming of the fairy tales examined earlier, the process of "disneyfication" also required an outright torquing of narrative facts. Among the most flagrant of those changes was the characterization of Jiminy Cricket himself. In the novel, the otherwise nameless Talking Cricket is a minor character who, early on, tries to instruct the proto-human puppet in just such a fashion as a creaturely embodiment of conscience might. Given wooden legs by his father-maker Gepetto, the boy-puppet has immediately run away and run amuck, and when, in the aftermath, the Talking Cricket voices the obvious lesson (that he should obey his father instead of heeding his own impulses), Pinocchio responds by hurling a hammer at this would-be moral mentor, smashing him to death against a wall.

So it is that in Collodi's savvy rendering of the graduating stages of emotional maturation, Pinocchio reacts like many toddlers do when, high on their newly won abilities to walk and talk, they are first confronted by annoying insects weaker than themselves and by annoying counselors who advise that freedom must be checked by an internalized caution. The willful two-year-old doesn't want to hear that his newly acquired "can-do" must be balanced by a carefully calibrated "preference *not* to."

Spared the hammer, endowed with a chipper first name, a mellifluous voice, and an official designation that transforms his symbolic role as Pinocchio's conscience into a literal office, Disney's version of Collodi's Talking Cricket has been elevated to the status of both a major character and the story's narrator. That dramatic shift in the role's quantity is more than matched by a revision in its quality. As a major character, this embodiment of conscience has now been revised from earnestly annoying to comically ingratiating. Within the story, Jiminy is a friendly, winsome, tag-along sort of fellow: someone who rarely raises his voice to criticize; who, more buddy than mentor, calls his moral charge "Pinoc"; and whose small size and general ineffectuality as moral guide serve as reliable triggers for a host of visual jokes.

As it turns out, however, *this* talking cricket is not without persuasive authority, for in his entirely new role as narrator, Jiminy serves as our conscience as well, and far more effectively. He not only literally opens the story's book (the visual frame that cleverly enacts the transformation of the story's medium from Collodi's print to Disney's film); much more importantly, his signature song "When You Wish Upon a Star" has first and last say on what *Pinocchio* means. Both as we enter this make-believe world and as we leave, his closed couplets pronounce, patly and exactly, the moral of the story—the moral, that is, as radically revised by Disney's imagineers.

As a literary artist, Collodi had discerned within the cricket a credible image to fit one specific phase of the very human story he aspired to tell. Mythical reasoning has its own standards of accuracy which, because its work must bridge the differences between our sensory-physical and our moral-psychological selves, are those of apt likeness rather than exact equivalence. Its natural medium is associative rather than abstract (metaphor over math), and it is always striving to discover a secret sharing between apparently disparate things. Collodi's selection met that standard of accuracy in that he located a true secret sharing between our outer and inner worlds. A cricket does metaphorically resemble the earliest stage in the evolution of a child's conscience because it is an insect that "talks" (and conscience is a kind of internalized voice), and because it is just the sort of vulnerable creature that little boys love to crush (just as they love to blot out the initial voice of moral inhibition). And these likenesses hold despite the literal fact that a cricket is a cricket and not a toddler's proto-conscience.

But Disney's animators were not simply artists—they were imagineers, and as such, they were obliged to heed the virtue claims of the mood merchantry who paid their wages. By translating the engagement of literary experience into the diversion of light entertainment, they radically revised the characterization of conscience itself, transforming its tenor from anxiously self-correcting toward soothingly self-endorsing. The same image (cricket) remained, but its meaning and feeling had so radically changed that it constituted an almost total reversal of Collodi's intent. This masquerade worked, in part, because the Disney team did succeed in locating another, if very different sort of secret sharing within the original metaphor. Drawing on a separate dimension of "cricketness," their personified creature was more akin to that persistent musician whose hypnotic compositions (techno on Darvon) seesaw us to sleep on lazy August evenings. Conscience, as it spoke and sang directly to Disney's prewar audience, was now assuming the psychological function of the lullaby.

Let's step back to consider the relevance of that shift. This book's title is *The Demise of Virtue in Virtual America*, and it would be difficult to find a more vivid example of that demise—"the transfer of sovereignty" from one set of virtues to another—than Disney's radical revision of Collodi's Talking Cricket. Read the book, then watch the animated film and, abracadabra, the character of conscience is transformed from the inner voice that chastises, urging us to corrective action, to the inner voice that anesthetizes, even while endorsing our most extreme desires. The sociological context also matters here, for this reconfiguration of the American conscience wasn't being pushed by a radical intelligentsia but by our mainstream entertainment industry. Notable as well: the film was released some six years before the first Aquarians were born.

The broad acceptance of this new ethical compass required the effective extinction of its predecessor. In the mechanical chime of Jiminy's rhymes, we can hear the death knell of the spiritual urgency that had once spurred the Judeo-Christian conscience. With its new mythos of innocent entitlement extinguishing the old anxieties about right and wrong, the cricket's song was putting to sleep, in the nurseries of the nation, any cautionary belief in forbidden fruit and, with it, any inclination to "prefer not to." The lyrics did mention love once in passing, yet the emphasis was now turning away from Chesterton's tough imperative to "love the world without trusting it"—which is precisely what Collodi's Pinocchio suffers to learn— toward something nearly the opposite. Kids were being encouraged instead to trust in both their own desires and the world's imminent (if mysterious) compliance with them. They were being told to believe, just believe in a truth reconfigured by the Magic Moment and in a goodness redefined by the Fable of Innocence. "When you wish upon a star / Makes no difference who you are / Anything your heart desires / Will come to you": the promise could not have been more explicit. As expressed by the literal conscience of the Disney mythos, all desires were now good desires, plausible desires if (wishing upon a star) we just desired fervently enough.

To have been sold on the notion, in 1940 of all years, that no dream is too extreme and (later in the song) that "fate is kind" might now seem the cruelest of quackeries to the historically-minded. But it is just the sort of spiritual mood music that, focusing on the stars and so diverting attention from who and where they really are, keep the mice smiling, passively expecting that "out of the blue . . . [their] dreams will come true." And if we return to that touchstone question of ultimate intentions cited at the start, asking what this new moral mindscape was finally for, a plausible purpose quickly appears: one couldn't imagine a climate of thought more conducive to the evangelical claims of Mammon's marketeers.

Disney's Land: The Sanctification of Fantasy's "Place"

Saturation, as I defined it last chapter, refers to that conversion of our everyday ethical environment that supplied the necessary psychological precedent for our whole society of salesmanship. It marks the historic reversal when a once marginal set of human behaviors—"the due prurient insincerity, open voracity for profit and closed sense for truth" characterized by Carlyle's Quack and Dupe—became the norm for our mainstream economy, revising both the stories that we were telling our kids and the places where we chose to congregate. And this revision in the moral nature of our social spaces can be traced not just to the emergence of the enclosed mall but also to the conversion of the old carnival into the new theme park that was occurring simultaneously. Here, too, Disney proved to be a transformational figure.

In *Fables of Abundance*, Jackson Lears traces the origins of modern marketeering back to the showmanship of the various itinerant entertainers, peddlers, and patent-medicine men who crisscrossed agrarian America in the eighteenth and nineteenth centuries. Prior to urbanization, modern transportation, and electronic entertainment, most Americans lived in rural isolation, within small and culturally homogenous communities where they were land-rich in comparison to their European counterparts but diversion-poor. The movable store of the Yankee peddler with his melodramatic rhetoric and newfangled products, the medicine man's wagon with its portable theater for pitching miraculous cures, the seasonal grounds of a market fair where economic exchange assumed the exultant air of the ancient harvest festival—for rural Americans, these were the sorts of evanescent places whose tents, stalls, and improvised stages "specialized in 'what was strange, absent, and not mine.'"[12] There, briefly and in relative safety, a rationalizing, utilitarian, still largely Protestant nation could experience the otherwise proscribed: the outrageous claim, the hedonistic pitch, the amazing yet economically useless skill, the exotic (read *erotic*) display, the pagan belief, or game of chance.

Eventually, in a kind of consolidation whose funhouse mirror both mimicked and mocked the historical growth of the national corporation, the merged Barnum & Bailey Circuses acquired a representative variety of these boundary-testing acts and shows. Within their tents and booths could be found the dwarfs, giants, and bearded ladies who broke the normative bounds of body and gender; the clowns whose pratfalls and costumes transgressed the requirements of a dignified decorum; the trapeze artists, sword swallowers, and lion tamers who challenged the limits of safe behavior; the gypsies, exotic dancers from the East, and Wild Men from Borneo who flagrantly broke the Calvinist mold with a tarted-up show of the cultural other; and, too, the fortune-tellers, hypnotists, and games-of-chance pitchmen whose claims defied the official consensus on scientific causality. Here, for a weekend or a week on the margins of town, one was supplied the rare gift of public permission: to *be* superstitious, to gamble, to overeat, to scream like a child with fear or delight, to stare unabashed at the freak or at the sexually attractive man or woman dressed in tights. Here was a place where adults and kids alike could be "taken for a ride" beyond the bounds of gravity and gravitas, above the rules of reason and the restraints of status, and then returned to the ground of one's everyday life without loss of face or significant fortune.

These diversions bore within them a serious purpose. Insomuch as the self-sustaining vitality of any human society balances precariously between the potential anarchy of individual appetites and the potential tyranny of communal rules—between a return to the "animal" and a reduction to the "mechanical," with danger lurking on either side—it is a crucial function of the mythic imagination to explore the dynamic border between the sinful and the civil. Because the most effective forms of virtuous self-discipline, the most lasting and adaptive, are those that admit both the desires that have called them into being and the dangers of rote obedience to any rulebound scheme, moral vigilance requires that the forbidden, too, be actively imagined. In gauging the best way to conduct ourselves, the voracious wolf is as necessary to our collective thinking as the prudent pig, the illicit carnival as crucial as the solemn civic ritual or sacred rite.

What happens, though, when the spaces reserved for the illicit go legit and the carnal is airbrushed from the carnival's grounds? What happens when, "for the good of the kids," the transient spectacle of the forbidden is converted into a permanent playground of virtual innocence? Early on, as a metaphor for the psychic sources of Virtual America, I cited the anecdote of the little boy who tried to step inside his favorite storybook. Recognizing that desire's universal appeal, Walt Disney grasped in the early fifties that his band of imagineers already had the skills in hand to do just that. They *could* transform the virtual fantasies of their animated cartoons into a permanent and publicly accessible space, a life-sized Magic Kingdom.

As is often the case with the entertainment industry, two stories coexist as to the motives for building Disneyland: one public and inspirational, the other private and commercial. The first emphasizes the primacy of creativity as magically supplied by "the talent"; the second stresses the imperative of profitability as mercilessly pursued by "the management." The financial motives for building Disneyland were as simple as they were perennial: then as now, the movie business was a boom-or-bust affair, and the Disney brothers, Walt and Roy, were seeking new ways to generate a steadier stream of corporate profits. By contrast, the inspirational story casts Walt as a concerned parent who, finding no suitable entertainment for his family, built a better alternative on his own initiative. As the immortal prophet of a civic religion whose spiritual premise is the moral innocence of American materialism, Walt still narrates this myth of origin in the theater on Main Street in his Magic Kingdom. There, he plays an avuncular version of the moral visionary, someone who aspired to reform the seedy carnival by replacing its freak shows, scam artists, and amateurish illusions with a new theater of family-friendly fun, expertly rendered.

And so it came to pass that on forty-five acres in Anaheim, the prophet imagineered fantasy into a "land," a pseudo-place of a sort once only staged in romantic tableaux for kingly courts but of a scope and perfection never seen before and democratically accessible to the paying public. Inside that land, not just the company's cartoons but the nation's past and future had been uplifted into the venues and vehicles of sheer amusement, both history and science conveyed via a state-of-the-art entertainment that was suitable for all ages. In Disneyland's theater, the fourth wall between stage and audience had been dissolved. The old static diorama of the Western settlement, the sort once found in dusty museums behind prohibitive glass or in the shoebox projects of grammar school kids, had given way to a Frontierland one could actually traverse in a life-size stage coach. Later, thanks to the ingenuity of Walt's robotics engineers, the terrifying crime spree of the buccaneer was also recast into a genial ride, mom and the kids safely floating in little boats past serial scenes of maritime plunder, as mechanically simulated by "animatronic" pirates.

Across the way, tomorrow too became a land. There, the exhibits confirmed the American Dream as it had been revised to fit the utopian creed of Evangelical Mammonism, reassuring the postwar crowd that a material upgrade equaled moral improvement and that (if not every day, then every decade) technology would make us better and better. In yet another "jux-taposition of the incongruous," this promise of a perpetually better tomor-row—human progress as brought to us by consumer commerce—coexisted with depictions of an Edenic past whose perfection was based, at least in part, on the very absence of such high-tech products.

Entering the park, families passed through Main Street USA: a movie-set version of a turn-of-the-century Midwest hamlet, supposedly based on Walt's hometown. This warm and fuzzy nub of civic nostalgia included quaint shops and a general store, and it was overflowing with sweets from soda fountain drinks and old-fashioned candy, as sold by friendly employ-ees in period costume. Here, as in Frontierland, the exclusion of unpleas-ant historical facts (along with any signs of dirt, litter, decay, or discord) was as essential to the overall theatrical effect as the obsessive inclusion of period-authentic architectural details. In Disney's sunny version of 1900, Jim Crow did not exist, nor the suffragette movement, nor the problem of public drunkenness that would lead to prohibition, nor the anxieties of an encroaching modernity that was already on the verge of extinguishing the ethos of small-town life.

This process by which an intensely sophisticated artifice (the obsessive engineering of theatrical effects) evoked the apparently simple and natural place (democracy's Eden) was characteristic of all Disney's infoproducts, beginning with the first. Main Street's relation to an actual turn-of-the-cen-tury American town was metaphorically equivalent to Mickey's relation to a real—that is, dirty, vermin-laden, sexually prolific—mouse. Likewise, the Disney cartoon's apparent recovery of totemic anim*ism* (that ritual which permitted the preliterate person to become one with Nature by assuming the potent identity of a particular creature) fronted instead for the postmod-ern triumph of anim*ation*. Where the magic of the former supplied a mythic means to bridge and so test the critical boundary between the preliterate psyche and the wilderness on which its survival depended, the new magic of imagineering mediated the division between the postmodern psyche and *its* environment: that highly mechanized "social absolute" which was taking Nature's place in everyday life.

In the totemic myths and rituals of the anim*istic* imagination, natural creature and tribal person traded places. Bears and salmon resembled peo-ple, assuming human voices and motives, while clan members merged with their affiliated animal, wearing a bear's fur, say, or imitating the motions of a spawning salmon in a stylized dance. But in the anim*ated* imagination, as first fully realized by pomo shaman Walt Disney, persons swapped identities with their now fully mechanized representations, wearing the abstracted ears and imitating the stylized cheer of the virtual mouse. In the new ritual transformation, the two-way metamorphosis was between the humane and the robotic. The park created an imaginative space where machines aspired to become ever more lifelike (Walt's imagineers as corporate Gepettos relentlessly pursuing a better Pinocchio) and where, reciprocally, people aspired to become cartoon-like, receiving in return a uniform, predictable, and repeatable experience: a reliable ride to "the sunny side of things."

Inside Disney's enclosed land, this reciprocal simulation of the robotic and the humane proliferated. Just as Walt's animatronic figures were fashioned to simulate people in the Pirates of the Caribbean ride, real people were refashioned (costumed and scripted) to simulate the company's cartoon creatures. The park was (and is) patrolled by actors playing Mickey, Minnie, Goofy, and Pluto, their costumes complete with neutered bodies and fully enclosed head-pieces molded with their characters' perpetual smiles. Waving and mutely interacting with the kids, these animated persons (impersonations of animations?) were meant to convince Walt's youngest "guests" that they had actually stepped inside the cinematic storybook, its animated fantasy now their own immediate, interactive, and circumscribing reality.

This commitment to a global reenactment of the Disney film experience was so complete that all the park's employees were dubbed "cast members." Each had been trained at Walt Disney University in the fixed protocols of customer relations, especially in the theatrical imperative of never "breaking character." In the self-proclaimed Happiest Place on Earth, social interaction between employees and customers must itself be mechanically animated, spontaneity expunged on behalf of a uniform, predictable, and repeatable sequence of staged behaviors. Further, given the fragility of the fantasy, the mask must never slip. To sustain Tomorrowland's future-without-fear and Main Street's past-without-regret, the show and its cast had to stick to a ritualized script as strictly determined as those in Deuteronomy, but one whose prevailing intention had now become fun for profit instead of piety for God.

Here, too, then, the moral end of the new civic religion of Disneyism could be found in its beginning. For all its range and technical sophistication, the Magic Kingdom was, at heart, but a recapitulation of Disney's first successful cartoon series: a multimirrored reflection, animatronic extension, and architectural projection of its monotonic cheer. To enter this new ecosphere of fantasy was to absorb the old mindscape of Walt's animated mouse. From the public's perspective this chiropractic mood adjustment was the ultimate lure—what Disneyland was finally *for*. Americans would pay not only top dollar but highest homage to the man who could make them believe in the specific make-believe of this Magic Kingdom.

Henry Ford had been the most popular and influential entrepreneur of the early twentieth century. By refining the extraordinary productivity of late industrialism and applying it to the mass manufacture of the automobile, Ford, more than any corporate figure of his time, pushed the economy toward today's consumerism. But by 1928 when "Steamboat Willie" appeared, Ford was no longer at the forefront of commercial innovation. America's economic future would be shaped more by the "software" of commodified experience, as brought to the nation by the gregarious invasion of cinema, radio, and then TV. Walt Disney became the great entrepreneur and populist hero of this second revolution and, as such, arguably the most important commercial figure of the mid-twentieth century. His empire of the Mouse both exemplified and accelerated the economy's switch in emphasis from the industrial manufacture of utilitarian tools to the postindustrial animation of desirable moods. With consumerism's new emphasis on marketing, many corporations began using the images and narratives of seductive fantasy (updated versions of Lears's "fables of abundance") to pitch their products. But in a distillation of postmodernity's emerging ethos, Disney was selling fantasy itself.

The subsequent transformation of this fantasy into a land symbolically marked, then, a critical shift in the nation's character. When it opened in 1955, the Magic Kingdom rendered literal and physical our ongoing enclosure within a new "social absolute" of commercially-controlled civic spaces and electronic entertainment. As with nearly every Disney project, the quality and thoroughness of the simulations were exceptional, even amazing, but not the general nature of the ambition or the overall strategy for staging it. To the contrary, Disneyland was completely attuned to the populist dreams and corporate techniques of the era, as they have been described in my first two chapters. The park opened just as the nation's first truly enclosed mall (Southdale Shopping Center in Edina, Minnesota) was being built, and both would operate on the same profit-driven principle of sensory enclosure for seductive control.

As armpits and mouths were being cleansed of their unpleasant smells in these postwar years, as Living's Town itself was being stripped of most visible signs of death, disease, and poverty, the new-and-improved amusement park would also be freed of the unhappy, unwholesome, unfit, and unclean. According to the new Deuteronomy of fastidious normalcy, Nature's real and disturbing "freak show" had been banished from view, replaced by the comforting conjurings of a Nature 2.0. Bodily oddities had now been reduced to the amusing modeling of Walt's cartooned creatures, moral deviancy niftily transferred to the electronic puppetry of his harmless robots. The help, too, had been carefully recast and industrially animated. The old lowlife carnies who had worked the games and rides of the traditional American amusement park, and whose frankly hostile and lustful stares (on beyond objectifying the female body) could have peeled the paint off a parsonage, were replaced by college students trained in the emotive robotics of customer relations—trained, that is, to "put on a happy face."

Through techniques similar to the ones used in Northgate Shopping Center, the park's customer base was also sanitized and homogenized. Just like the castle of old, Walt's kingdom had been enclosed for security and control. An admission fee excluded the sociological riffraff while inside the park's walls an invisible but omnipresent security staff monitored the crowd for any sign of undisneyfied behavior: a category that could range from drinking, to inappropriate displays of affection, to protesting the cost of a Main Street hamburger. Because they, too. were part of the masquerade, the customers, like the help, mustn't ever be seen breaking character.

Someone like the early American Puritan—who was, ideally, always earnest, always focusing on the grimmer side of human nature, and who was trained, therefore, to recognize (within that child-in-all-of-us) not an immaculate Pollyanna but a corruptible Eve—might have benefited from an occasional vacation into a disneyfied levity: a day off, with the kids, from his anxious preparations for the Day of Wrath. But by 1955, when a nominal allegiance to Judeo-Christian belief was masking a broad conversion to the ritual behaviors and core beliefs of Evangelical Mammonism, Disneyland did not provide anything like a transient escape from the ruling ethos of the day. Whereas a trip to the carnival had supplied a seasonal chance to test the boundaries of the forbidden and the strange, a visit to Walt's park provided a passage into the ideological center of a consumer economy that increasingly depended on adults behaving like kids, "wishing upon a star" and routinely chasing the pixie-dust promises of a million marketeers.

That crucial distinction between the marginal and the conventional highlights why the historian's claim that Disneyism has become our civic religion is not as extreme as it first might seem. Insomuch as carnivals supply an escape from normative beliefs where temples offer an intimate engagement with their spiritual core, Walt's theme parks do, after all, serve a churchly function: they are shrines to those beliefs, the Magic Moment and the Fable of Innocence, that have gradually reshaped the soul of our republic.

Disney's World:
The Demise of Democracy in the "Community of Tomorrow"

"Why should I run for mayor [of Los Angeles] when I'm already king?"[13]

—Walt Disney

The political danger of idealizing marketplace Mammonism is a cautionary tale also deeply encoded within Disney's own history. As noted last section, the company's theme parks practice a kind of tacitly emasculating internal governance similar to that favored by the enclosed mall, and the growth of this preference for behavioral control can be traced throughout every stage of the company's spectacular growth. In the rapid evolution of Disney's product line from a ten minute cartoon to a full-length feature film, to a forty-five acre "land," to a 27,000 acre "world," we can spy that same progressive flip in scale from moral figure to moral ground—in this case, from virtuality as *diversion* to virtuality as *dominion*—which has driven the broader shift in our nation's values. As highly compressed models of Virtual America's moral logic, Disney's theme parks exemplify that shift in the cultural ecology which, under the guise of celebrating our democracy, has been rendering freedom an endangered species. And like so much of the self-induced misery that characterized the last century, this enclosure and erosion of freedom's native ground have proceeded under the banner of utopian progress.

Cultures can improve or degrade by degree, but emotional pain, social deviancy, and existential suffering (not to mention vanity, envy, gluttony, sexual jealousy, and other unsunny tempers and moods) cannot be solved like a geometric proof or cured by a dose of the latest elixir mixed by the folks at Pharmaceuticals, Inc.—yet out of a blend of aesthetic, psychological, and political motives, the various regimes of modernity have often tried to affect just such a cure. With a wave of their authoritarian wand, whole groups—the defiant, the deformed, the morally unclean, the conspicuously poor—have been swept from view; they have been imprisoned, committed to asylums, evicted to the rural margins, confined to urban ghettos, or excluded from the crimeless yards and crackless streets of the gated community.

But one mustn't confuse the cosmetic manipulation of public appearances (*seeming*) with an actual revision of either the body politic or the human condition (*being*). Given the falsity of its premises, each such purified "virtual reality" must periodically break character, revealing the full and messy range of human motives and behaviors, as well as exposing the very social classes whom the elite would exclude but whose labor has been required to keep the illusion afloat.

So it was that despite the immediate popularity and profitability of Disneyland, the principal imagineer of the Happiest Place on Earth was not himself entirely happy when, in the early sixties, he surveyed what he had wrought. Although the Magic Kingdom's original land had been agricultural, the site of orange groves, the theme park's unparalleled success had spurred the construction of multiple low-end businesses—cheap motels, souvenir shops, bars, and fast-food restaurants—all mustered to serve the sudden influx of visitors, which had already reached five million annually by 1960.[14] Walt was trebly offended by this "juxtaposition of the incongruous": the tawdry sprawl of overt commercial avarice pressing up against the storybook walls within whose realm he had so fastidiously staged his Fable of Innocence. Not only did he find this new encircling neon junkyard aesthetically ugly and both physically and morally unclean (sins that always blurred in Disney's new Deuteronomy of Mammonite purity); worse, its proprietors were making a buck off Disney's own so-called guests, siphoning profits that were rightfully his.

Orlando was the company's aggressive response: over 27,000 acres, bought secretly and on the cheap in 1964 and 1965, which would supply enough space to build other and far larger theme parks while still providing a huge greenbelt buffer to keep the unclean competition both out of sight (for the sake of the show) and away from the customer (for the bottom line). The sheer size of the purchase would also serve, however, a third and far more audacious purpose: it would help justify seizing *political* control over this new and enormous commercial venture. The virtual space of the Magic Kingdom was about to acquire actual sovereignty. Once again Disney was on the fringe of cultural change. Just as, in the ethical and spiritual realm, Disney's "land" had supplied a ritual intensification of Virtual America's postwar investment in Mammonite values, Disney's "world" would become one of the earliest and most audacious examples of privatization.

As drafted in its entirety by Disney's lawyers, scarcely amended by Florida's regulators and lawmakers, and passed in an astonishingly irresponsible twelve days with but a single dissenting vote, the legislation that licensed the new park allowed the company to form what was, in effect, its own private government. As Richard E. Foglesong observed in his detailed history of Disney's relations with the Orlando region, *Married to the Mouse*, this newly conceived state within a state bore an ironic resemblance to Vatican City inside Rome, thus further confirming the spiritual status achieved by the Mouse. Powers ceded by Florida's elected officials to this governing entity, eventually called Reedy Creek Improvement District (R.C.I.D.), included:

the authority to provide its own fire and police services as well as levy taxes and issue its own tax-free bonds; immunity from building, zoning, and land-use regulations; the rights to pave roads and lay sewer lines, to manufacture liquor and license its sale, to construct its own international airport and even a nuclear power plant. Other, administrative agreements dramatically lowered the tax evaluation of the Disney properties. And all these concessions were granted without any compensatory obligation on the part of the company to help support the enormous public costs in infrastructure and social services that inevitably follow such huge developments.[15]

It would be inaccurate to call the discussions that preceded these agreements negotiations. After a careful corporate study conducted in utmost secrecy and in avid pursuit its own self-interest, the company dictated the terms of its own legislative charter, after which, with no careful study, those terms were immediately, passively, even gratefully accepted by Florida's officials. If we ask how the full host of democracy's public servants could have been reduced to such docility, we find two reasons.

The first is financial and all too common in today's privatizing scene. Local communities, desperate for economic development, compete among each other by offering infrastructure improvements and tax incentives to attract large companies that, loyal only to their own ledger, will expand or relocate to the most compliant region. (A civil war of this sort was conducted in 2001 when Boeing announced that it was moving its corporate headquarters out of Seattle and overtly invited competitive bids.) In the current political environment, this compliance to corporate needs is understandable if often misguided. By winning Disney World, for example, the Orlando region attracted development on a scale beyond even the company's wildest predictions, yet the legislation was so one-sided that Disney now draws most of the profits while local government remains stuck with the social consequences and associated costs in roads, schools, hospitals, and prisons.

But while Florida's financial generosity, if ill-advised, was a common tactical response to economic need, its political concessions were historically unique. When a beaming Gov. Claude Kirk ceremoniously signed the legislation on May 12, 1967, with Roy Disney on one side and his own young daughter on the other, he was ceding sovereignty over some forty-two square miles of Floridian territory to a non-democratic commercial enterprise, and one that wasn't even locally based. With a scratch of the pen, representative local government was gone. Only Walt Disney—whose carefully crafted public image of moral innocence and patriotic allegiance had made him the most trusted figure of his day—could have won such a set of dramatic concessions while still making it seem a hopeful occasion: the surrender of democracy but one more product of postwar progress, enacted (as the photo op with Kirk's cute blonde daughter overtly suggested) "for the good of the kids."

Yet the proper provinces for make-believe are amusement parks and movie theaters, not governor's seats and legislatures, where a scrupulous pursuit of the public interest demands that pixie-dust optimism give way to a mature skepticism about human intentions. Fantasy can entertain delightfully, but as a favorite tool of demagogues, quacks, and cons, it can also gull maliciously, and Disney's legislative proposal proved to be one of the greatest (and most revealing) cons of the postwar era. Like most con games, this one arrived wrapped in a utopian appeal. In graduating from "land" to "world," the claims of the next generation of Disney's 3-D virtual realities were also upgraded, the earlier guarantees of a safe diversion now enhanced by intimations of a serene dominion: a new-and-improved *political* order.

In a promotional film shown after Walt's unexpected death on December 15, 1966, Walt posthumously promised to build, with the legislators' help, not only a new Magic Kingdom five times the size of the original wonder but also a second theme park, to be called Epcot (Experimental Prototype Community of Tomorrow), which he praised as "the most exciting and by far most important part of our Florida project." Epcot was a response, Walt added, appealing to a widely held concern in the aftermath of the Watts riots in 1965, "to the problems of our cities." In approaching this crisis, the company aimed to start "from scratch on virgin land and build a special kind of new community." "Taking its cue . . . from the creative centers of American industry," this brave new world would apply the latest ideas and technologies to the day's social problems. Warming to the pitch in familiar Disney terms, Walt assured his audience that "everything in Epcot [would] be dedicated to the happiness of the people who live, work, and play there." A voice-over then described the community's radial design, its industrial center surrounded by playgrounds, churches, and schools, and by a mixed set of high and low density residences that would eventually house some 20,000 lucky citizens.[16]

This was Walt's final performance, his posthumous pitching of an actual and not just virtual community, one where the cinematic promise of happily ever after would step off the screen to be imagineered into a real and permanent form. The appeal of such a utopian project was deeply seated in the American character. Some 340 years earlier, the Pilgrims had landed in New England where, "start[ing] from scratch on virgin land," they intended to build their own City on a Hill as a beacon to the world and a fulfillment of biblical prophecy. The specs had been dramatically revised—from a Protestant theocracy preparing itself for Christ's second coming to a Mammonite technocracy promising salvation via the "creative centers of industry"—but the desire to believe in an imminent and happy "end of history" had remained undimmed in the American psyche. Drawing on that hope, Walt insisted that, with a wave of his wand, he could not only imaginatively conjure but materially construct a New World never-never land on the sandy soil of central Florida—if only the area's elected officials (like Peter Pan and his siblings to Tinkerbelle's plea) would believe, just believe . . .

And they did—Claude, the grown-up governor, no less than Claudia, his namesake daughter. The extraordinary sovereignty awarded the company was based on the officials' childlike trust in Walt's pixie-dust promises: their trust in the man (to whom, after all, they had already entrusted their children's care), and their trust in the project's utopian prospects, which harmonized completely with the ethos of commercial salesmanship that ruled the day.

In the classic configuration of the seductive con, a gullible hope for a fantasy future—the gold in a mine that doesn't exist, the wedding bells whose ceremonial sound will never ring—is induced to justify a tangible surrender in the here-and-now. Florida's officials ceded all that they possessed, their political authority over "virgin land," on the presumption that once Epcot had been constructed, its 20,000 citizens would naturally reassert democratic control. But as Foglesong shows in a survey of consultants' reports and intraoffice memos, the company never really intended to have Epcot occupied by permanent citizens.[17] Here, too, as in the first Magic Kingdom, the population would remain transient, divided between "cast members" and "guests"—that is, compliant employees and consuming tourists—all compelled or seduced into staying "in character" during their temporary residence. If we watch what the Disney team did rather than what they said, *their* creative solution to "the problems of our cities" was, in fact, the permanent substitution of corporate authority for communal democracy: the municipal mayor was being replaced by the managerial king.

So it was that, in his final performance, the most trusted figure and prominent patriot of the postwar period misled the American public, with the aim of usurping political authority. Walt Disney's lifelong mastery of evoking sentiment through American symbolism was put to use subverting the very core of American principles—our strongly voiced, foundational preference for democratic governance. After their leader's death, the remaining corporate team, headed by Roy Disney, continued the con, misleading legislators, regulators, journalists, and the public about their intentions for this "most important part of [their] Florida project." Yet it wasn't the nose that eventually grew on this vast animatronic Pinocchio but the corporate bottom line—an outcome which wouldn't have surprised Florida's officials if they had chosen to analyze the moral logic of "the management" rather than believe the magic spell cast by "the talent." The growth of their own income and not the welfare of our kids or the health of American democracy was what the Disney Company, then as now, was finally *for*.

With their constitutional charter passed, the founding fathers of Disney World then set up a complex shell of a governance structure, one in which two pseudo-residential communities provided the legal cover for their corporate sovereignty and where (in a reactionary return to property rights over egalitarian empowerment) voting power was directly linked to acreage owned. The charade persists to this day: two official municipalities—Bay Lake and Lake Buena Vista, with just sixty or so residents, mostly the company's own executives and their families—whose virtual existence justifies R.C.I.D.'s actual governance. And so it goes in the real Magic Kingdom of Disney's rule, the happy face of a paper democracy "put on" to justify the corporate monarchy of upper management.

Metafiction: Mapping the Moral of Disney's Double Story

Because even true revolutionaries don't create their new social orders ex nihilo, we mustn't lose sight of the cultural context that favored the success of the Magic Kingdom. Just as Henry Ford had consolidated the emerging ideas of late industrialism to reorganize production in ways that would license the consumer economy, Walt Disney formalized and purified principles of showmanship already present in the new electronic entertainment industry. The perpetual buoyancy of Mickey Mouse was, for example, a true temperamental rhyme to the teen roles played by Mickey Rooney in the 1930s, even as the broader worship of childhood's innocence made Shirley Temple a top box-office draw at roughly the same time. Disney's was not an alien schooling, then, but one jointly discovered by the impresario and his mass audience inside an already emergent marketing culture whose first inclination was to blur economic value with ethical value, the pose of innocence with the urge to buy.

Nor should we limit the historical roots of this new civic religion to American shores. Walt's Fable of Innocence clearly echoes the voices of numerous European predecessors, including those Victorians who helped to compensate for their own ruthlessly rationalizing economy with a sentimentalized view of both childhood and agrarian life. And the Victorian prettifications of the child and the preindustrial hamlet were themselves drawn from earlier ones: those Romantic complaints against modernity that had stressed, as the cost of rational-materialist progress, a tragic loss of simplicity and harmony in Western life. Once upon a time, the happy guileless tribe and the happy sinless child were both at one with a benign Nature, only to be estranged by the astringent fruit of modern knowledge with its tendencies toward a corroding skepticism, an alienating self-consciousness, and an industrial despoiling of the natural order. The unGrimming of the human story, it seems, was a compensatory fantasy that reliably arose wherever and whenever industrial modernity took hold.

But this story of a tragically lost innocence is never one that can resonate alone for long in the conventional American consciousness. Here, the Romantic stance was constantly skewed by other powerful features of the national character, especially the can-do optimism born of both the immigrant experience and a Cartesian belief in utopian solutions to the human predicament. In the American mind, lamenting a lost past had to coexist somehow with an inexhaustible belief in a perfectible future—a Phoenix-like faith that human happiness could be engineered. Disneyism became our civic religion primarily because its core aesthetic appeared to resolve this inherent contradiction, the stresses of which were becoming all the more pressing as the rationalized economy enclosed and invaded nearly every domain of American life, including the homestead of the nuclear family.

Those stresses expressed the darker side of our consumer's economy's astonishing abundance. For all the material progress that scientific capitalism had produced by 1928, its relentless project of rationalizing our most intimate beliefs and traditional practices had also served to disenchant the world. Its atomized assembly lines had sucked the joy out of work while its underlying philosophy had reduced the human spirit to a "ghost in the machine." Even as it became a rationalized industry itself, American entertainment would have to provide a diverting compensation for an economic order whose sheer scale and intrusive control were reducing once self-reliant men into mechanized mice, and no one pursued that ironic mind cure more fiercely or profitably than Walt Disney.

Under the aegis of his imagineering, the factory techniques of animation would labor to reproduce the fairylands of old. In a clever reversal, the actual machine would now hide behind its virtual ghosts, invisibly generating a whole pleasing host of fantastic creatures—of fairy godmothers, antic sorcerers, and daffy talking dogs—all following the tracks of pixie-dust plots. Under Walt's leadership, mechanism itself would re-enchant the world as the "miracle of science," in its last ironic phase, labored to resuscitate a superstitious worldview: that same *buena vista* (beautiful view) which, blending the Magic Moment with the Fable of Innocence, was evident in his subversive revision of Pinocchio's conscience.

Nowhere has the pedagogical power of that Magic Moment been more perfectly staged than in Disney's parks. There, just as the carved wooden toy becomes the real little boy whom Gepetto wished for "upon a star," Mickey steps off the flat screen to become a 3-D walking creature who meets and greets America's children. As the ritual climax of an expensive pilgrimage to our nation's Mecca, the easy instancy of this transubstantiation reinforces the belief that the metaphorical and mythical can "come true" literally and materially "out of the blue" at any given moment. Such a lesson inscribes, at the earliest age inside Anaheim and Orlando's shrines to childhood's lasting innocence, the truthfulness of magical thinking—the dubious belief that our favorite fantasies are always on the verge of becoming material realities.

As befits the shrine of a civic religion, that message is one that acutely minds our current place. Disney's Magic Kingdom *is* "good for the kids" in this sense at least: its rituals of initiation do prepare them to participate in the political economy of artful deception and willful self-deception, of quackery and dupery, that they are bound to enter once coming of age. It teaches them to believe in the many magic kingdoms of today's fantasy-driven consumer marketplace. As a warrior society trains its children to the moral imperatives of soldiering, preferring such traits as rote obedience, tribal allegiance, and a stoic acceptance of physical danger, our marketing culture has, over time, logically scripted a moral primer keyed to those habits of mind—seductive affability, superstitious gullibility, and unbounded self-indulgence—that are best suited to serve its own preferred activities of buying and selling.

But this schooling is only good for our kids in the larger sense if we accept the primary principles driving it. The virtue of its moral logic depends, finally, on the truth of its Mammonite claim that *more* (profits for the seller, consumption for the buyer) *must equal better*. It requires that we agree to believe in the Magic Moment and in the Fable of Innocence, and that we heed the crooning voice of its animated conscience that "no request is too extreme." Yet look where you will within the wisdom literature of the world, Eastern or Western, pagan or Judeo-Christian, look even in our collected fairy tales before they were unGrimmed by both sides of our culture wars, and you will find that the judgment pronounced on those beliefs is remarkably consistent. In tale after tale, history after history, the consequences for such wishful thinking are, well, unrelievedly grim. And as our own recent descent into the fraud and folly of economic ruin suggests, any story whose moral insists otherwise is just a myth.

4

The Pharmacy of Pain Dissuasion

"I cheerfully repeat that the Samaritan Pain Dissuader,
which I hold here in my hand, will either cure or ease any pain
you please, within ten minutes after its application."
"Does it produce insensibility?"
"By no means. Not the least of its merits is that it is not an
opiate. It kills pain without killing feeling."
"You lie! Some pains cannot be eased but by producing
insensibility, and cannot be cured but by producing death."[1]

—Herman Melville
The Confidence-Man: His Masquerade

THE PRIMARY PURPOSE OF all designed enclosures is control—the careful composition of physical structures, sensory cues, and social rules to educe a specific set of preferred sensations and endorsed behaviors. Because our emotions powerfully influence our behavior, such artificial environments aim to shape how we feel as well as what we think, and in Virtual America's inner spaces this sort of "mood management," once primarily the province of art and religion, has become the object of intense scientific scrutiny, most often for the purposes of commercial exploitation. Which color schemes, patterns of product displays, seductive sales-pitch narratives, which mix of scents and medley of sounds subtly effused, will keep the customer inside your store and activate a buying mood?

Commerce may be funding most of the findings of these new applied sciences for its own narrow purposes, but a deeper moral premise has been driving our broader attempts at behavioral control through environmental enclosure—a sincere belief, separate from the aims of seductive salesmanship, about what is best for us as human beings. Dating back to the Enlightenment, this moral premise was most purely articulated by Jeremy Bentham's utilitarian claim that pain is "the only evil," from which it follows that the eradication of pain—the pursuit of analgesia, broadly conceived—should be an unambiguous good. These virtue claims, when combined with our collective faith in scientific progress, have led to the presumption that the chambers of our hearts, like the rooms in our houses, might eventually be kept within a thermostatic comfort zone: the mood equivalent of a tropical isle's 72. They have led to the belief that "happily ever after," the ending that sweetens so many of our most popular narratives, is not, after all, a goal too extreme. Not if our heads as well as our hearts are in the dream. Not for a nation that has invented and perfected so many machines. If our digital devices can get better and better, then why not our selves or souls, our innermost tempers?

The TV laugh track that both tells us when to laugh and then keeps us company when, alone before our sets, we do; the piped-in music whose "audio architecture" (the actual term used by Muzak) structures and instructs a soothing mood; the multiple-screen, surround-sound video of my airport entrapment, its bubble of seemingly benign distraction; the Disney imagineer's litterless, crimeless, theme-park village, the sunny stasis of its perpetually grinning cartoon faces, and all the casinos and arcades and total-experience restaurants that mimic its methods to model their spaces: together these designs, allied in their attempt to engineer a kind of happiness lite, enclose our minds and recalibrate our moods with increasing frequency.

Still, of all the many ways we now try to regulate our mental states, none is more invasive and elusive, more difficult to gauge scientifically or introspectively, than our use of psychoactive drugs. Forget for now both alcohol and illegal drug use, our private attempts at mood regulation. My concern here instead is with official diagnoses and legal remedies. Two recent studies starkly quantify our nation's ironic addiction to "pain dissuasion." Sales of prescription painkillers tripled from 1999 to 2010, with a sufficient number dispensed in the final year alone to medicate every adult for a month[2]; more relevant here, one in ten Americans over the age of twelve is now taking an antidepressant drug, with Prozac, Paxil, and Zoloft the most commonly prescribed.[3]

This trend of redefining painful mental states as biological diseases best treated with powerful psychoactive drugs begs a thoughtful scrutiny, as does the related search for the sort of psychic steroids that can boost our everyday emotional performance. *Can* our moods, like our seasonal machines, become "new and improved," and if so, what would such an improvement mean?

Better Living through Chemistry

The hope for a chemically cushioned comfort zone is hardly new. As my opening quotation attests, the desire to "kill pain without killing feeling" is perennial, as is the attempt to exploit it commercially. In the cited passage, Melville's con man, acutely aware of the multiple ways in which irrational hope can be converted into hard coin, has assumed the disguise of an "herb-doctor" to hawk his "Samaritan Pain Dissuader," which he claims can salve all human suffering, mental as well as physical. Against the skeptic's furious rebuttal (which is also clearly Melville's own view) that certain pains are intrinsic to our lives, some of today's bona fide herb doctors—such as Brown University psychiatrist Peter D. Kramer, a long-time proselytizer of Prozac's benefits—turn to hard data wrested from clinical trials. Citing that evidence, they conclude that what we once could only address superstitiously or morally, with either snake oil elixirs or sermons on the virtues of stoic endurance, we now can treat rationally and materially through the proven products of biochemical research—products which, over time, are bound to improve.

Certainly those claims are not without their historical precedents. Our management of physical pain—from ether, aspirin, and Novocain to today's more sophisticated forms of analgesia and anesthesia—has improved dramatically since Melville's day, and in the case of some severe forms of mental illness, such as schizophrenia and manic-depression, strong drugs have at least moderated symptoms if not enacted cures. The appeal of Prozac and the other "selective serotonin reuptake inhibitors" (SSRIs) has been precisely their claim that they kill emotional pain without killing feeling—that they "dissuade" mental suffering, especially the crushing symptoms of depression, without otherwise distorting our perception of the world. Unlike previously prescribed mood-altering drugs, which one by one fell out of favor as their serious side effects became evident, the SSRIs have been advertised as nonaddictive and (just as important to a society driven by the sober regimens of economic efficiency) neither sedating nor intoxicating. Like the smart weaponry that the Pentagon has been developing, this family of drugs is said by its supporters to target the enemy—depression, now mechanistically defined as a "chemical imbalance"—without causing any statistically significant collateral damage.

The postwar American public had twice before fallen in love with a particular family of medically prescribed psychoactive drugs, even as the nation's Beatniks and hippies were touting the redemptive powers of their illicit ones. In a process accelerated by the new electronic media, as soon as Miltown and Librium were released, in 1955 and 1960 respectively, ordinary citizens—both homemakers and businessmen—began demanding prescriptions. In the year following Miltown's release, one of twenty Americans was taking some form of tranquilizer, a term cleverly coined by Miltown's creator, Frank Berger. By 1969, even as efforts were under way to further criminalize marijuana and LSD, Librium's successor Valium had become the most heavily prescribed psychoactive drug in America. A year later, an astonishing one of five American women and one of every thirteen American men were on some form of tranquilizer or sedative. In each case, the new drug's popularity was based on the broadly held presumption that the miracle of medical science could ease or erase life's emotional woes— that tranquility could be bottled and then safely imbibed—and both crazes inspired a flurry of articles and TV debates about the moral implications of "happiness pills."[4]

Although now the specific form of unhappiness to be targeted was depression rather than anxiety, "blues" instead of "nerves," this cultural pattern repeated itself with Prozac's release in 1988: the same broad publicity, the near instant popularity, the subsequent debates about the ethics of "cosmetic psychopharmacology"—a term coined by Kramer in his 1992 international bestseller *Listening to Prozac*.[5] With his Brown affiliation, medical degree, transparent prose style, and access to individual patients whose cases dramatized the subject at hand, Kramer became the perfect vehicle for Prozac's proliferation among the nation's educated classes. He didn't appear to be either a corporate shill or a daffy academic radical like Timothy Leary; he showed real concern for the patients in his care; and he worried dutifully about the ethical issues of prescribing drugs for the moderate woes of everyday living, even as he was reporting radical and largely cost-free improvements in his patients' mental states.

Given the drug's transformative powers, the primary question, as Kramer posed it then, was this: should he continue to prescribe Prozac to patients whose immediate emotional problems had disappeared but who wanted to stay on the drug, or even increase its dosage, because it made them feel, they reported, "better than well"? That concern notwithstanding, Kramer concluded his book as follows:

> Is Prozac a good thing? By now, asking about the virtue of Pro-
> zac—and I am referring here not to its use in severely depressed

patients but, rather, its availability to alter personality—may seem like asking whether it was a good thing for Freud to discover the unconscious. Once we are aware of the unconscious, once we have witnessed the effects of Prozac, it is impossible to imagine the modern world without them.[6]

By equating the SSRIs with Freud's discovery of the unconscious, a foundational event in the history of psychiatry, Kramer was clearly promoting a paradigm shift within the profession, one in which the therapist's pursuit of effective care would be pharmacologically based. That such an apparently sensitive professional could, with some hedging, define the powers of Prozac in these grand terms—the subtitle of the paperback edition included the phrase *Antidepressant Drugs and the Remaking of the Self*—was reassuring in a way that, say, a celebrity's glib endorsement could never have been. A movie star could quickly popularize a medical treatment (and indeed pharmaceutical companies would soon be paying stars to do so), but only a sober and sensitive doctor like Kramer could render that treatment respectable by framing it within the mainstream culture's meta-narrative of self-improvement through scientific progress.

Tied to the radically transformative experiences of both New World immigration and spiritual conversion (the Protestant emphasis on being born again), the necessity and allure of "remaking the self" had long been an indispensable theme of American aspiration. Kramer's meditation on the extra-therapeutic uses of the new antidepressants served to link those old moral and spiritual imperatives to technology's scheme of linear progress. It now seemed possible, through the agency of a lab-crafted pill, to become "better than well," and for wellness itself to become better and better.

The subtle differences and hidden similarities between America's bohemian fringe and its bourgeois center on this subject bear noting here. The sixties' counterculture had playfully hijacked DuPont's corporate motto "Better Things for Better Living through Chemistry" to proselytize the redemptive powers of the psychedelic drugs they strongly preferred. They were claiming then, as some of Kramer's patients on Prozac would later, that they felt better than well after smoking grass or dropping acid, and they were suggesting, as Kramer himself would, that the ingestion of psychoactive drugs could result in the birth of a new and explicitly better self. The differences were profound, though, as to what each group thought "better" meant, and those differences were keyed not only to the unique effects of each particular drug but also to the ethos of the era in which they were being taken or prescribed.

The counterculture, as the term itself implies, associated "better" with a radical transformation of the nation's primary institutions and ruling beliefs. Echoing Wordsworth's initial complaint against industrialization, this group's endorsement of drug-taking was inseparable from its critique of postwar capitalism's accelerating emphasis on "getting and spending," and its call to "turn on" was closely allied with its advice to "tune in" and "drop out." This soft revolt against the rigid work regimens and avid acquisitiveness of the time was simultaneous with significant political revolts against the ruling system, including the civil rights movement, the Vietnam War protests, and feminism. To tune in and drop out was to reject that system's ethos of competitive individualism, and so drug-taking was reframed as an activity to be shared, if often furtively due to the drugs' illegality, and one that assumed a ritualistic, even sacred status, for some groups. Like the phrase "better living through chemistry" itself, the term "righteous," as applied to a powerful batch of psychedelic drugs, was at once ironic and sincere.

The collapse of the counterculture as a credible alternative to consumer capitalism is a now familiar story, its global failure linked not only to the most unrealistic of its Romantic expectations but also, ironically, to its specific successes in transforming American values. In the aftermath of the sixties, the pursuit of pleasure was fully out of the closet, redefined as righteous, and ready to be serviced by hundreds of thousands of new commodities, as pitched by aging Aquarians who had once scorned "the man" and his marketplace methods. Meanwhile, American women were being liberated from the home only to enter a workplace whose ruling ethos was even more committed to the hyper-rationalism and avid materialism that the counterculture had critiqued—a fact that dress-down Fridays, corporate gyms, and the occasional offer of on-site day care couldn't quite conceal. And, as has been the case throughout history, the results of the era's romance with drug-taking had proven less sacred than profane, less redemptive than destructive, leading to a host of twelve-step programs and to a new public culture characterized by talk-show confessions of lives gone desperately awry through drug dependency.

By the time Prozac was released in 1988, the cultural environment had completely changed, the poles of virtue in the public domain nearly reversed. With the Berlin Wall about to fall, American capitalism's main global opponent had been completely discredited. Freed of regulation and idealized rather than demonized, corporate culture increasingly dominated civic culture, recasting the public domain after its own image: life itself as a free market in which the fittest thrived while the slow and the dim went out of business. In such a radically privatizing society, the meaning of "better living" was inevitably recast. Like the early proponents of LSD, some of whom had also borne Ivy League credentials, Prozac's expert advocates were proselytizing the virtues of a psychoactive drug, but now they promised an internal transformation that would boost the self's performance separate from any reformation of the sociopolitical scene. Rather than sanctified and communalized, the "remaking of the self" via psychoactive drug-taking was medicalized and privatized. The drugs in question weren't to be shared in a ritualistic setting but taken alone, as part of one's preparations to succeed in the workaday world—the psychic arming of scientific capitalism's would-be Achilles.

Kramer's reports of patients becoming "better than well" on Prozac[7] offered the boon of a personal advantage in an exceptionally competitive cultural environment, one in which traditional roles, especially for women, were rapidly changing, their associated networks of social support dissolving in the process. The new economy was producing extraordinary opportunities for wealth and career advancement, but the endemic uncertainty of its boom-or-bust ethos and the pressures it placed on family life were also generating inner moral conflicts and emotional exhaustion.

The good news announced by Prozac's expert advocates was doubly reassuring, then, for not only did the new SSRIs promise a cure to postmodern life's psychic woes; that cure was also emerging from within the system itself. Private corporations, exploiting the latest techniques and technologies, had competed to produce these new drugs, proving once again that scientific capitalism was inherently self-correcting. A patented commodity would itself ease any emotional damage collaterally generated by a culture now fully committed to the production and consumption of new commodities. More than heal these heartsick selves, such a drug might even make them "better than well," reassuring them that they could now keep pace with our rapidly changing political economy and maintain their place on its escalator of perpetual progress.

By highlighting the cultural relativity of "better living" here, I don't intend to imply that there are not significant differences in the drugs themselves—only that both the endorsement of those drugs and the evaluations of their psychic effects can never be fully separated from the shifting matrices of social meaning. Nor in noting a generational divide do I want to ignore some potent likenesses. For all their meaningful differences, the counterculture of the sixties and the corporate culture of the eighties and nineties were alike in this: both believed in the traditional American imperative of remaking the self, and both were binding that refashioning to psychoactive drug-taking—as indeed the so-called Great Generation had done before them when they rushed to be tranquilized by Miltown in 1955. Viewed from an anthropological distance, postwar Americans of all stripes were linking material progress to the inner project of mood enhancement. The drugs preferred could vary widely, along with the cultural context within which they were taken, but the populace as a whole—rationalists along with romantics, Rotarians as well as radicals—was adopting a belief in better living through chemistry.

Not unanimously, of course. Kramer's upbeat views did not go unchallenged. Years of controversy ensued and continue to this day, arguments similar in type to those that occurred after Miltown's release some thirty years earlier. In the initial phases at least, this debate was occurring under the broad presumption that a significant number of patients *were* becoming "better than well" on the SSRIs—that cosmetic psychopharmacology was either an immediate or imminent social reality. Although some experts thought otherwise, their efforts drew far less publicity than TV newsman Mike Wallace's personal endorsement of Zoloft or the *Newsweek* cover story, "Beyond Prozac: How Science Will Let You Change Your Personality with a Pill."[8]

Yale surgeon and noted author Sherwin Nuland savaged such claims as "preposterous" when reviewing *Listening to Prozac* in the *New York Review of Books*,[9] and Dr. Peter Breggin, author of *Talking Back to Prozac*,[10] and Thomas Moore, a health policy analyst,[11] challenged both the effectiveness and harmlessness of the SSRIs. Later, Dr. David Healy, an expert on the history of psychopharmacology, and Harvard-affiliated psychiatrist Dr. Joseph Glenmullen updated those skeptics' arguments in well-documented books. Often using the drug-makers' own clinical trials and internal memos, some of which only came to light through "wrongful death" law suits, these critics asserted that, contrary public perception, the SSRIs could have multiple serious side effects, a list that included nausea, insomnia, facial and body tics (indicating possible brain damage), withdrawal syndromes, sexual dysfunction, and (in rare cases) suicidal or homicidal behavior.[12]

Along with disturbing accounts of the duplicity of the drug industry and the regulatory impotence of the Federal Drug Administration (FDA), these authors revealed the degree to which the most common problems— love affairs gone wrong, work-home conflicts, performance anxiety in graduate school, even obsessive nail-biting—were being treated as "chemical imbalances." The disturbing news that these drugs might be implicated in violent psychotic episodes, inciting rather than "dissuading" pain, was intensified by the fact that children were being given SSRIs without clinical trials to determine their safety and effectiveness on young bodies and minds, and for conditions as trivial as bed-wetting. More recently, some meta-studies have concluded that these same drugs are, on the whole, no more effective at treating mild to moderate depression than the placebo they were tested against.[13] Kramer and his allies have fought back, accusing their critics of romanticizing melancholy, misrepresenting the evidence, and scaring away patients in real need of treatment.[14]

Given that one of ten Americans over the age of twelve is now taking an antidepressant, the supporters of the SSRIs do appear to be winning the day. The sheer number of prescriptions, however, does not in itself verify their value, and the technical complexity of these debates presents certain obvious problems to laypersons like ourselves. Should we trust the highly trained specialist and sensitive caregiver Peter Kramer or the equally prestigious and apparently sensitive Joseph Glenmullen, doctors both? And behind the usual mystifications of medical research's scientific complexities, the same crucial philosophical questions apply. Is pain "the only evil," and to what extent is the elimination of emotional pain either a feasible or a desirable expectation? And if, after all, we *can* live better through this new chemistry, what will "better" actually mean? Which specific virtues will this projected "remaking of the self" redeem?

Anatomizing Melancholy

The utopian belief that we can find a physical solution to human suffering has its own history, and to frame our recent obsession with curing depression, we can turn to *The Anatomy of Melancholy* by Robert Burton, who was likewise obsessed. First published in 1621 and expanded over the next twenty years to over a half million words, Burton's *Anatomy* was one of the last books that aspired to comprehend the whole of Western learning in a single volume. A cleric and passionate bibliophile who was "writ[ing] of melancholy, by being busy to avoid [the] melancholy" he fitfully suffered, the author exploited his topic to analyze nearly every dimension of human experience, tying each in some way to the cause, course, or cure of the melancholic mood.[15] In a stunning if often mind-numbing display of retentive scholarship, Burton's analyses proceed through a relentless accretion of multilingual quotations and paraphrases. He is avid to retrieve—and, it sometimes seems, attribute equal value to—every opinion ever expressed on the subject at hand, from the earliest Greeks to his own contemporaries: a two-millennial miscellany of herbal and homiletic prescriptions, superstitious rituals, and commonsensical advice, much of it yoked together within hyperextended sentences.

At once impressive and absurd, both an unsurpassed expression of pedantic plenitude and an implicit plea for radical epistemological simplification, this motley mix exemplified the intellectual crisis of Burton's day—which, on reflection, bears considerable resemblance to the one we now face. Just as he lived at a crucial pivot point in the evolution of Western consciousness and culture, so now do we. As our transition out of the cultural forms of a decadent modernity is being driven by a technologically mediated information explosion, his era's transition out of a decaying feudalism was driven by an equivalent explosion—one fueled by the invention and proliferation of the printed book. As Burton's response to that crisis was an attempt to contain the new and disorienting abundance of book knowledge within a single, super-tolerant literary form, we now struggle to invent our own inclusive forms: musical fusion, political multiculturalism, interdisciplinary study, New Age religiosity, the hodgepodge mix of collage and montage. Finally, that Burton should be so obsessed with melancholia, and we with its contemporary equivalent depression, may say something profound about our species' characteristic response to these transitional times when, swamped by new knowledge, the old cultural common sense is losing both its descriptive accuracy and its prescriptive authority.

In "Mourning and Melancholia," Freud supplied the raw terms for just such an explanation when comparing the psychopathology of depression to the normal condition of grief. Realistic and transitional, mourning's deep but temporary sadness emerged from the conscious loss of either a beloved person or "an abstraction that has taken the place of one, such as fatherland, liberty, an ideal." Although alike in kind, Freud observed, the sadness of melancholy differed from mourning not only in its duration but also in the confusion that often accompanied the mood: the inability of both the patient and his analyst to "consciously perceive what it is he has lost": the mysterious absence that, unnamable and thus incurable, evoked a grief that would not stop.[16]

This cluster of acute observations pointed to a possible conclusion about the causes of melancholia that Freud, given his fixation on sexual instinct, did not discern. For unlike the loss of one's fatherland or one's liberty by military conquest, or the radical extinction of ideals that occurs when a preliterate tribe is invaded by modernity, an internally driven obsolescence of cultural meanings is hard to spy. When the aggressive agency of change is native rather than alien, when it arrives in the guise of a technological progress that may also supply material improvements and military victory, when our old beloved ideals are not expressly forbidden but co-opted instead—when, for example, a hero like Abraham Lincoln is nominally honored (if actually demeaned) by having his name bestowed on a luxury automobile—then it becomes much harder for us to "consciously perceive what it is [we] have lost."

We salute the same flag, chant the same prayers, and mouth many of the same old aphorisms even as those time-honored markers of meaning cease to describe what we are doing in our economic, political, and domestic lives. And as our daily behavior deviates from our ongoing profession of traditional beliefs, we begin to suffer in many of the same ways that the defeated nation or invaded tribe suffers. We display the same tendencies toward moral confusion and social dissolution, but we do so absent the clarity of their historical explanation. Grieving for this largely unconscious loss of effective higher meaning, many grow melancholic but few know why.

Such a hypothetical diagnosis would suggest that the current prevalence of depression in America—to the extent that it is not the consequence of corporate moneys corrupting psychiatry and hampering regulators—is, primarily, an historical phenomenon: a social disease whose first cause can be found in cultural rather than chemical "imbalances." Contra Freud's emphasis, this diagnosis also points us away from the private dynamics of personality formation toward the public drama of culture-making—or, rather, it reverses the authority of their interrelation. It directs our attention toward the communal mind's ongoing mediation between tradition and innovation, and to the mental forms which that mediation strives to maintain: all those myths, rituals, symbols, and credos that coordinate our immediate practices with ultimate purposes, and that align the mundane economy of our material acts with a profound ecology of moral values and metaphysical beliefs.

Both this potential diagnosis and the sorts of cures it implies, however, lack credibility in contemporary America. If we ask why, the obvious response—that such an approach to mental suffering is not "scientific"—merely raises the linked questions of how that once broadly defined word became so specialized and how that same reductive definition then came to monopolize our self-understanding. Key characteristics of Burton's *Anatomy* do suggest some plausible answers here. To begin with, the sheer excess of his project demonstrated the West's need for some form of radical epistemological simplification. Two centuries after Gutenberg, the Renaissance project of recovering knowledge from many cultures and epochs was being challenged by the confusing profusion of its own success. In such times, as we now experience all too commonly when surfing the web, the virtue of intellectual inclusiveness can easily tip into a virtual incoherence, an appetite for diversity into an addiction to distraction.

To recast W. B. Yeats's famous prophecy backward in time: the epistemological center of the late Renaissance could not hold. The near-chaotic plenitude of new book knowledge, conspicuously on display in Burton's literary mosaic, would have to give way to some order of value that could reliably discriminate the most credible "news" from the new print culture's superabundance of ambient "noise." An alternative already existed in the radical Protestant sects of the day—witness the rationalist rigor of Puritan theology and the spartan self-discipline of their "plain style" in all things. And during the very period when the Pilgrims were founding a new society in America shaped according to that style, René Descartes was crafting a new epistemology modeled after the rigorous geometry in which he excelled.

With the ensuing triumph of this newly "scientific" method for assessing the world, the West would, thankfully, come to reject the superstitious cures (bleeding by leeches) and trivial categorizations ("Windy Hypochondriacal Melancholy") that abound in Burton's *Anatomy*—but not without a substantial cost to the unity of its self-conception. The impractical plenitude of his book rapidly gave way to its intellectual foil: the instrumental parsimony of Cartesian-Baconian science and, eventually, to the *social* science of utilitarian progress, within which even morality became rationalized and materialized for programmatic reform. This extension of the scientific approach logically led to the expectation that we could correct our social and psychological states in the same ways that we were asserting our control over the material world.

On the diversely populated European continent, with its long history of tribal, ethnic, and denominational conflicts, this utopian promise took the compensatory form of the perfectly designed communal order: at its most extreme, either the workers' paradise of the Marxists, with its promised erasure of all class differences, or the Nazis' physiological perfection of the species via industrialized genocide and eugenic breeding. In the exceptional circumstances of the New World, however, with its open spaces, immigrant population, democratic inclinations, and subsequent emphasis on individual performance, the utopia promised was individualized as well: not an end to the discord of European history (which our immigration had already achieved) but to the anxieties of individuality (which that immigration had greatly intensified.) Here, the expectation of a final solution turned away from the utopian state and aimed instead to the perfection of the single self—the same goal that Kramer and his allies have now claimed as their own.

That history of applied ideas brings us back to the new enclosures of Virtual America, for all our current versions of the comfort zone—whether physically constructed, rhetorically buffered, cybernetically programmed, or pharmaceutically induced—have their roots in this avid pursuit of a personal and happy "end of history": a triumphantly final "remaking of the self." Idealizing pleasure and demonizing pain, boosting self-esteem over the virtue of humility, promoting "celebration" over moral self-reflection: these current preferences of Virtual America are rooted in a particular philosophy, a utopian rational materialism, as it has been adapted to fit the unique circumstances of the American settlement.

Defining all reality as reducible to a calculable sum of chemical and mechanical processes, this Evangelical Mammonism presumes that each person is in essence an elaborate machine—a computer atop an engine—whose every malfunction can be redressed and every improvement enacted by either rational redesign or material intervention.[17] The expansion of these beliefs into pharmaceutical mood enhancement thus completes a four-hundred-year process of conversion by redefining even the most subjective aspects of our individuality, along with the means by which they might be improved, in utilitarian terms. As should be obvious, this reductive approach also tends to ignore or dismiss more traditional responses to human unhappiness, such as moral reformation, political engagement, artistic self-expression, and spiritual regeneration, along with the complex character skills required to enact them. Whether such a redefinition of our innermost nature can actually bring us closer to perfecting the self is the crucial question I will turn to next.

The Purposes and Perils of Pain Dissuasion

Grief is itself a medicine.[18]

—William Cowper

The historical record of colonial America catalogues concretely the appalling prevalence of early mortality in a pre-scientific era: families with seven out of eight children dead, the serial loss of spouses, the early passing of friends and leaders, a life punctuated by funerals and by the wrenching adjustments—emotional, spiritual, political, economic—to so much loss. In a book focusing on the ways in which our rational-materialist heritage may have led us astray, periodic reminders of its considerable achievements are a necessary counterpoint, and no achievement has been more significant than our dramatic increase in life expectancy. In Burton's century, grief was a near constant condition of colonial life. By the 1950s, however, it had become something more like what G. K. Chesterton thought melancholy ought to be—"a tender and fugitive frame of mind"—and only the most morbidly romantic sensibility, in love with suffering for its own sake, would rue the change.[19]

I have cited doubts about the effectiveness of the SSRIs, but what about the goal itself? What if Melville was wrong and the real progress we have achieved in both increasing life expectancy and "dissuading" physical pain could, in fact, be duplicated with mental suffering? What if the stoic virtues *are* archaic, just a middling and muddling phase in our evolutionary development toward a material self-mastery, one of whose key ingredients would be the pharmacy of mood enhancement? Would we be, as Kramer complained, romanticizing melancholy if we chose to shun this chemically-induced remaking of the self?

In posing these questions, I am testing our belief in the utilitarian ethics that now calibrate our pursuit of the self's perfection. And, to evaluate that system's aggressive assertion that "pain is, without exception, the only evil," I now raise for consideration a counterclaim by Bentham's contemporary, the poet William Cowper, that even grief, the most agonizing of inner states, can be seen as medicinal. To what extent is emotional pain a kind of moral disease, against which all the armory of scientific technique should be mustered, and to what extent might it be instead an initiating cure—a transfiguring message or means of passage between the shifting realities of the human condition?

To address that question requires that we consider first the ultimate purposes such pains might serve—what *they* are finally for—and what they are for, I would say, is roughly analogous to the survival function of physical pain. As a sharp stab in the foot warns us that the physical integrity of our body has been violated, painful emotions such as jealousy, guilt, and grief are alarms that warn us of immediate or imminent violations to our psychological well-being—they tell us "where we are" in the social dimensions of human experience. Jealousy sharply alerts us to a gap between whom or what we desire and what we have achieved; it not only identifies, it vivifies our most pressing and personal unsatisfied needs. In a similar fashion, guilt assails us when our actions have trespassed the norms of society; it not only clarifies, it intensifies our current estrangement from the values of the tribe. Precisely because they are so painful, these social emotions stir us into action, spurring us to redress situations injurious to ourselves or to those we care about.

The obvious problem with reductively identifying emotional pain with evil and prescribing drugs to eliminate that evil is that we might dull or mask the sensation without ever changing the danger it signals. As the chemistry of comfort prescriptively replaces the practice of self-reflection, we might kill the messenger without ever addressing the bad news it bears. Yet, as most of us have experienced, emotions like jealousy or guilt, can themselves sometimes obscure the truth. Their alarms can be completely false, or persist long beyond their usefulness, or surge out of scale with the events they report. To fail to grieve for one's dead spouse seems inhuman, but to grieve at the same pitch for twenty years, or with a similar intensity over the loss of a pet parakeet, or, worse still, for no apparent reason at all—these are occasions when pain does seem, if not evil, then indisputably and perversely harmful. As with diseases like lupus, where the body's immune system turns against its host, this key feature of the psychosocial self's defenses has become instead that self's own enemy. When emotional pain radically distorts the actual meaning of "where we are," it undermines its own reason for being, and the "medicine" itself, whether grief or guilt, requires a cure.

In these extreme cases—when, say, grieving turns suicidal or anxiety pushes a patient toward a total breakdown—the argument for seeking chemical comfort becomes compelling indeed. Compassion demands immediate intervention, which is why reasonable critics of the Prozac solution such as Glenmullen accept the strategic use of psychoactive drugs as a means of stabilizing patients in crisis. It also seems clear that a lifelong dependence on such drugs may be the only current treatment for some severe forms of mental illness, the serious side effects of treatment often still preferable to the hellish state of the disease itself. In fairness, too, one has to wonder about Cowper, who suffered bouts of melancholia so severe that he periodically had to surrender himself to another's care. *His* grieving was not "tender and fugitive" but torturous and perennial, and although he was able to find some meaning in his suffering through the medium of his poetry and the practice of his religion, would Cowper really have rejected an even marginally effective "pain dissuader" if one have been available?

The danger does not lie, then, in the pharmacy of mood management per se but in the increasing promiscuity of its official use to the exclusion of other approaches to the perennial problem of human suffering. The trend is now clear. Not only, as Healy notes, have the official estimates of depression increased a *thousandfold* since the 1950s[20]; antidepressant drugs are increasingly being given as substitutes for, rather than supplements to, professional counseling, and often for problems never before defined as mental illness. By the late nineties, SSRIs were being prescribed for shyness, bed-wetting, and family disputes, as well as for menopause and compulsive shopping. Along with Ritalin, they were being given to boys who "act out" in school and, as *New York Times* columnist Maureen Dowd wryly reported, offered to women who are "between relationships."[21]

When the shy adult and the aggressive middle-schooler, the Super Mom and the single woman, the anxious grad student and the lonely geriatric, are all being offered some version of the Prozac solution, and when so many outside the system choose to self-medicate in other ways, the cumulative effect suggests the breadth of our conversion to a utopian materialism that promises a strictly technical fix to unhappiness. Implicitly in our actions at the individual level and explicitly in our policies at the institutional one, America appears to be accepting a rapid expansion of that applied philosophy's value system into the most intimate domains of our daily lives. And because this science, unlike Burton's, avoids both ethical and metaphysical self-reflection, we as a nation are failing to ponder some crucial questions about our apparent epidemic of depression.

Can the "badness" of human sadness really be eradicated by our smart pharmaceutical weaponry without causing potentially catastrophic collateral damage to the integrity of the whole self and to the moral health of society? (There are already, for example, those walking among us who have solved the problem of guilt's discomforts: they are called sociopaths.) To what extent has the statistical surge in depression been induced by the climate of unreal expectations generated by our marketing culture and its closest ally, the dream machine of mass entertainment? Might some of our mental anguish be arising from our adoption of a political economy whose ambitions are becoming both inconsistent with fundamental truths about the human condition and inhospitable to the finest elements of our human nature, as those elements have been refined by our own civic, spiritual, and political traditions? Might, then, our growing belief in drug-induced mood enhancement itself be a symptom, a sign of disease that begs a cure?

In confronting these questions, we might recall, too, that some of humanity's finest creations—our artistic forms, our civic and religious rituals—deliberately induce the experience of emotional pain. In Yeats's words, they *ask* "for mournful melodies."[22] What these cultural forms at their best supply is precisely what Evangelical Mammonism, in all its variations, does not: meanings beyond the rational sum of our material sensations. Rather than deny suffering, they invite it inside their shapely domains, weaving it within the novel's plot, the painting's frame, the ritual recitations at the graveyard, battle site, or communion rail. They do so, however, with the aim of making sense of suffering's various occasions by enfolding them within the nesting structures and scripted rhythms of communal sharing. And although we do retreat from the real world to enter these carefully crafted spaces, *their* virtual domains aim to ready us for a return to reality's ongoing trials.

By contrast, the pharmaceutical goal of becoming "better than well" seeks to change the way we interpret any location. A mirror image of pain gone wrong, it promises us its own kind of emotional solipsism, with

THE DEMISE OF VIRTUE IN VIRTUAL AMERICA

undeflatable cheer replacing unremitting suffering irrespective of where we actually are.

Our Medical-Industrial Complex

Reason panders will.

—Shakespeare, *Hamlet*

Following Cowper's claim, I have tried to show the ways in which emotional suffering can "itself be a med'cine," but my approach so far, favoring the collective over the individual perspective and focusing on social issues rather than clinical ones, would seem a luxury, and a cruel one at that, to anyone suffering from severe depression. For conditions like bed-wetting, nail-biting, performance anxiety, or mild cases of the blues triggered by job losses or love gone wrong, reminders of both our social context and the ultimate limits to human happiness seem reasonable cautions against the dangers of over-medication. Severely depressed people, however, need immediate relief, not sweeping cultural analysis. The public debate for them narrows to just two crucial questions: are these drugs effective and, if so, are they safe?

Alas, the answers to both questions appear to be considerably less sanguine than Kramer's musings and *Newsweek*'s two cover stories suggested. Breggin, Moore, Healy, and Glenmullen each insist that the science endorsing the broadest claims of the Prozac solution—science, that is, in the strictly modern sense—cannot withstand objective scrutiny. It is from their work, and not Kramer's books or Eli Lilly's websites, that one learns that Prozac failed its initial clinical trials on severely depressed patients, and only marginally passed muster as a treatment for the mildly depressed.[23] Although the SSRIs are clearly psychoactive, their actual impact, these critics insist, is more global than "selective" and includes the serious potential side effects cited earlier. Is it really possible, then, as these claims would suggest, that our objective procedures for approving prescription drugs no longer merit our trust?

We are not bereft of examples of how such corruption might occur. President Eisenhower identified a similar concern when he warned against the growing influence of what he dubbed our "military-industrial complex." What worried Ike then was an evolving pattern of corrupted judgment, an institutionalized process whereby our technical analyses of military needs were routinely skewed to mask the venal intentions of a politically-connected armaments industry. The sheer complexity of the new weapons made it all the easier for experts to conceal their tainted motives, and the combination of primitive emotions that everyone felt (fear of one's enemy and, in those days especially, of a nuclear holocaust) with complex calculations that only a few could comprehend led to the procurement of unnecessary and even ineffective weapons systems. That same pattern of primal fears exploited by a privileged priesthood of specialists now threatens the approval process for prescription drugs.

We do have a system in place to prevent the sort of abuse that Ike decried. According to its original design, corporations research new drugs, independent scientists conduct clinical trials to test them, and then the FDA reviews the results to reject or approve their use. The presumption has been that the checks and balances of this three-pronged approach will protect the public interest, but in actual fact an aggressive infusion of commercial models, motives, and moneys has radically altered the balance of power between those parties, skewing the system's overall judgment. Only by closely examining this new *medical*-industrial complex can we begin to understand how and why a drug of limited merit can gain the seal of approval. Eight of the key causal agents are briefly sketched below.

1. Companies seeking FDA approval for a drug do not have to argue their case based on the preponderance of available evidence (the usual standard in science) but merely supply two studies that demonstrate a "statistically significant difference" in their drug's safety and effectiveness when compared to a placebo. This lower standard allows them to fund multiple studies in search of favorable results. Theoretically, a company could fund twenty such studies, eighteen of which showed no measurable effect, and still win approval.

2. The nature of the organizations that drug companies turn to for those favorable results has changed dramatically. In an article in the *New England Journal of Medicine* (*NEJM*), Dr. Thomas Bodenheimer showed that from 1991 to 1998 the share of industry money for clinical trials that went to academic medical centers plummeted from 80 to 40 percent.[24] During roughly the same period, Glenmullen has estimated that 75 percent of all such trials on SSRIs and their relatives were conducted instead by commercial "testing mills," whose continued existence was directly dependent on their pleasing the pharmaceutical companies that hired them.[25] (This is the same ethically dubious economic model that, on Wall Street, had rating services like Standard & Poor's granting AAA status to those actually "toxic" mortgage securities.)

3. Given the reduction in federal support for research, even clinical trials conducted at academic medical centers are mostly funded by corporate interests these days. They are also being led by researchers who often have multiple ties to the very firms whose drugs they are testing. According to Dr. Marcia Angell—in an editorial entitled "Is Academic Medicine for Sale?" that appeared in the same issue as Bodenheimer's report—these entanglements include not only the grant support, which is the lifeline for any research laboratory, but many personal financial perks as well, including consulting and speaking fees, patent and royalty arrangements, and expensive gifts.[26] These ties have affected *NEJM's* own practices in significant ways. Three months before Bodenheimer's piece appeared, the journal's editors acknowledged that they had failed to meet their own ethical standards by allowing nineteen of forty drug reviews they had published in the previous three years to be authored by researchers with undisclosed financial ties to the corporations that made the drugs being tested.[27]

4. When pharmaceutical firms fund the trials of their new drugs, they usually insist on retaining strict contractual control over publication rights. Six of the independent researchers interviewed for Bodenheimer's article reported that either publication had been halted or their findings altered when the results did not fit the marketing interests of the funding corporation. Combine those facts with Healy's estimate that as much as 50 percent of the therapeutics literature is now ghostwritten—that is, leading clinicians lending their names to articles composed by "writing mills" also hired by pharmaceutical companies—and one quickly loses faith in the objectivity of today's published research. As offensive as liability law suits can sometimes seem, such cases are now often the only legal means to gain access to the full clinical trial record of any given prescription drug.

5. Once a drug has been approved, the FDA has few funds to support the follow-up studies necessary to reveal the sorts of serious long-term side effects that have often been a problem with psychoactive drugs.

6. After a new drug has received FDA approval for treating one condition, any physician is legally entitled to prescribe it for other conditions as he or she sees fit. This license to diversify a drug's therapeutic uses, strongly encouraged by Big Pharm's salesmen, explains why a woman can go to her doctor with a complaint about migraine headaches or menstrual mood swings and emerge with a prescription for a drug only formally approved for mild depression.

7. Aiming to increase their customer base, drug companies have not only used "disease awareness" campaigns to tout our so-called epidemic of untreated depression;[28] they have also aggressively pitched new diseases that those same SSRIs can treat. Eli Lilly, for example, began selling a different version of Prozac (Sarafem) as a treatment for something called "premenstrual dysphoric disorder"—a condition which seems little more than severe PMS redefined for marketing purposes. Likewise, SmithKline broadened the appeal of Paxil by touting it as a cure for both "social anxiety disorder" (SAD) and "general anxiety disorder" (GAD), two newly minted diagnoses. But after reviewing the whole process, it is hard not to conclude that this syndrome of finding new syndromes that their drugs can treat is a primary symptom of PAD ("profit anxiety disorder"): that ethical disease which, boosting corporate income irrespective of social consequences, is truly epidemic in our time.

8. Finally, we have to add the practical realities of today's privatizing political climate, including intense lobbying of the FDA by politicians receiving contributions from drug companies and, too, the reductions in government-funded research that have induced both academic science departments and medical schools to form financial partnerships with corporate interests. Once "on the payroll," such institutions are unlikely to hire industry critics—a fact that Healy discovered when a job offer at the University of Toronto was promptly rescinded after he gave a lecture there that linked Prozac use to suicidal ideation.[29]

So it is that a whole series of institutional biases built into this new medical-industrial complex has favored the adoption and proliferation of the SSRIs irrespective of their actual safety and effectiveness. None of this has to be the case. With a truly independent review process that adheres to the highest standards of scientific proof while forbidding the censorship of any clinical trial's results, and with regulations that strictly separate corporate interests from medical training and practice, pharmaceutical treatment could begin to resume its rightful place in a complementary approach to mental suffering. But in the land of Evangelical Mammonism, where "reason" routinely "panders will" in pursuit of profit, one has to wonder if such reforms are possible.

Surely critics like Healy and Glenmullen will keep questioning the approval process. But if drug firms continue to own the rights to clinical trials, and the current attempt to restrict liability law suits succeeds, will there be any available cautionary data for them to uncover? Ten years from now, will there be any medical schools that haven't gone into partnership with commercial interests? Any researchers who aren't, in some way, on the corporate payroll? Any medical journals worthy of the public's trust?

The trends have not been encouraging. Shortly after publishing "Is Academic Medicine for Sale?," Dr. Angell retired as editor-in-chief of *NEJM*. At the time of his appointment, her replacement, Dr. Jeffrey M. Drazen, had received grants and consultation fees from nine pharmaceutical firms. Soon, noting that "not all financial associations are the same," and asserting that, given a lack of qualified reviewers who had no ties to industry, the journal's "ability to provide comprehensive, up-to-date information, especially on recent therapeutics, [had] been constrained," Drazen announced a formal change in their ethical guidelines for authorship. The strict prohibition of financial ties to any corporation with a stake in the analysis had been revised to no "significant" financial ties.[30]

With the addition of that single word, a little influence-peddling had become a permissible practice. As in so many other instances of virtue's demise inside Virtual America, a once dubious ethical activity was now recast as conventionally acceptable. Through their saturation of nearly all the venues for clinical research and care, the customs of crony capitalism had co-opted the protocols of psychiatric science.

Ship of Fools

Grasping that the American character's "affable air" was being hijacked to mask an implicit loathing of human beings as they actually are, Melville coined the perfect phrase for his nation's emerging pursuit of painlessness. He called it "genial misanthropy," and showed it to be, at heart, a scam, one whose multiple variations he relentlessly explored in *The Confidence-Man*.[31] This scam wasn't simply foisted on the innocent citizen by the clever charlatan but emerged from a complicity far deeper than the superficial exchange of real money for bogus product. Melville's confidence-man succeeded only insomuch as he could conjure up what his victim truly wanted: a renewed "confidence" that the highly improbable—whether in the form of the free lunch, the sure bet, or the certain cure for pain and death—was both possible and purchasable.

The very name Samaritan Pain Dissuader satirized that process, suggesting how under the aegis of Samaritan compassion we are rhetorically converted ("dissuaded" or conned) rather than actually cured of life's intrinsic sufferings. Despite the variety of bogus schemes being pitched, the product being sold time and again was the same *psychological* opiate: the numbing faith that allows us to forget that "some pains cannot be eased except by producing insensibility, and cannot be cured except by producing death." What was being sold was a willful insensibility to the human condition. Set on April Fools' Day on the steamer *Fidèle*, the novel depicted a "ship of fools" in constant flight from the harder truths of that condition. As if bowing to the bleakness of his own message, Melville ceased writing fiction at the peak of his powers after completing this dark book, and the final words of this, his final novel—"Something further may follow of this Masquerade"—voiced an exquisitely understated prophecy to the public he was leaving behind.[32]

Today, with the motives and methods of the Masquerade invading nearly every cranny of the American mind and every corner of the American place, we are nearing the climax of that conversion Melville foresaw: the projection of that same disingenuous "confidence" into the operating logic of our entire political economy. To the degree that the chemical cocoon of pain dissuasion serves to mask the emotional meaning of both "where we are" and how we behave there, it constitutes an especially insidious development in our ongoing enclosure within the venues of virtuality; for our depression, anxieties, and deeply felt yet baffling griefs—the whole emotional tenor and texture of postmodern life—might be bearing the messages we most need to heed. We don't to have to *ask* for these mournful melodies, but when they repeatedly arise, we should at least pause to reflect on what they might imply about the current state of our real fate and place.

Some of the ground rules of that real place were revealed all too cruelly by the terrorist attacks of 9/11, when the presumptive safety of the comfort zone was obliterated with the twin towers, and the country was moved as one by the powerfully painful emotions of fear, rage, and grief. The claim was quickly made then that America had changed forever, yet the limits of our communal self-reckoning under the pressures of such pains were quickly suggested by an American leadership whose advice to the home front, after a mere ten days of patriotic mourning, was a return to economic normalcy. It was our duty, we were told, to take a trip, to see a show, to reenter the dulcet domains of the comfort zone and, for God and country, resume consuming. It was our duty, the President advised, to continue the American way of life by taking the family to the Magic Kingdom.

To be fair, he was acting on the counsel of economic experts. Reacquainted with the psychological basis of consumerism but unaware of the Melvillean irony that attaches to the phrase, these advisers were concerned with boosting "consumer confidence" and, with it, the gross measures of consumption that defined their conception of national prosperity. But insomuch as periods of mourning painfully remind us that we are born to a condition whose inevitable end is not the self's perfection but its physical extinction, they should challenge us to reconsider all our previous prescriptions: the fitness of what we, collectively and personally, have come to value.

Rather than serving to reaffirm economic normalcy, our national grief might have moved us to ask then how it had come to pass in American history that the righteous response to infamy was to go on yet another shopping spree. It might have prompted us to consider how the meaning of prosperity had been radically reduced to the rationalized measures of material consumption, and to ask why metaphysical realism and the stoic virtues it commends have been banished to the margins of conventional belief. Burton's anatomy of melancholy may have been rife with factual errors, but *his* science could at least pose these uncomfortable questions: ours, apparently, could not.

Instead, doing as we were told, we returned to the shrine of Virtual America's soul in even greater numbers and, reaffirming our faith in the immunity supplied by its Fable of Innocence, went on a debt-driven shopping binge. More than restored after 9/11, the nation's confidence soared. Because their hearts were in the dream, millions of Americans consented to believe that, thanks to Wall Street's magical Samaritan Debt Dissuaders, they could possess the deed to their own dream castle. And although the foreclosures, evictions, and trillion-dollar bailouts following that spree all conveyed the same brutal message, reminding us that what had passed for economic normalcy was actually a form of collective lunacy, we shouldn't presume that such lunacy won't soon reemerge. Without a profound revision in the moral logic of our conventional thinking, you can bet on this: a new set of schemes will soon be pitched promising to fulfill the utopian dreams of Evangelical Mammonism.

To believe in those schemes requires, however, that we remain inside a Virtual America where nearly every day is April Fools' Day, every passage a voyage on the steamer *Fidèle*. Driven by its engines and directed by its charts, we are all encouraged to play there, at alternate times, the complicit roles of the con man and his mark. We are trained both to pitch and to catch the many versions of genial misanthropy's perpetual lies: its sunny faith in the moral Eden of materialist plenty, its willingness to believe in a technical fix to life's perennial predicaments—that cruise missile soon to come which will surgically remove from reality's text all the interwoven themes of pain and risk.

And the more we play, the more we believe the message we sell. Through conning the mark, we con ourselves. In the midst of the Masquerade, its colloquy of spin, most quickly forget what they ought to become, and almost no one is who he seems to be. On this ship, as that sly demagogue Huey

Long understood, the fascist arrives in the guise of the anti-fascist,[33] the misanthrope speaks from the dais of the philanthropist, and (as we shall see next) the aggrieved conservative consumes unto death the very values he claims to revere. On this ship, the self-promoting conformist believes herself to be a righteous mutineer while the agenda of Dr. Feel-Good is actually driven by the tremors of an unappeasable fear. Surely *something* further will follow all these masquerades, but its moral, political, and spiritual meanings are unlikely to be apprehended by a nation addicted to pain dissuasion.

5

The Politics of Pain Dissuasion

"Yes, we golden boys, the moderns, have geniality every-
where—a bounty broadcast like moonlight."
"True, true . . . We have genial senators, genial authors,
genial lecturers, genial doctors, genial clergymen, genial sur-
geons and the next thing we will have genial hangmen."[1]

—Herman Melville, *The Confidence-Man: His Masquerade*

ALTHOUGH MELVILLE'S WORK IN the 1850s did illuminate the moral con-
tradictions implicit in the nation's emergent money economy, his explora-
tion of modernizing America focused less on the new social structures than
on those subtle shifts in the American psyche required to justify their im-
position—especially on the conversion of the Puritan's "cosmic optimism"
into the Yankee's earthly confidence. He traced with passionate acuity the
process by which the once deferred promise of heavenly ascension was giving way to the scheduled expectations of a here-and-now perfection: one
rationally designed, materially manufactured, and individually possessed.
Most of Melville's best fiction after *Moby Dick* was obsessed with testing the
self-protective seal of this new confidence, which offered all the apparent
benefits of "pain dissuasion" without the physical dangers or social stigma
of drug-taking. In a series of prophetic stories, he drew a set of portraits of
likeable, upbeat fellows whose innocence, on inspection, was shown to be
an artifact of willful moral and metaphysical ignorance—a global denial of
bad news.

The boss in "Bartleby, the Scrivener," who is eager to do anything to
ease his employee's suffering *except* acknowledge the inhumanity of the very
economy that funds his own prosperity; Capt. Amasa Delano in "Benito

Cereno," whose wholesale rejection of the grimmer side of human nature prevents him from recognizing a slave mutiny in progress; the destitute family in "Cockle-Doodle-Doo!" whose members die almost cheerfully: in all stations, classes, and professions of life, Melville found the inner hyping of a hope that admitted no corrections. And though totalizing in its own way, this New World version of modernity's optimism was not authoritarian (as in the continental theorist's utopian program) but genial (as in the traveling salesman's upbeat patter).

For Melville, the process of modernization on American shores was inseparable from what he wryly called the "progress of genialization,"[2] and his biting critique of the purblind optimism that he witnessed all around him proves significant to this book's argument in that it anticipates the two forms of pain dissuasion studied so far: the unGrimming of the nation's mythos, beginning with its fairy tales, and the avid pursuit of a drug-induced comfort zone. Crafted in 1856 and exaggerated then for satirical effect, Melville's list of "genialized" professions has proven all too predictive in the literal sense. Certainly, we can recognize our own versions of his genial clergymen in all those evangelical preachers who have traded in their sermons against original sin for the jackpot guarantees of a prosperity theology. And who could deny that we are now awash in a sea of genial authors who, for a fee, are ready to supply us with their surefire techniques for our imminent sexual-spiritual-professional triumph? Even the comic climax of his list has proven merely descriptive in the journalistic sense, for in George W. Bush we were given an unparalleled example of the genial hangman: a Texas governor whose aw-shucks, black-slapping leadership style presided over the execution of 152 prisoners, and who, in a scene more appropriate to *Animal House* than the state house, was caught making fun of a condemned prisoner's televised plea for clemency.[3]

As a failed oil entrepreneur and mostly powerless frontman for a professional baseball team, Bush's two primary qualifications when first running for governor were his family name and his bonhomie. That they should have proven sufficient for victory is hardly surprising, however, in an age of relentless branding when most Americans receive their leaders via some form of video screen, assessing them there as they do Super Bowl ads, talk-show hosts, and anchors for the evening news. In the electronic age, elections have become indistinguishable from ratings sweeps, reduced to occasions where, as on late-night TV, "likeability" rules. And in using his affability to win political authority, including finally the presidency itself, Bush was following the example of the two most effective politicians of the post-sixties era, Bill Clinton and Ronald Reagan.

Clinton did possess a formidable analytical intelligence, but his wonk-ishness was less essential to his electoral success than his ability to emote in various modes of genial fellow feeling. Tearing up, with bit lip, for the ladies, he could affect on cue that all too rare sympathetic male listener, always ready to pass a Kleenex with one hand while undoing a garter strap with the other. Winking for the boys, he could instantly morph into your basic backyard, barbecuin', beer-swillin' huntin' buddy (via Georgetown, Yale, and Oxford). Reagan's election, however, was the true pivotal event. In the ongoing legacy of his pseudo-conservative presidency, characterized by massive indebtedness, incoherent policies, and a cynicism masked by sheer sentimentality, Melville's dark vision of a nation bent on genial self-delusion has proven all too true.

Sunny Jim: The Rise of the American Disingenue

He strove, by ignoring the symptoms, to get rid of the malady.[4]

— Herman Melville, "Benito Cereno"

Given his long career in the entertainment industry, it was not surprising that Ronald Reagan could deliver a political speech so effectively, but he also proved consistently charming face to face, even to those who opposed his policies. The immediate sources of that charm weren't hard to spy. A *temperamental* egalitarian, Reagan blended an apparent modesty (that rarest of traits in both politicians and actors) with an ever-buoyant mood and a desire to amuse. As someone who served jelly beans at cabinet meetings and who was far more likely to go for a laugh through the recitation of a memorized joke than pursue a hard answer through a cross-examination of aides or petitioners, this global leader aimed to entertain rather than intimidate those he met. And although intellectually lazy and largely disengaged from the nuts and bolts of policy-making, he compensated for his lack of knowledge with an almost radiant sincerity—like the children in *Peter Pan* and the Gipper on his deathbed, like Jimmy Stewart rallying America's townsfolk against the transgressions of a corrupt elite, he believed, he believed . . .

Although this apparent sincerity would seem the opposite of Clinton's winking duplicity, it only served to mask an even greater scope of deceit and self-deception. While Clinton's Slick Willy was a fudger, a corner-cutter, an equivocator of exquisitely sensitive two-mindedness who, following the GPS of his narcissistic self-interest, could land on either side of an issue with an instant, gyroscopic precision, the misrepresentations of Reagan's Sunny Jim were seamless and categorical. The totally consistent medium of his message was in almost complete disjuncture to its actual effects. Nearly every value, trait, or political theme projected by Reagan's persona was subverted by the reality of the man as either person or politician.

"Boyish," he was the oldest sitting president in American history. "A nice guy," he was, in practice, a distant and thoughtless boss who showed little interest in even his closest aides' private lives—someone whose niceness lacked the inner resources of acute compassion and whose geniality, so inviting to those he barely knew, became a screen to avoid the obligations of intimacy to those he should have known well.[5] An "embodiment of America's small-town, Christian family values," Reagan was a mostly non-churchgoing adult, the first divorced president, an indifferent father often estranged from *two* sets of children, and the man who reintroduced the pomp of high office and the preening of high society to the White House scene. Physically courageous all his life, he was nevertheless something of a social coward, a man who assiduously dodged face-to-face conflicts. A notorious "tough guy" on foreign policy who was fond of quoting Dirty Harry to make his points, he often acted instead like an egregious sentimentalist: a chief of state so desperate to rescue American hostages that he was suckered by Oliver North (the Maxwell Smart of American intelligence) into something very close to impeachable behavior. A "populist" campaigner who spoke directly to and for the small guy, winning his vote time and again, Reagan put into place policies that strongly favored large corporations and financiers while actively attacking those laws, unions, and regulatory agencies that protected the small guy's interests in the economic sphere.

On all these matters, the image confounded the fact, and although Reagan was dubbed the Teflon president, the quality of his slipperiness was of another and grander order than that of Clinton's Slick Willy. For, in a sense, everything stuck to Clinton—his egregious but nevertheless private sexual behavior, his pathetically innocuous college drug experience, a real estate deal gone sour whose monetary value was scarcely more than the cost of a K Street lobbyist's Italian suit—and the theater of *his* slickness involved an endless evasion of formal consequences, with all the verbal jujitsu of strategic admissions, counter accusations, and ambiguous denials. If Clinton's oily evasiveness bore a resemblance to the cosmopolitan con man on Melville's "ship of fools," Reagan's character proved an eerily exact recapitulation of that other key figure in Melville's critique of the nation's modernizing psyche. His was a true reflection of those immediately likeable but ultimately dangerous authority figures: that leader of industry (Bartleby's boss) and captain of state (Amasa Delano) whose commitment to an upbeat innocence prescriptively rejects all contradictory evidence.

Heavily invested in sustaining a status quo of genial news, such a person tends to miss (as Delano did) imminent threats from the outside world even while he ignores (as did Bartleby's boss) the moral dangers ever present in himself. Contravening those cautionary readings of the human condition supplied by the West's Greco-Hebraic wisdom literature, this decadent version of the American character denies both the tragic sense of life and the inward risk of sin. Tempered by a mix of apparent sincerity and affable egalitarianism, this character's vanity avoids both the self-conscious rebelliousness of the Hebraic sinner and the overt hubris of the Greeks' fallen hero. In response to the shifting course of events, Achilles boasts, pouts, then grieves and rages; Satan frontally attacks and then surreptitiously schemes. But America's Sunny Jim never changes. Inwardly as well as outwardly, he beams the benevolence of his geniality, a "bounty broadcast like moonlight" on every occasion.

Insomuch as this figure lacks the sort of name that efficiently defines the modern con man or the ancient trickster, rhetorical convenience begs the invention of one, and so I have dubbed this uniquely American character type the Disingenue.

Reagan's contemporary, the poet Delmore Schwartz, captured the actual acquisitiveness behind the Disingenue's apparent innocence in his comic lyric "The True-Blue American." Brought to an ice cream parlor, the poem's boy protagonist, Jeremiah Dickson, is asked to choose between a banana split and a chocolate sundae. But "denying dilemma," he "refus[es] to believe the choice of between," and as a "true-blue American" who embraces instead "the infinite and the gold / of the endless frontier, the deathless West," he defiantly declares "I will have them both!"[6]

Schwartz's lines inscribe a farcical portrait of American exceptionalism, the inner mapping of its most infantile temper. They satirize the sweet-tooth hope of that ever boyish, New-World self whose glad-handing philosophy reliably transforms the anxiety of free choice into the surety of a free lunch. Here, the landscape of opportunity (in the form of the superabundant soda fountain) justifies a gluttony whose manifest destiny, doubly blessed by God and Nature, is placed beyond question: the right to have *both!* without guilt or indigestion.

Along with fearmongering, the most common strategy of the demagogue is to dangle that promise of *both!* before the voting public. Although Reagan made tactical use of fear by conjuring the communist menace to secure the nomination for president, his popularity among the broader electorate was primarily secured through pitching his personal belief in that same unchecked prosperity: the imminent arrival of "the infinite and the gold." He appeared to transcend partisan politics by asserting the manifest destiny of an exceptional nation to which we all (theoretically) belonged. By the mere fact of our membership—by the virtue, that is, of simply being true-blue Americans like Jeremiah Dickson—we citizens, haloed in the glow of the nation's moral grandeur and material might, were bequeathed the same set of immeasurable rights.

That Reagan's two terms were simultaneous with the emergence of both identity politics and the self-esteem movement is no accident, for those enemies of the political and cultural right were offering their adherents a mix of moral immunity and self-congratulation very similar to that which characterized Reagan's own disingenuous vision of American life. His was an identity politics on the grandest of scales, a self-esteem therapy for the entire republic—or, rather, for those who identified truly and bluely with the republic recast as an ice cream parlor. As in Schwartz's poem, however, Reagan's "electing absolute affirmation" was always built on his lifelong habit of "denying dilemma." As in the poem, too, that denial was primarily serving the greediest of fantasies: the boyish insistence that he, now conveniently recast as the communal *we*, both could have and should have the sundae and the split.

The fundamental theme of Reagan's personality—and so, too, of his incoherent presidency—was this overriding temperamental lie, this genialization, which repeatedly preached the bounty of *both!* Both the idealization of the old West and the commercialization of its spaces. Both the preaching of individual self-reliance and the licensing of the mega-corporation. Because he refused to believe in "the choice of between," we could drastically cut taxes *and* balance the budget; we could shrink the federal government while (voila!) dramatically expanding the nation's defenses.

To the amazement of his aides, Reagan didn't merely adopt these contradictory stances out of political necessity; he gave every appearance of believing their blarney. The old political schemer would have chosen supply-side theory with a cynical self-consciousness, well aware that its claim to balance the budget through cutting taxes was largely hokum. But Reagan lacked both the fierce self-awareness and the sociopathic indifference of the Machiavellian leader. As a company man masked by the mere costume of cowboy-individualism, he could neither a Iago nor a Hamlet be. He represented instead a new kind of demagogue, one better fashioned to exploit the tenor of his time. As a supreme example of the electronic age's post-literate persona, he assumed power not through rational analysis but emotional mimicry. The old calculating cynic had been superseded by the genial sentimentalist, the shameless liar by a new form of egotist: the conveniently self-deluding Disingenue.

Cowboy's "Nice Place":
The Cinematic Origins of the Genial Demagogue

I looked toward the movie, the common dream,
. . . .
And I accepted such things as they seem . . .

—Delmore Schwartz, "Metro-Goldwyn-Mayer"[7]

TRAINED BY HIS SERIAL successes as radio announcer, movie actor, TV host, and corporate speaker, Ronald Reagan didn't simply exploit the skills he had acquired in his thirty years as a professional entertainer; his private personality had been molded by them as well. As the biographies by Lou Cannon and Gary Wills attest, the pervasive PR of the movie industry was especially influential in modeling how to stage a convincing pretense of perpetual innocence. From the earliest days of the cinema, the sexual allure of its stars had fueled its profitability. Yet, just as the rapacity of greed was frequently concealed in modernizing America by the fig leaf of philanthropy (the *more* money given, the *better* the person, no matter how his money had been earned), Eros in these older movies was often disguised by a saintly costume of chaste concern, and the studios developed, in Wills's apt phrase, an elaborate system of "omnidirectional feigning" to sustain that masquerade.[8]

There were notable exceptions, of course, the likes of Valentino, Jean Harlow, and Mae West. But from Mary Pickford, the first female movie star, who was perpetually cast in girlish roles, through Doris Day who was still playing cute in daddy's pajamas as she broached middle age; from the genial Jimmy Stewarts to the gruff John Waynes who, so brutally blunt when facing down outlaws, were reduced to blushing stutters before their rescued ladies, the pretense of a sexual innocence became one crucial theme of the "common dream" produced by the studios and beloved by the public. Soon after he arrived at MGM in 1937, Ronald Reagan enlisted as an enthusiastic participant in staging this pretense. Although he never quite made the a-team, he became a successful studio actor of the chaste sort, immediately handsome yet immaculately harmless. Wills cites the line that captures in comic extremity the nature of that role. Playing "Cowpoke" in the 1955 movie, *Tennessee's Partner,* Reagan compliments his hostess with the observation, "nice place you have here, ma'am," apparently unaware that the place in question is a whorehouse.[9]

The studios' investment in this staged innocence extended beyond the theater proper. In one of the clearest signs of the persuasive power of the electronic media, the public expected that the stars they adored were actually living the roles played: fans not only "accepted," they demanded that "such things" remain "as they seem[ed]" on the silver screen. That illusion was then sustained by a studio-fed network of newsreels, gossip columns, and fan magazines. Even as actors were forced to play the same role over and over, their private lives were fictionalized into exact reflections of their cinematic stereotypes. Mary Pickford had to dress the part of the virginal girl whenever in public despite her multiple marriages. Later, to mask his homosexuality and so maintain his allure as a leading man, Rock Hudson agreed to an arranged marriage.

For most of the early studio stars, the obligation to sustain this campaign of "omnidirectional feigning" was a burden they accepted for the sake of their very profitable careers. Publicly, they played by the rules—posing for the rigged photo opportunities, allowing agents and studio flacks to submit false copy about their private lives under their own names—while privately nursing the sort of cynicism that necessarily emerges in any profession that comes to depend on wholesale deception as a matter of course: the same smoldering derision that has now come to prevail throughout a Virtual America bent on disguising avarice as innocence. But Ronald Reagan nurtured no such privately subversive thoughts. Where the old Machiavellian prince had composed his deceptions self-consciously, our new genial schemer, the Disingenue, was enacting his lies as *un*consciously as possible.

Always the compliant company man, Reagan gladly volunteered to share this gift for selective amnesia with the public at large. A past president of Eureka College's Booster Club, he evinced from the start that key characteristic of the political personality: an urge to speak both to and for the community as a whole. In these public relations speeches given on behalf of the movie industry, Reagan would complain that Hollywood had been unfairly cast by unknowing critics as a sinkhole of immorality.[10] In his retelling, the so-called community of movie land reemerged, boosted, into a West Coast version of Main Street USA, where a gang of swell guys and gals had gathered to make a better life for their children. Here was yet one more tranquil, tree-lined nexus of civic duty and familial love, built on the bourgeois bedrock of good schools, stable marriages, and neighborly regard. Reagan's pitch never changed a whit. As Lou Cannon notes, even after he was divorced by his first wife, Jane Wyman (a fact he seemed to forget, along with his own indifferent performance as a Main Street dad), Reagan's speeches still stressed the stability of the Hollywood marriage.[11]

One couldn't have guessed from his account that the business of Hollywood *was* business, and that the primary motive for settling there was not the excellent school system but a very human hankering after wealth and fame. Nor, "refusing to believe the choice of between," did his speechifying ever acknowledge that such hankering might conflict with the performance

of civic duties or the sustaining of stable marriages. In fact, as today's del-
uge of cut-throat corporate bios and screw-and-tell memoirs reveals all too
gladly, Hollywood was a lot more like a brothel than the fabled cradle of
Cowboy's "nice place." Which is to say, simply, that its central reason for
being was the production of fantasies—often, though not exclusively, erotic
fantasies—in pursuit of hard cash.

The "common dream" preferred by Cowpoke dictated the neighborly
generosity of pitching in together for barn raisings and quilting bees, and
sketched happy family scenes of gift exchange on hearth-lit Christmas Eves.
The memoirs reveal instead a sphere of intense ambition and competition,
where studios stole each other's stars, actors each other's lines (as Errol
Flynn did to Reagan in *Santa Fe Trail*), and where the effrontery of actual
independence could lead to career extinction, as in the virtual blacklisting
of Orson Welles. They unveil as well tales of counter-Dickensian holiday
traditions, such as the annual celebration of William Holden and Shelley
Winters, who committed adultery together each Christmas Eve for seven
straight years.[12]

Seen from a distance and as a whole, American public culture during
the Reagan years exhibited just such a theater of complementary duplicities. Even as his popular speeches evoked a nation with a sinless past and
a riskless future, outside the fences of that fantasyland, TV's talk-show culture was coming into its own, casting the shadows of another and counter
"common dream" of the republic. According to Sunny Jim's identity politics
of metaphysical exemption, America was all material sweetness and moral
light, the home of the utterly free and the unfailingly brave. Meanwhile,
daytime TV was projecting a counter image of our republic, one rife with
enslaved addicts and whimpering victims—a Noah's Ark of abused or abusing men and women who were now ready to come clean and tell it all on the
Phil-prah-raldo Show.

Rather than contradictory, however, these two versions of America
were, like Carlyle's Quack and Dupe, "upper-side and under of the self-same
substance." They were interdependent and even interchangeable visions,
elected and selected by the same voting, viewing public. Sharing an "open
voracity for profit and closed sense for truth," their simultaneous visions of
the American character falsified the good and the bad alike. Here, too, the
public was choosing the bounty of *both!*, demanding the rich banana split
of decadence along with the cherry-topped sundae of innocence. We could
binge on sordid sin while basking in civic righteousness.

The revisionism of the Reagan presidency, in which the *job* of the chief
executive was radically retooled into the *role* of the Great Communicator,
was precalibrated in those early days of his studio employment when he

volunteered as an industry spokesman. Working, in fact, then for the material good of the company—for Hollywood constituted a company town no less than Henry Ford's Detroit or the hillbilly hamlets indentured to big coal—Reagan spoke instead of the moral good of the community. In doing so, he was enlisting as a trooper in the second stage of that mutual dupery which, swapping money for make-believe, constituted the complex relationship between the ticket-buying public and the movie-making industry. To succeed in the precincts of make-believe, most of Hollywood's actors had to go along with the pretense that their actual lives mirrored their fictional roles. But Reagan, in his secondary role as industry spokesman, boosted the private pretense into a collective fantasy. Stepping off the screen yet staying in character, he insisted that the "common dream" was a political as well as personal reality. Not only was the individual sex symbol really chaste; the entire brothel was Cowpoke's nice place. "As you like it" *was* "the way we were."

From the start, then, Reagan's political message, as honed by the public relations desks of the studio system, pitched the collective fantasy of genialization. Later, this defender of Hollywood simply expanded the definition of that fictive community, at once marvelous and maligned, to include the village square of the entire nation. Once again, there were unfair critics—intellectual pessimists, big government bureaucrats, civil rights activists—who missed the inviolable goodness of the communal enterprise to which we all (theoretically) belonged. Once again, the fantasies of optimism would mask the avidity of egotism while the image of tough-guy self-reliance would reliably deliver the treacle of self-esteem: according to Reagan, it was always about to be "Morning Again in America," his re-election campaign's upbeat theme.

"There You Go Again": The Political Savvy of the Genial Demagogue

Not only did the same message, with its meta-narrative of a happily-ever-after ending, persist from Hollywood to Sacramento to Washington, D.C.; so did the organizational structure that delivered and defended it. Once a screen actor achieved star status in the old studio system, his primary job, other than the acting itself, was to protect the public image that stoked his popularity. He and "his people" strove to make sure that both the roles he was given and the publicity he received were of the quality and character that would safely sustain his box office appeal. Then as now, the star's bond with the public, his or her capacity to embody the "common dream," proved crucial in the marketing of a film. But most of the decision-making that went into the actual creation of those older movies was left to the studio's corporate executives.

When he moved into politics, Reagan naturally borrowed his model of governance from this familiar system. He was exceptionally adept and, for him, uncommonly active in those aspects of political leadership that harmonized with the role of an actor-entertainer in the electronic age: box office draw was not *that* different from electoral appeal. And those separate skills that he had honed on the PR circuit as a spokesman for Hollywood and then General Electric, both of which involved learning to communicate in ways that pleased a mainstream crowd, made him an exceptional campaigner, so long as he had a script prepared and the self-discipline to stick to it. He became especially adept at staging that artifice of innocence that has always driven the "progress of genialization."

A crucial example of this highly honed skill occurred during the campaign of 1980 in his only debate with President Jimmy Carter. In truth, given the economy's double-digit inflation and the humiliating hostage crisis in Iran, the incumbent had already lost by the time the debate occurred just a week before election day. Still, Reagan's performance then exemplified his strengths as a political contestant in the TV era. A number of the two candidates' exchanges were analyzed in the following days, but the essence of the event was eventually reduced in the collective memory to a single line. After receiving from Carter a detailed attack on his health care and Medicare policies, Reagan simply and famously replied, "There you go again."

To see the bare words on the page is to be amazed that they should have proven so effective, for they appear to be pithed of any actual content. But Reagan wasn't making an argument: he was playing a role. And the line wasn't merely spoken, it was theatrically delivered, with the deliberate intention of redirecting attention away from the two candidates' diverging policies (and they *were* divergent on health care) and toward their contrasting personalities. With an expertly enacted ruefulness, a sad slight smile and a dipping of his head, Reagan was instantly evoking any number of cinema's nice-guy leads. We were back in the Bijou, and there on its screen was the familiar fetching image of democracy's swellest fella, Jimmy Stewart redux, affably tolerating the town's crackpot grump—a role that fit the moralistic Carter just well enough.

Delivered that way, the line succeeded in contrasting the incumbent's aggressiveness (and so *un*likeability) with Reagan's affability. Masking condescension with a show of compassion, the reply was a subtly crafted act of passive aggression, one that succeeded in personally criticizing Carter for Carter's own tendency to personally criticize. Although (it announced)

Reagan was man enough to take the punch, the blow (it implied) had been below the belt—beneath the fair-play standards of American geniality. In political rhetoric, it was the equivalent of Ali's rope-a-dope strategy and supplied the knockout intended as Reagan's poll numbers climbed every day after the debate.

The effectiveness of the strategy depended precisely on the perception that it wasn't a strategy but the spontaneous reaction of a real and decent man to an unfair attack. This impression went to the heart of the archetypal role that Reagan had assumed as his own: that of the genial everyman whose effectiveness avoids any immodest displays of overt cleverness. The Disingenue must never be seen to scheme on his own behalf, much less indulge in lawyer-like trickery. He reacts instead, and his reactions are—like those of the frontier hero who is his mythic father—simply and natively good, even as they just happen to serve his own political interests.

But the line *was* planned, and a fine example of Reagan's own brand of super slick cleverness: that of the actor's manipulation of emotions rather than the lawyer's manipulation of reasons. To the consternation of his handlers during the predebate practice sessions, Reagan had focused less on mastering complex arguments than on scripting memorable theatrical moments, and "there you go again" had been one of the lines he had coined at that time, storing it away for later use.[13] What appeared to be so natural, then, was itself an artifice—the instinctive reaction, a clever ploy staged through heeding the old script of the "common dream." In doing so, Reagan showed that he had mastered Hollywood's means of denying dilemma, pursuing a career of unchecked and (in the case of running against his party's incumbent president in 1976) *unseemly* ambition under the Teflon cover of the small-town hero. Only if you paid attention to what he actually did instead of who he unfailingly *seemed* to be did the true nature of his character become clear. Economist Martin Anderson was one of the few advisers who, keeping his eyes on the prize of political power, read his leader correctly when he concluded, admiringly, that Reagan was a "warmly ruthless" man.[14]

This ruthless calculus behind the aw-shucks smile was evident long before he finally secured the presidency. Although Reagan always bridled at the accusation of racism, he was not above tacitly appealing to racist voters, a tactic that began as early as the 1968 presidential campaign when he refused to criticize George Wallace, the nation's most notorious segregationist governor. And later, during the 1980 campaign, he angrily rejected the advice of his pollster Richard Wirthlin by accepting an invitation to speak at a county fair near Philadelphia, Mississippi: the very town where, in 1964, three civil rights activists were murdered with the complicity of local officials. It was his first speech after receiving the nomination, the kick-off to his fall campaign, and there can be little doubt about his motivation. Then Mississippi Congressman Trent Lott had promised Reagan that making an appearance would tip the state his way.[15] But for a man who, above all else, understood the symbolic nature of the political enterprise, the pretense that delivering his standard state-rights speech in such a place should not be construed as pandering to racist votes was disingenuous in the extreme.

In every election he entered with the exception of the last, Reagan was underestimated by opponents who tended to find him intellectually dim and sentimentally naive, unaware that he was exceptionally clever (and far more experienced than they) in the ways that mattered most when campaigning in an electronic age. Nor did they discern until it was too late that his genial persona, so carefully staged, was the primary source of his uncanny immunity to political attack. The Mississippi speech provides a clear example, for even he as nearly swept the South with his states-rights stance, completing the so-called Southern strategy first envisioned by Republican operatives in the late 1960s, the accusation of pandering to racist voters never really stuck. After decades of loathing FDR's legacy, the Republican right finally had a candidate with equivalent political charm, the populist touch par excellence.

Failure to Execute: Studio Stardom as Managerial Template

The personal traits that prove successful when running for office are not simply equal to those required to run that office once victory has been won. Although political charm can help pass policies, it can't supply the character necessary to design and execute effective ones, and as it turned out, the studio system that provided the organizational chart for Reagan's managerial style proved an inadequate model for political leadership. America's president *is* the government's chief executive officer. Because he is not only the star of the show but also the equivalent of the old studio boss, an effective president must "administrate" as well as "communicate," and Reagan lacked the native skills, training, and necessary will to fully take charge of the office he held.

The problem went deeper than his well-known disinterest in policy detail; he was also dangerously disengaged from the duties of personnel management. Reagan preferred, he insisted, to delegate rather than micromanage, but his form of delegation was always more like that of the studio's star than the studio's boss. Effective delegation in executive office still requires managing one's appointees, including intervening to assert authority and enforce consensus, but because Reagan loathed personal conflict, substantial disputes between his key aides (such as the ongoing feud between Secretary of State George Shultz and Secretary of Defense Caspar Weinberger) were left unresolved, paralyzing his administration on important issues. Rather than choose between the two men's policies, Reagan withdrew, and decision-making too often devolved to backroom maneuvering, including a penchant for secret initiatives that eventually led to the Iran-contra scandal.[16]

Although detrimental to his authority, this withdrawal was necessary to sustain the sunny worldview that had won him the office in the first place. Because, despite the promises of genialization, we can't always trust the world or even our selves; because not only do bad things happen to good people, good people sometimes do bad things; because alternatives do exclude and dilemmas are real, so that we can never really reap the bounty of *both!*—because, in short, the human condition is not "a major motion picture" produced by Metro-Goldwyn-Mayer, the maintenance of Reagan's sunny personality demanded a constant campaign of mystification and self-mystification, lie after lie in the genial mode. It required the same "omnidirectional feigning" that had prevailed in Hollywood's company town.

Forever deaf to the drumming of his own darker ambitions, forever fudging or simply "forgetting" the facts, always busy deflecting attention away from the hard realities of political difference and toward the soft geniality of personal presence ("There you go again."): Reagan, the inner man, had been thinned to those roles he had played on the screen, and his administrative aides then co-dependently took on the same tactics of make-believe.[17] His lies were for us, their lies for him, so he could keep lying for us, so we all might continue to believe in the cinematic dream that it was "Morning Again in America."

The left still angrily assails, while the right giddily praises, Reagan's so-called conservative philosophy, and yet, despite his administration's lasting impact on American governance, Reagan himself wasn't really a political ideologue any more than he was really a chief executive officer. With all the offices he held transformed into roles, policies for Reagan were more like costumes—to be donned or changed (from union leader to union buster, from budget balancer to supply-sider, from hawkish missile-builder to radical disarmer) as the "scene" required, and all in the service, first, of his own political ambition and, second, of a story line whose ultimate intention was not political coherence but psychological analgesia. Special interests certainly profited plenty from Reagan's confidence-game conservatism, but ideas as such were incidental to the meaning of the man as a public leader. Ronald Reaganism, like Coca-Colaism, was primarily "a feeling" and that feeling was perpetually "up."

The deep psychic need to stay up, the imperative of mood enhancement, trumped every other consideration in Reagan's life. His characteristic emotional detachment, which was both masked and enforced by his superficial warmth, constituted a formidable defense against true intimacy.[18] Intimacy was bad because it would, inevitably, bear bad news about himself and the world: the persistence of pain, the reality of failure, the moral consequences of his ambition on family and friends, the fragility of human happiness. As a leader, Reagan preferred to delegate partially because stars communicate rather than administrate, but also because his hands-off management style supplied him with the same psychic distance that he so assiduously cultivated in his private life.[19]

So, too, with his habitual avoidance of analysis.[20] Wishing to exclude cognitive as well as emotional dissonance, Reagan was notorious for failing to read policy proposals, his preparation on most subjects reduced to dumbed-down oral briefings that were heavy with visual aids, including cartoons. One vivid instance of this leader's approach to absorbing policy can represent the rest. In 1983, on the afternoon before an economic summit being hosted by America at Colonial Williamsburg, James Baker, Reagan's chief of staff, left the president a thick binder of relevant materials to study. When he returned the next morning, Baker observed that the briefing book hadn't been touched: the Reagans, it turned out, had watched *The Sound of Music* instead.[21]

Political enemies, and not a few of his allies, thought such behavior proof of a fundamental laziness. But the choice of the entertaining movie over policy homework, and an oldie he had likely seen before, was just as indicative of the constant emotional buffering that was required to keep his sunny side up. Reagan may have been as intellectually lazy as he was politically ambitious and physically active, and he may have possessed a mind natively keyed to a narrative rather than an analytical understanding of the world,[22] but his aversion to detailed analysis was also being driven by the same denial that prevailed in every other aspect of his life. Better to hear the sound of the same happy music again and again than to read troublesome budget numbers or confront painful policy options. Better to stay inside the "common dream" than to venture into a reality that was rife with disturbing ambiguities.

Golden Goose: The Genialization of American Prosperity

Most of Reagan's political authority evolved from his unmatched capacity to connect with what his aides called "mythic America." But the myths he drew on were precisely the ones that the studio system had aggressively un-Grimmed, reducing them to sentimental mush, and as a result of constantly searching for the electoral equivalent of box office draw, Reagan quickly adopted a series of policies which, taken together and "denying dilemma," made no more sense than the standard plot line of a Hollywood thriller.

Nowhere was this more evident than in the sheer unreality of the first Reagan budget, whose economic and political impact is felt to this day. A late but total convert to the happy-talk news of supply-side theory, Reagan proposed drastically cutting taxes (especially for the rich) while significantly increasing defense spending, even as he maintained the traditional conservative promises of balancing the budget and shrinking the federal government. How could such a seemingly self-contradictory agenda succeed? The eventual magic of supply-side's golden goose (its paradoxical promise to generate more tax revenues through cutting tax rates), when combined with a commitment to eliminate waste, was supposed to bridge the already enormous gap between income and expenditures. But following the politics of the ice cream parlor, Reagan (like every president before him) wouldn't touch the gargantuan entitlements of Social Security and Medicare which, along with defense spending, were the primary engines of federal indebtedness. He even rejected an exceptionally rare proposal by Republican senators to trim those popular programs' cost-of-living increases. Instead, his budgetary efficiencies focused on cuts in social services for the poor, which, whatever one thinks about them politically and morally, were entirely insufficient to the daunting task of controlling the federal deficit.

In a show of impressive political salesmanship, Reagan managed to sway enough Democrats to pass his economic program, but the results quickly belied the pot-'o-gold promises Sunny Jim had made. Although he had won the election in large part because the country was already suffering from severe economic trouble, his policies only intensified the pain. Supply-side's goose, federally endorsed, laid an egg all right—but it wasn't a golden one. The deficit soared; Reagan's more pragmatic aides began to insist that some of his tax cuts needed to be reversed; and the country suffered its worst economic downturn since the Great Depression.[23]

The general result, if not its specific parameters, shouldn't have been surprising, for, in precisely the terms we have been using here, Reagan's first budget was a con. It was a manifestly fraudulent proposal which, enriching the relative few, could only be sold to Congress and the public by boosting their "confidence" in its impossible dream of an imminent and painless prosperity for all. Reagan, the son of small-town Dixon, Illinois, was proposing an economic program whose core logic was worthy instead of Delmore Schwartz's Jeremiah Dickson. Indeed, he one-upped the boy prophet of *both!* by promising *all three!*: reduced taxes, increased security, and an end to deficit-spending.

But the con worked, and largely because Reagan *was* the Great Communicator: just the sort of genial demagogue who could subvert common sense on behalf of make-believe. Eventually, given the near unanimity of his aides' concerns and the manifest gravity of the bad news, Reagan relented, and small shifts in policy were made, including the passage of "revenue enhancements." The economy would return to prosperity, and just in time to secure his re-election, yet the route back wasn't the painless one promised, nor even the moderate "soft landing" that most realists aim for in times of economic downturn. Rather than the abracadabra of supply-side's magic, the harsh medicine of controlling the money supply (as enforced by Federal Reserve Chairman Paul Volcker) and the crash-landing of a brutal recession, along with a serendipitous easing of the oil crisis, reduced inflation and recalibrated the economy for renewed expansion. The size of that expansion would prove impressive, but thanks to Reagan's policies on taxes, unions, and regulation, its benefits were as unevenly distributed as the economic suffering that preceded and primed its eventual surge.[24] This accelerating inequality has been one of the clearest legacies of the Reagan years.

Further, because they felt compelled to deny the unreality of their original premises, the Reagan team never admitted, much less addressed, the full severity of the federal deficit. Arriving as a self-proclaimed antidote to liberal fiscal irresponsibility, Reagan ended up submitting to Congress eight consecutive unbalanced budgets.[25] Rather than check the liberal penchant to overspend, he adopted it himself (if toward different ends), so much so that national debt was nearly tripled under his rule. Here, too, Reagan was at one with his people, for individual behavior quickly came to mirror the economic values of his administration. The new prosperity, it turned out, was being driven in part by a radical increase in both personal and governmental indebtedness. One of the secret sources of the Reagan expansion was not so secret, after all. It was the same practice favored by every profligate since the invention of money: consumption on credit.

The premises for this historic shift, whose recklessness would eventually help trigger the financial collapse of 2008, were long in the making. In the past, however, that temptation had been at least partially checked by various strands of our cultural heritage, including a show-me conservatism especially strong in the Midwest. In yet another instance of his adept demagoguery, Reagan drew on that very tradition to cover the true implications of his economic policies. His voice, gestures, and dress, the modesty of his manner and the innocence of his humor, all evoked the prudent ethos of Dixon, Illinois. Personally, Reagan projected the character of that small-town Midwesterner who, as decent and humble as he was democrati-cally accessible, always dressed and spoke plainly, paid his bills on time, and saved what remained for the proverbial rainy day.

Yet, as on the subject of race, Reagan's budget policies completely con-tradicted his personal image. A strong argument can be made that America would have arrived there eventually anyway, but it was under the cover of Reaganism that the nation rapidly completed its conversion to a debt-based vision of prosperity. Consume now, pay later because, well, "the infinite and the gold" were sure to come to the exceptional nation. Beneath the Jimmy Stewart mask, this was the actual legacy of the new "conservative" econom-ics, based as it was on the dubious husbandry of the golden goose.

Maginot Line: The Genialization of Military Danger

Reagan could ignore the federal deficit because, buffered by his own psychic self-defenses and sheltered from bad news by his overprotective wife and aides, he was able to sustain an unsinkable confidence that "the infinite and the gold" were soon to come. Like the little boy in one of his favorite jokes, he could be surrounded by a pile of horse manure and still remark hope-fully, "I know there's a pony in here someplace." And so it was that, despite the financial fiasco generated by his first budget, the imaginary pony of a painless prosperity was soon followed in 1983 by the winged steed of a per-fect security. The same up mood that licensed the magic of the golden goose conjured the prospect of a space-age version of the Maginot Line.

Although, as the truest of true-blue believers, the president had to be held accountable for his budgetary policies, Reaganomics was still a con with many culpable conspirators. But the Strategic Defense Initiative (SDI)—a plan to install a space-based missile defense system that would prevent a surprise nuclear attack—was Reagan's own baby; it was adopted by him without the consultation of many of his most knowledgeable aides, including his secretaries of state and defense.[26] Such an end-around was precisely what some of Reagan's most fervent backers had been hoping for all along. Resenting the influence of pragmatists like Baker and Shultz, and blind to the essentially *non*political coordinates of their leader's true compass, right-wing dogmatists were perpetually grousing, "Let Reagan be Reagan." With SDI, their wish came true, and almost literally out of the blue. The program represented Reaganism in its purest form—that is, it was a policy unimpinged by even the glint of a hint of pragmatism. Given the Kafkaesque maze of the defense budget, the true numbers may never be known, but after absorbing tens of billion dollars, SDI (scornfully dubbed

Star Wars by its critics) did not produce a single viable weapon system for either ground- or space-based missile defense.

This simple sum of the program's failure needs to be stressed because its adoption has been rationalized by Reagan's hagiographers as a primary cause of the Soviet Union's fall. Rather than a con on the American people that wasted tax dollars on an epic scale, SDI has been recast as a masterful duping of the Kremlin's strategists. Forced to keep pace in this new realm of the arms race, the argument goes, the already failing Soviet economy was gravely threatened, and the new communist leaders, driven to adapt to that grim reality, began authoring reforms that quickly led to their empire's collapse.

This much is true: SDI did play a prominent part in the final rounds of arms negotiations that preceded that collapse, and Reagan's national security adviser, Robert McFarlane, did plan to use the program to force concessions at the bargaining table—a ploy he sometimes called "The Sting." But the ploy was not Reagan's, nor did McFarlane ever mention it to him.[27] And although SDI did help bring the Russians to the table (Gorbachev, attempting to rescue the sclerotic Soviet system, had multiple reasons for pursuing détente), Reagan's fierce attachment to the program's utopian fantasy of a failsafe security became the final impediment to a radical reduction in nuclear arms.

For McFarlane, SDI *was* Star Wars: a fantastic scheme with little plausibility beyond its scare value in Moscow. He helped to engineer its initial adoption inside the White House with the specific intention of giving it up, plotting to enact a classic con by trading SDI's worthless promise for the tangible reality of the Soviet's superiority in long-range missiles with multiple warheads. McFarlane had to resign due to the Iran-contra scandal before a key summit with the Soviets at Reykjavik, but when Gorbachev arrived there with a similar proposal in mind, it seemed that the grand scheme might succeed even in his absence. McFarlane's sting, however, was fatally flawed from the start in that its author misunderstood the character of the president who would have to sign off on such a deal. Reagan wasn't, after all, a Machiavel (someone who could self-consciously deceive for his side's advantage) but a Disingenue, and true to that character's investment in self-dupery, Reagan's commitment to SDI's fantasy was so complete that he refused to give it up under any conditions. To his credit, and in contrast to most of the cold warriors in both parties, Reagan really did desire a radical disarmament, but when brought to the brink of its eventuality, he rejected a huge reduction in nuclear arms in favor of the imminent pony of SDI.

What was so attractive about this program's promise that Reagan was willing to forgo such a dramatic achievement? To answer that question we need only to return to the narrative of the "common dream" which, whenever circumstances let Reagan be Reagan, always prevailed in his decision-making over both *real politik* and right-wing ideology. Buffing his populist image as a citizen-politician, Reagan loved to say that he was just an actor on loan to public service, and insomuch as these statements were being used to discount his political ambition, they deserve to be dismissed as yet one more feature of his carefully crafted disingenuousness. But it is also true that the primary coordinates of Reagan's private worldview were fatefully fixed in Hollywood, and as a consequence of being an-actor-on-loan-to-public-service in this global sense, he naturally assessed his two terms in office as he would the plot line of any Hollywood script.

As I already noted, the star's primary concern in the studio system was to assure that the roles assigned to him were worthy of his winning image, and SDI's script, in Reagan's experience, had all the makings of a bona fide hit. In it, he could play the classic American hero: that natural man whose native genius, uncluttered by the blinding details and cautious limits of nerdy expertise, would save the day. As it happened, this was a role he was especially prepared to play, for on the complex subject of nuclear armaments, like that of financing the federal budget, Reagan's mind was uncluttered in the extreme. Freed of such niggling complexities, he surveyed the big picture and spied a solution to the mutual terror which, alone in those days, secured a fragile peace.

He left the details to the experts, but the basic idea, Reagan insisted, had been his alone: we would create a defensive bubble or shield that "could protect us from nuclear missiles just as a roof protects a family from rain."[28] Whether space-based, ground-based, or both, new technologies would be implemented, and these miraculous instruments would then form an all-enclosing perimeter of defensive weaponry that could instantly zap any rocketing invader before its warhead could be delivered. Once that shield was in place in "the deathless West," the threat of nuclear war would become obsolete.

As an actor-on-loan-to-public-service, Reagan found this cinematic climax hard to resist. Like a willful studio star who knew the vehicles that would serve him best, he clung to SDI because it alone could supply the sort of happily-ever-after ending that all such major motion pictures required. Only with SDI's promise of eternal peace actively in place, and not bartered away for some mundane advantage in kill capacity, could he complete this role of a lifetime. It didn't matter that most of the scientific establishment, with the conspicuous exception of those who would directly profit by SDI's adoption, opposed the program as completely implausible. Skeptics could satirize and experts analyze by brandishing their wit and mustering their data, but, in the realm of polemics, the demagogue knew better. He knew that, in a nation raised on the "common dream," the likeability of hope would reliably trump the credibility of fact. So it was that just as he had convinced Congress to invest in supply side's golden goose, Reagan closed the sale on this space-age version of the Maginot Line. Under the guise of a conservative revival, the grounds for security, like those for prosperity, were genialized.

SDI finally proves to be the most personally revealing of Reagan's key policies. Its vision of a safe inner haven, one whose perimeter would be guarded by sensitive satellites that could instantly shoot down any harmful invader, not only supplies an accurate chart of Reagan's managerial style—one in which a set of super-protective aides was expected to take the "initiative" by "strategically defending" their boss's peace of mind from all incoming bad news; such a system was also an accurate projection of the principles commanding Reagan's own psyche.

This was the president's climactic inspiration, the final gift that he wished to bequeath to the American nation: our military defense would now be modeled after the lifelong success of his psychic self-defenses—a system whose vigilant instruments of fantasy and forgetfulness dissuaded all pain, and within which even the rankest ambition could masquerade as well-intentioned. The sun might eventually set on our postwar republic, but within the self-sealing sphere of such a defense, it would always *seem* like morning again in America. The harsher storms of history, its perennial pains and hurtful sins, might continue to lash down, but the flawless deflection of SDI's "roof" would turn the very sound of their assault into the muffled proof of safety itself. Meanwhile, those of us inside, having pushed aside the briefing book of life, could hear the hills come alive (again and again) with *The Sound of Music*.

Virtual Conservative: The Genial Demise of the Protestant Self

The broad allure of the cinematic fantasies that sold both the golden goose of supply-side theory and the Maginot Line of SDI reveals the actual significance of the Reagan presidency—how he both reflected and accelerated a pattern of change in the national character that was long in the making. Born in 1911, the year when the first Hollywood studio was erected, Reagan was a true child of the electronic age and the new entertainment economy it spawned. His was the first generation for whom the primary mode of populist storytelling was cinematic rather than literary, and crucially, too, the first to become accustomed to a profusion of consumer products, along with the marketing that relentlessly pitched them.

As a result of these changes in the shape, pace, and material expectations of everyday life, the practical compass of American virtue was also shifting. In a mainstream economy that now touted comfort as an ideal; that used flattery, envy, and tacit sexuality to "push our buttons" for boosting sales; and that increasingly relied on personal indebtedness, the old Protestant ethic had to be debunked, for its cautionary emphases on simplicity, humility, abstinence, and frugality—as well as its insistence on an introspective self-criticism to enforce them all—were incompatible with the ethos required by corporate consumerism. But since those traditional virtues were interwoven into the nest of habits, hopes, and covenants that had fashioned the nation's ideal sense of self, the threat of their loss was potentially traumatic. And so the old virtues had to lose their appeal quietly, behind a mirage of conservative continuity designed to comfort the anxious, while blame for the ethical changes that were bound to ensue was deflected instead onto alien sources.

As we have seen, this tacit assault on traditional morality became a central feature of Hollywood's productions, an agenda most evident in Disney's emasculation of Pinocchio's conscience "for the good of the kids." Mimicking the soul and substance of *that* "mythic America," Reagan then projected a similar strategy into the political sphere. Just as in the heyday of the studio system when the disingenuous role of the nice-guy hero, playing chaste and making nice, fronted for the crudity of the studio boss who had a starlet on his couch and his eyes laser-locked on the bottom line, Reagan's sentimental persona covered for the cynical reality of scientific capitalism in the 1980s. It hid that economy's promiscuous intention to reduce every virtue, conservative or liberal, republican or religious, to its market value— all agencies of meaning-making into vehicles for money-making. Behind the make-nice masquerade staged by Sunny Jim, "Mammon led [us] on— / Mammon, the least erected spirit that fell / from heaven."

Reagan's election did mark, then, a symbolic divide in the evolution of the nation's character, but it was one utterly different from the triumphant return to conservative values that his hagiographers now like to imagine. A leader steeped in the classical versions of the conservative temperament, one who believed in the tragic sense of life and in the salience of sin—a leader, for example, like Abraham Lincoln—would have demanded self-sacrifice and embraced self-criticism. Instead, we were promised the bounty of *both!* and fed the sentimental hubris of the true-blue American.

We are now living with the wreckage that always lurked behind that genial message. Massive federal indebtedness, rampant economic inequality, a thoroughly corrupted financial industry, an ongoing addiction to golden-goose notions that recently led to the housing bubble: these toxic conditions are the "something further" that followed the Masquerade which Melville first predicted and, after thirty years of training on the large and small screen, Ronald Reagan perfected. Completing a process more than a century in the making, his ascendancy to the highest office in the land signaled the effective demise of the old Protestant self under the "progress of genialization."

And, irony of ironies, Reagan enacted this symbolic demise of the once super-effective Protestant self through a strategy very similar to one favored by the pomo aesthetes whose sudden success was exactly simultaneous to his unanticipated rise to political prominence. Like those first Pop artists of the New York scene (whom cultural conservatives have so loved to loathe—often rightly, I believe) and like the more recent cultural "transgressors" whose faux rebellions we shall turn to next, Reagan appropriated the imagery of a revered tradition, borrowing the look-feel of the old Protestant character, only to subvert the virtues that defined its essence. His virtual conservatism was the Trojan horse that snuck the confidence game of pain dissuasion into the apex of political power.

6

The Masquerade of Faux Rebellion

In almost any society . . . the quality of the nonconformists
is likely to be just as good as, and no better than that of the
conformists.[1]

—Margaret Mead

IF AMERICA'S SHIP OF state has begun to resemble Melville's ship of fools, a
social space where the poses of the Masquerade and the colloquies of Quack
and Dupe have been replacing the older rituals and scripts of civil exchange,
what does that mean for the artist, whose truth-telling has traditionally proceeded through a mastery of masks, all the subtle simulations of metaphorical imagery and symbolic role-playing?

The painter's mission of conjuring images to evoke lasting essences
becomes problematic, doesn't it, in a society saturated by millions of images, most of which serve the hawking of products? If the poet's task is,
in Emily Dickinson's subtle phrase, to "tell all the Truth but tell it slant,"[2]
how does she succeed within a public conversation most of whose phrases
have already been spun to serve an angle? How to "make it new"[3] when
oddity itself has become a seasonal commodity? How to cast a jaundiced
eye on officialdom's lies when the once reliably subversive tactic of irony so
suffuses the body politic that it actually serves to immunize deceit from effective critique? And when relentless marketeering now demands of us daily
a "willing suspension of disbelief,"[4] can theater or cinema possibly make a
difference?

As a kind of prefatory credo in chapter 1, I announced my intention
to rebel against this political economy's insinuating sway. One might have
thought then that, as a working artist, I practiced the perfect profession for

125

a principled resistance to those values I disdain. Mutiny, after all, has long been acknowledged as a righteous tack for the *literary* sailor. Yet one of the most prominent features of the aging of Aquarius has been the co-opting of resistance. With increasing shamelessness, the simulation of rebellion has become both a favorite shtick in the vaudeville of salesmanship and the plastic prize promised at the bottom of the box of consumer confection. Yes, don the right brand and you, too, can exude transgression. Although such toothless poses can seem mightily amusing, Virtual America's strategy of enclosure for control is much enhanced by its ability to stage these phony exits from its ruling ethos. The time has come, then, for a closer look at how the appearance of a daring deviancy has concealed a broader submission to the core beliefs of Evangelical Mammonism.

I. The Art of Faux Rebellion

One unanticipated change in the years following World War II was the proliferation of private lessons, summer camps, and college degree programs in the fine arts. As families once sent second sons into the ministry, parents were starting to accept the arts as a quasi-respectable profession for their children to pursue. This new social sanctioning couldn't be confused, though, with an actual appreciation of aesthetic truths. Then as now, not a single mode of serious art could be said to serve as a pole star for conventional thought. Leaders never cited literary classics; paintings became newsworthy only in the guise of commodities when auctioned to oil barons at astonishing rates; and artists were left to debate among themselves their raison d'etre while their wealthy nation smiled down with obtuse benevolence, deaf to their arguments, no matter how loud.

This postwar attitude, with its oddly commingled portions of endorsement and indifference, solidified into policy in 1965 with the creation of the National Endowment for the Arts (NEA). Because art was "good," individual artists were to be supported by federal revenues, and because no one else really understood (or cared to examine) why or how that might be so, the awarding of moneys would be left primarily to artists themselves. What seems astonishing in retrospect is not the government's eventual interference in this purportedly objective process but the lengthy term of its benign neglect. And so, although artists had something to fear in 1989 when questions first arose about the NEA's funding of certain projects, one might have hoped then that a serious discussion on the quality of art and its public function, so long deferred, would finally take place. The urge to criticize, after all, at least acknowledged that art might have a potency and purpose beyond elevating one's social status. Better to be scrutinized than to remain a boutonniere in the buttonhole of the merchant's good life.

What took the place of that enlightening debate, what artists revealed about themselves as would-be rebels when drawn out of their isolation at last, and what their critics revealed about the actual moral stature of their conservative stance all made for a darkly funny, if finally disturbing, story. In the debasement of the NEA debate, we were witnessing on both sides the same mustering of a preening moralism to mask a corrosive cynicism that would characterize so many later rounds of our cultural wars.

Hypocrisy Check: The Artist's Civil Liberties Index

The story began with an act of cynicism when the minions of Senator Jesse Helms, who would never enter a gallery themselves, began closely examining the NEA's list of grant-winning projects, hoping to be outraged by what they found. The agency didn't disappoint them. Pudenda-shaped plates, a photo of a piss-pickled Jesus enshrined in a jar, propagandist prettifications of sado-masochistic homosexual acts: obscenity to the left of him, blasphemy to the right of him, into the valley of spotlights and sound bites, the "offended" (but secretly smiling) senator charged. He had found at last an issue to stoke his constituents' ire.

And not just his usual constituency, that was the shocker. The so-called Moral Majority, which has never been a majority and has rarely spoken for the moderate center of American culture on matters moral or otherwise, had grasped a new way to define debate on its own narrow terms. Moderate politicians were quick to express their personal outrage that public moneys had supported such work, and liberals were once again placed in the impossible position of defending the principle of free expression while having to decry a few of its most publicized products. John Frohnmayer, the new head of the NEA, was forced into negotiations with Helms's aides; the entire budget supporting individual artists was threatened; and new guidelines were drawn up, including an anti-obscenity pledge which all recipients were required to sign. Meanwhile, the broader public, whose contact with the art world was normally limited then to airport bookstalls and video-rental stores, seemed fed up. They sensed, if not the gross offense to civilization that Helms claimed, another rip-off by a privileged group, more of their own money squandered on a pampered few.

Although stunned at first and nearly routed politically, individual artists, their professional organizations and political allies did mount a vigorous campaign of resistance. Letters to the editor, news releases, and essays

on the threat to artistic free expression proliferated. A few notable organizations, such as *The Paris Review*, refused NEA grants rather than sign the
anti-obscenity pledge; others, more aggressive, chose to sue. Inevitably, the
drama of a confrontation so dominated by extremist factions wore on the
patience of the powers-that-be. In late 1990, with an unexpected war loom-
ing and the fall elections finally over, Congress passed a compromise bill
that would, it was hoped, end this unseemly show.

Given the alternatives, the new law was largely favorable to artists: individual grants were kept, and without the burden of an obscenity pledge;
"peer review" panels were retained (although some non-artists would sit on
them now); in an artful dodge, the courts were left to define censurable art;
and the NEA chair was newly charged with somehow ensuring that both
"general standards of decency" and "respect for the diverse beliefs and values of the American public" were taken into consideration when dispensing
funds. The vagueness of that last provision, nervously balancing "decency"
with "diversity" in a high wire act of compromise,[5] worried both sides, and
eventually led to Frohnmayer's resignation, but the NEA did survive, if on
a shorter leash and a skimpier budget, and later assaults resembled the first.

Other than the range of his initial success, this controversy revealed
nothing new about Jesse Helms. The reaction of too many artists, however,
was also predictable. To an extent, I shared their concerns then. I, too, get
nervous when legislators flirt with defining permissible art; like many authors and artists of my generation, I had been supported by the NEA, and,
as a counterbalance to commercialization, I did believe in public financing
for the arts. High principle and lowly self-interest thus apparently joined, it
was tempting to read the conflict as a finally hopeful story, one where the
artistic community rose up to resist the Helmsian Hun. "Hey," one might
say, slipping into the folksy-ironical accent of the football commentator, "it
wasn't pretty, but the good guys won."

Or did they? Yes, former Dixiecrat Jesse Helms was a nasty politician,
and should his point of view have ever extended from cutting funds to active censorship, he could have become a dangerous one for artists. But, that
said, how accurate or ethical was the response of the art world to Helms's
attack? We did survive the funding battle then, but what about the moral
debate? To what degree was our position then more principled than cynical,
one that spoke to the public good rather than to private gain?

One heard at first excited accusations of censorship and grave concerns about First Amendment rights, but as numerous commentators, too
few of them artists, were quick to point out, that simply wasn't true. The
anti-obscenity pledge wasn't restricting free speech but *paid* speech, the
sorts of projects the government was willing to fund. There followed, then,

claims about the dangers of a "chill factor" and "self-censorship," of artists muzzling themselves or avoiding controversial subjects. We would lose, it was said, a diversity of opinion. Decisions about art, it was said, should be above politics, the artist's imagination remaining unfettered. Bureaucratic functionaries were not competent, after all, to judge the redemptive qualities of the aesthetic enterprise. And anyway, art was for art's sake—a higher good, a pure end in itself.

This was where I began to get confused. Weren't these the same artists who, over beers with me, would tout their own fierce political commitment and who would proselytize, often eloquently, on the necessity of a politically centered art? Weren't these the same people who, when sitting on panels dispensing prizes, used their own political compass unabashedly, unashamedly, to select the winners? And what about the fear of being muzzled, of self-censorship? Almost every response by an artist to this issue made a reference to the heroic status of the artist as righteous rebel and social critic, one of those precious few who dares to speak truth to power. I don't want to mock that ideal—I believe in it, aspire to it—but what sort of hero censors himself out of fear of losing a government grant? We weren't talking about execution or imprisonment, as is the case in too many nations even today; we weren't even talking about actual censorship then. The issue at hand was the removal of artists from the public payroll—which, after all, seems a strange place for a truly rebellious artist to be.

Perhaps, then, this was but another example of the sexually repressed (and repressive) middlebrow majority attempting to assert its puritanical morality on the daring few? Then as now, however, even the briefest glance into our bookstores, galleries, theaters, and movie houses would have killed that notion. Many adjectives might accurately describe America's post-sixties cultural scene—puritanical is not among them. One possibility remains, and it returns us conveniently to the source of the controversy. Work our artists made and our panels selected spurred this controversy. It's just possible, isn't it, that some of what ensued was the art world's own fault?

If not simply the various projects' flagrant content, what was it about the artists' position that so offended the public? Let's begin with what seemed to some our most sanctified proposition—the notion that art is for art's sake and hence above or beyond the political pale. To the average citizen, this insistence on the piety of professional self-centeredness must have seemed a peculiar argument for the artist to muster to induce support, leading to some unattractive comparisons: medicine for medicine's sake, say, or the government for the government's sake. Would anyone really rally to support a doctor or politician who espoused such a cause?

Likewise, artists' resistance to any restrictions may have reminded the public of the logic that had recently been used to push through the dubious agenda of financial deregulation. The Reaganistas, after all, had also laid claim to the revolutionary, and like all revolutionaries, they had their exalted ideals by which they planned to reorder the world. A day didn't pass then without a new sermon on the saving grace of the liberated marketplace: how setting corporate commerce loose would magically produce a moral as well as a material Eden, and how, by contrast, Big Government would suck vitality from the all-wise, all-knowing, beneficent Free Market. Horrible to relate, all those anecdotal tales of voracious welfare mothers bankrupting the system, thirty bucks at a time, via food stamp fraud.

Fraud should be expunged wherever it is found, and the welfare system needed reform, but with the exposure of the Savings & Loan scandal during that same period, we quickly learned which economic class was really bent on sucking the blood from the body politic. (A lesson, alas, that we soon forgot.) Coauthored by the Reagan administration and a Democratic Congress under the righteous masquerade of deregulation, this shameless scam eventually cost the public some 341 billion dollars.[6] And as almost all of that scandal's well-heeled bankers escaped prosecution, retiring behind the gates of their walled estates with their accounts intact and their high-tech toys in tow, it was their hypocrisy that grated as much as their thievery.

But on the subject of hypocrisy, how well did artists of the same period compare? How true were we then to the principles we still espouse? When *our* work was demeaned, our pockets pinched through the forfeiture of grants, we preached indignantly on the evils of censorship, but in our own domain—in our theaters, on our campuses, and on our grant-awarding peer panels—how much freedom of speech were we tolerating then, and how much do we tolerate now? The following is a test—let's call it the Artist's Civil Liberties Index. It might prove instructive to see how you fare.

Were you one of the people who wanted smash-mouth comedian Andrew Dice Clay kept off the air? Where did you stand on the Actor's Equity vote that banned a white actor from playing the part of a Eurasian in a Broadway play? Are you one of the academics who voted for a campus code that redefined specified kinds of offensive speech as violent behavior, allowing faculty, staff, and students to be punished for what they said? Here are some questions in a more speculative mode. What if the art funded by the NEA had mocked or condemned homosexual acts? Would you still support the artist's right to free expression and the panel's right to independent assessment? What if the icon dropped into the jar of urine had been not a crucifix but an image of the leader you hold most dear: Nelson Mandela? Cesar Chavez? Golda Meir? And what if the passive recipient of the "golden shower" in Robert Mapplethorpe's controversial photo (two men, one standing, the other prone, the former urinating into the gladly gaping mouth of the latter) were, in fact, a woman—would you object? What if the man were white and the woman a woman of color? Would you be protesting censorship if, say, a liberal senator had risen to the forum to demand a review of the NEA's funding?

Peer Review

As with so many of the skirmishes in our culture wars, the initial NEA debate was characterized by a lot less principle than met the eye or assaulted the ear. Like the libertarian right's highly vocal romance with deregulation (which is the businessman's version of free expression), too many artists making noise on these subjects seemed to honor tolerance only when they could profit from it. Take, for example, the idealization of freedom and individuality that has been characteristic of both camps. Although their primary spheres of interest differ, each group makes an extreme claim as to the value of creativity within that sphere, and each embodies that heady principle within an archetypal heroic figure—the entrepreneur in the first instance and the true (which is to say *revolutionary*) artist, in the second—the two of whom, on closer scrutiny, lead analogous lives. Both the entrepreneur and the true artist, for example, are supposed to be, above all else, independent people, gifted with an intelligence so rare and fecund that it must eventually breed invention. Following Ezra Pound's dictum, they "make it new," and at great personal risk, for as people uncannily ahead of their times, both the entrepreneur and the ground-breaking novelist are likely to be scorned at first for their new ideas. Public mockery and material privation must be suffered first, the romantic story goes, before they win their just rewards—*if*, that is, the new fictive form or high-tech product proves valuable to the culture at large.

Again, I don't want to mock the ideal itself but note instead how that mythic story has been disneyfied by both sides, the *if* removed from its occasions. Real freedom is always conditional, but that anxious grammatical construction has become increasingly unspeakable in Virtual America, and nowhere was that erasure of risk more evident than in the S&L fiasco. For bankers in the know then, as well-connected as they were well-off, the *if* had been conveniently stripped from the market's equations. The risk on their increasingly reckless loans would now be insured, by Big Government no less, and at no cost to the so-called speculator. Like the CEOs of the same era whose dismissals for poor performance were being rewarded with golden parachutes, these venture capitalists couldn't fail for failing. Like the wizards of Wall Street in 2008, the profit was theirs, the liability the public's.

What did Neil Bush, Boy Banker, protesting his innocence, have to do with performance artists protesting the oppressiveness of obscenity pledges?[7] More, I fear, than either side cared to admit then. As always, the artist's economic reward was microscopic in comparison, but the betrayal of principle seemed all too similar. Again we had a philosophy of bold creativity concealing a Tammany Hall actuality. The avant-garde artist wanted to shock the public even as he was being subsidized by it. These daring entrepreneurs of thought wanted to dress for the part and reap the reward, free from the risks inherent in the work; they too wanted to remain, in the manner of those bankers, "deregulated." The public would pay, but it must not judge. How to assure quality, then? Artists, like bankers, would regulate themselves: "panels of peers" would review applications and justly divvy up the public's purse.

Word choices in debates often illuminate hidden motives. Note, for example, what happens to *peer* when it is used, as it was by so many artists then, to resist any outside scrutiny of the grants dispensed. If one is inside the artists' coterie, the word appears to retain its democratic denotation of "an equal before the law." But if one is outside the club, peer seems to refer instead to its second meaning, "a noble; especially a British duke or marquis." To an outsider, a panel of peers becomes a kind of House of Lords where nobility is granted an authority that the peasantry is denied.

That one of the key positions of artists on this issue was inherently elitist does clarify why, despite their grants' initial survival, artists lost the moral debate by inviting contempt from the public at large.[8] When, in the spring of 1990, a coalition of artist groups submitted a response to Congress asserting once again the sanctity of the peer-review process, Rep. Dana Rohrabacher (whose own proposed restrictions on funded art were a robotic reflection of the Moral Majority's social agenda) was quick to sum up the art establishment's position in this very quotable fashion: "It seems like more of the same. It's just 'Give me your money and keep your mouth shut.'"[9] Unfortunately, that *was* what it seemed like, and to a public fed up with taxed-funded boondoggles and elitist arrogance, Rohrabacher's point of view, wrapped in the sheepskin of fiscal responsibility, began to seem the more reasonable of the two. So it came to pass that Helms and his allies had attracted enough public support by 1995 to eliminate *all* the NEA's individual grants while slashing its overall budget some 40 percent.

Some artists will protest that, irrespective of the issue of elitism, the public really isn't qualified to judge contemporary art. They will insist that art, like all branches of higher thought, has become too sophisticated for the mere layman to comprehend, and that fair decision-making requires a certain expertise best exercised by savvy and sensitive professionals in quiet consultation behind closed doors. Such a position sounds fine, however, only so long as the expertise under discussion is one's own. If our arguments are to stand on principle and not pork barrels, then the same should hold true for all constituencies seeking federal funds. Once it is conceded, for example, that we do need some sort of national defense, or that nuclear power should be regulated, do we really want all decisions on weapons systems and nuclear power plants to be made in secrecy by "experts in the field"? Isn't that precisely what Department of Defense experts have been doing for years—saying to the public, "Give me your money and keep your mouth shut"? Wasn't that what Congress tried to do with its S&L bailout plan? And let's remember, please, that the bank boards that approved all those bogus loans were, in fact, "panels of peers."

But we're better than bankers, those same artists might protest. You see, though, we're not. And to believe that we are is to believe—like so many surgeons, lawyers, and Wall Street financiers—what all elitists believe: that their group (race, sex, professional guild) is innately superior to any other. To believe so is to assert the dominion of the second definition of peer ("a noble") over the first ("an equal before the law.")

Pinprick Stigmata

The moral and intellectual tensions that characterize any free society are very real, and not all Americans bear them equally well. For some, the wide range of possible beliefs available here proves more daunting than exhilarating. They fear, and not entirely without reason, its confusion; they fear that they will lose the core of their identity, and so cling desperately instead to rigid definitions of the good and the true. Artists are quick to accept this analysis when it is applied to reactionaries like Helms. We scowl at the reflexive passion of their intolerance, hoot at their repressed sexuality, and note with contempt their willingness to ban a book that they have never read. Yet there are those inside art's own guild who, as soon as they become a teacher, editor, or director, assert their own rigid judgments—although always, of course, for "correct" higher ends. And how many artists, without ever viewing Mapplethorpe's photos, automatically and with a passion mirroring the opposition's exactly, supported their funding then? To some artists, merely posing the question of art's civic value is to commit a kind of categorical error, and one characteristic of the Philistine mind. For them—and I have heard this said more than once with pride—"no work of art can be objectionable."

Nothing objectionable? Surely that's a proposition to tempt the imagination. Is a snuff film okay so long as the camera angles are "Wellesian" and one can read a wry tribute to Buster Keaton in the victim's silent forlorn features?

The convenient judgment that no art can be objectionable (which is, in fact, an utter nullity of judgment) wouldn't be worth mentioning if it were simply one artist's opinion. But in the totality of its self-exemption, it reflects a faddish consensus in one key faction of the art world today. Back at the time of NEA controversy, the news had reached a certain Annie Sprinkle who, enlightened by the verities of progressive art, had transformed herself—in a metamorphosis that would have made Ovid proud—from a prostitute and porn star into a performance artist.[10] A hustler supreme, and thus heroic entrepreneur in the libertarian mode, Sprinkle had improved her commercial efficiency at least a hundredfold. Previously, she had serviced only one or two johns at a time, but now she could entertain a few hundred nouveau art connoisseurs simultaneously.

Her act, in which she billed herself as a Post Porn Modernist, consisted of sketches with snappy titles such as Bosom Ballet and Public Cervix Announcement, along with a slide show that "demystified" the porn industry. This touching reformation, reminiscent of a Dickens novel, included an implicit endorsement of safe sex (she only masturbated on stage), was ecologically sound (scarcely a Kleenex was used), and exhibited, as T. S. Eliot required, a purification of the language of the tribe; for whereas Sprinkle formerly had to moan hyperbolically insincere sexual compliments into the ears of her johns to earn her daily bread, she now needed only to murmur demurely postmodernist pieties into media microphones. "In [her] view," she conveniently echoed in a post-performance panel discussion, "there [were] no correct judgments."[11]

And we in the art world felt free to hoot at the Bible Brigade? But we "got it," some might say; we were winking, à la David Letterman, the whole way. That, however, is what most johns think. And for this baring of her soul, modeled so closely after all those feigned submissions of her body to previous johns, the Post Porn Modernist was the one who actually "got it"—real coin of the realm for a feigned experience. She received the ten or twenty bucks per head that might have gone instead to that local theater group or street musician, to that excellent but struggling literary press.

Annie Sprinkle does lead us back to the NEA controversy—not because she was funded (she wasn't), but because the attitudes she had learned to parrot so profitably explain why the public lost confidence in the funding process then. For if reigning "experts in field" truly believed that no art could be objectionable and no judgments correct, what did that say about the rigor of their review? Could we be too far from the notion that anything is commendable and, therefore, from that banality favored by couch-potato con men: everything is art? And doesn't the claim that no art is objection-able sound suspiciously akin to those other peer reviews that find no weap-on system unfundable, no doctor suspendable, no drug unprescribable, no loan insecurable, no golden parachute undeserving?

Such a rigid advocacy generates a curious sort of co-dependency be-tween the rebel artist and his pious critic. As with most fundamentalists, both sides are lost without a visible enemy to define themselves by opposi-tion. One sensed this in the blizzard of press conferences, panel discussions, and printed appeals that spewed from each camp as the controversy intensi-fied—the secret delight transfusing the outrage, the delicious opportunity it provided to preen, promote, shore up solidarity. Careers could be made on the dubious cross of the devil's condemnation; the enemy's hyperbole con-firmed one's own, granting one the boon of being martyred. And oh what gloating ensued over such miniscule wounds, gallons of Mercurochrome for pinprick stigmata.

As it turned out, both sides were in need of just such a boost. With two of its most prominent ministers caught up scandals, the religious right was in disarray.[12] They needed a Sodom to blast and found it in the NEA. Likewise, what were transgressive artists to do when no one seemed to mind the perpetual revolution they threw, when their most outrageous proposals might even win them an academic degree? The awful maw of respectabil-ity loomed; the future looked prosperous and therefore bleak. Enter Jesse Helms, stage right, wearing his black hat (which is, of course, literally white but we know who to read *that* "text"), sex-shooters ablazing. What a relief—to be accused again, to rally around the anarchist flag, to find a prude one could still offend.

Both right-wing revivalists and rebel artists thrived on a self-image of passionate extremity, believing themselves to be our society's most tren-chant critics, yet both groups were in danger of losing their zeal. Each fed on outrage, yet nothing is harder to sustain in Virtual America than true indignation. Our economy had worked its usual strategy of accommodation through commodification. If these folks had an audience, then they had to have products, and Virtual America was happy to sell them. This, after all, is Mammon's version of the Bill of Rights: even extremists are allowed their market share. How quickly minimalist music entered the commercial marketplace. How easily Jesus rock turned a profitable coin. How quietly the ministry of public works adopted the orphan of radical art, the government choosing, as it were, to hand-feed the mouth that bit it. So why wasn't everyone happy? Each extremist had a piece of the pie. One way or another, both factions were, as they used to say in gangster movies, "on the payroll." This was democracy at work, wasn't it? Perhaps not Jeffersonian but the ward politician's version thereof. Vaguely egalitarian. So where was the beef?

The beef was this: neither group was interested in being average or equal—elitists never are. Neither was content with a mere market share, and so each needed a cause to boost its sales. Hence their mutual delight in each other's apprehension. With reciprocal generosity, each could provide a provocative image—Jesus in a jar or Jesse's beefy visage—to keep the other's congregation enraged, engaged and (yes) contributing. Pass the hat and praise the ammunition.

II. The Commerce of Faux Rebellion

Baited Hooks and Born Gangstaz

"What [William Burroughs] was doing in literature was the equivalent of what Nike has done in the athletic world in terms of pushing the limits and taking risks and doing things differently."[13]

—Nike, on why it hired the author to sponsor an athletic shoe

Artists on the make haven't limited their pseudo-subversive maneuverings to government grants, nor has the tactic prevailed solely on the scale of individual ambition. Since the sixties at least, Pop Culture, Inc. has complemented its perennial investment in sugary sentiment with a bitter, badder line of staged rebellion. Using its almost total control over production and distribution, the postwar recording industry was quick to co-opt each authentic outburst of cultural disaffection, efficiently turning rock's perennial "rage against the machine" into a profitable greasing of the machine itself and converting rap's attack on the white man into sing-along CD's for the suburban set.

Like all rationalized sales techniques, faux rebellion in the pop music biz has its own costume kit of obligatory postures and gestures: the surly promo photo; the obscene interview; the veiled references to an edgy yea-even-unto criminal past; the video desecration of religious and patriotic symbols; a set of lyrics obsessed with alienation, hard drugs, bizarre sex, misogyny, misanthropy, mayhem, murder, and suicide—the whole package doctrinally wrapped (as a prophylactic against charges of hypocrisy) with indignant denouncements of those who "sell out."

Back in 1994, Brett Pulley of *The Wall Street Journal* found an egregious example of such entrepreneurial hucksterism in Boss Laws. Borrowing from gangsta rap's thuggish imagery and narratives, Laws's first album, *Born Gangstaz,* had featured cover photos of her striking bellicose poses with automatic weapons and gritty lyrics that celebrated cop-killing: "I loaded the clip and took the nine to the copper's brain." Fond of slugging down malt liquor from 40-ounce bottles, cursing out her audience, and boldly boasting of her desire to kill, Laws spoke often onstage about her days on the streets. Her menacing persona and the gritty art it produced had arisen, it seemed, from her grim experiences as a gang member, drug pusher, and prison inmate. As it happens, however, Laws had never been in jail, nor could her other mean-street stories be verified. She wasn't *born* a gangster but was delivered to two protective parents who raised her in a middle-class neighborhood, paying for her education in Catholic schools and for her private lessons in ballet, modern dance, and piano. Laws had attended church and gone to college, where she had majored in business and managed to become, in contradistinction to most gangstaz, a fraternity sweetheart.[14]

Majoring in business is probably the most significant detail in that privileged list. As Laws herself said to Pulley in defense of her new persona: "I'm both a gangster and a smart business person. I know what I'm doing." Indeed she did. And that, as a smart business person, she entitled her album *Born Gangstaz* (instead of something more biographically accurate, such as *Born Bourgeois*) exemplifies the selling of pop art though faux rebellion and the reinvention of self as commercial product, even as it confirms Melville's prophecy about the triumph of the con man's Masquerade.

The notion that personal rebelliousness, rather than threatening capitalism, might be exploited to expand its base, dates back to the origins of mass-market salesmanship in the early twentieth century. But it wasn't until the sixties that Madison Avenue, hoping to cultivate an enormous youth market, began to exploit political revolt as well. This strategy was most evident in the Virginia Slims campaign in the 1970s. Launching the first cigarette targeted exclusively for women, these highly successful ads featured two photos, in an ironically staged before-and-after scenario, dramatizing the change from pre- to post-liberation American womanhood. In the first, a young woman fettered in a frumpy Victorian dress has been caught attempting to sneak a cigarette by an oppressive husband-father figure—a veritable starched phallus of paternalism complete with wagging finger, stern stare, and Germanic walrus mustache. In the second, her contemporary and now liberated sister poses, sassy, slender, joyous, and free, her cigarette transformed into an elegant fashion accessory, her progress proclaimed in the now famous phrase: "You've come a long way, baby!"

With its arch tone, its hip address, its mockery of the past and of prudishness, its trivializing of political change into selfhood's triumph, and its blurring of active achievement with passive sexiness, this campaign exemplified three decades of advertising themes. Like most seductions, it played on the twin emotions of resentment and self-love, but its genius lay in locating the language of vanity best fitted to the age: the supposed empowerment of self-liberation. That by celebrating freedom these ads actually intended to enslave, the hook of a deadly addiction cleverly concealed by their flattery's bait, encodes a dark but instructive irony: how postmodern marketing's inducements to revolt have routinely masked its commandments to obey.

By the nineties, this co-opting of revolt had become pandemic. In their constant search for frontmen who could lend real-life authority to their meaningless commodities, consumer corporations were rapidly adding cultural rebels to their usual stable of athletes and actors. So it was that the GAP gladly bought the rights to Jack Kerouac's name and image, ghoulishly exploiting the deceased Beat author to hawk its line of khaki pants. This tactic of transforming the "mutinous scrivener" into a sponsor for the bourgeois product reached its extreme, however, when Nike hired Kerouac's old buddy William Burroughs to pitch its Air Max 2 athletic shoe. Unlike wannabe gansta Boss Laws, Burroughs had managed to overcome his wealthy background and Harvard education to earn all the street cred that any artist-outlaw could ever hope for. A real drug addict and drunk whose fiction had spawned an obscenity trial, the author had actually killed his common-law wife while attempting to shoot a shot glass off her head, William Tell style. As this tragicomic incident of failed marksmanship was Burroughs's only known attempt at athletic accomplishment, some critics questioned Nike's motivation for securing his sponsorship. ("Just do it, Bill?")

Their reply, cited at the start of this section, went beyond the product being pitched to associate the character of the corporation itself with the legendary Burroughs's transgressive spirit. The once secret bond between the daring entrepreneur and the rebellious artist was now out of the closet. The high-tech shoe salesman and the outlaw-author were "equivalent," it seemed, in their willingness to "take risks" and "push the limits." In Virtual America, where *more* (money) *must equal better*, bad had now become conventionally good—good for business and so a trait to be pursued by both shareholding grownups and their status-seeking kids.

Cannibals and Carnivals

The surprise of the nineties wasn't the pseudo-rebellion of transgressive artists, nor the adman's rush to transgression's furthest border. No, the real shocker was the adoption of rebellion by business itself as a key to conducting its internal management. Nike was hardly alone in citing transgression ("pushing the limits") as a core component of its identity; more than a style then, rebellion was becoming a guide for corporate self-rule.

A pop quiz for my readers. (Number 2 pencils only. Keep your eyes on your own desk.) Identify the sources of the following quotations, all cited in Thomas Frank's acute critique of postmodern Mammon's propaganda machine, *One Market Under God*:[15]

a) "They . . . think they know the right answers, which is never true because there are no right answers."[16]

b) "DECONSTRUCTION IS COOL!"[17]

c) "Cannibalize Yourself"[18]

You will be forgiven your confusion, but if you named the usual suspects on the cultural left, you have flunked the test. The adamant denier of essentialist morality was not a touchy-feely educational reformer, nor a Post Porn Modernist like Annie Sprinkle, but a clothing CEO who was criticizing the arrogance of old-school competitors. The emphatic endorsement of deconstruction was not a lit student's pseudo-ironic bumper sticker but the sincere advice of America's most popular management theorist, Tom Peters.

Most surprising of all, the prescription to cannibalize oneself was not ripped from the title page of some performance artist's grant proposal, in which she planned to slice off pieces of her own flesh and eat them on stage as a statement against Third World poverty or the patriarchy's assault on the female body. It was snatched instead from the cover of *Fortune*, and represented management theory's surprise response to the new economy's radical assault on the *corporate* body. In an ironic inversion of the usual Darwinian, eat-or-be-eaten ethos, the with-it executive was now being advised by one of corporate America's favorite publications to prey on his own company: to dismantle departments, dismiss employees, discontinue product lines—to lunch, as it were, on his own infrastructure—before the merciless Market did it for him. Once again an American leadership would have to destroy a social structure in order to save it.

The astute reader will note a shared theme here. According to these theorists, the new secret to commercial success was an unrelenting, unrepentant, and largely unreflective commitment to destabilizing change. Two titles by Peters, *Thriving on Chaos* (1987) and *Liberation Management*

(1992), captured the spirit of the movement.[19] The first book insisted that the new prescription for management was nothing short of revolution, and its binding was red, as if to suggest that little book of sayings which had so happily guided those cannibalizing cadres in Mao's China. By 1992, however, Peters was chastising himself for not being radical enough. Having gone through the process of self-criticism necessary to all great thinkers, he realized that what the revolution required was not a transitory phase but a perennial state of mind. Deconstruction was not only *COOL!*—it needed to be *CONTINUAL!* For the liberated corporation, the edgy mission of transgressing tradition could have no end, demanding instead a total commitment to what Peters called (oxymoron approaching) the "permanently ephemeral."[20]

The message that Peters and like-minded theorists were bringing back from the anarchic gold rush of the new economy was at once terrifying and exhilarating. As they now saw it, even just-in-time manufacturing was an insufficient commitment to the punishing pace of the postmodern marketplace: one had to practice just-in-time management as well. The corporate leader's mind, like his postindustrial warehouses, had to be fruitfully empty of preformed products—especially all those puritanical notions of command-and-control and patriarchal commitments to the corporate family that had once served the Organization Man at IBM so well.

The new corporate leader had to be quick on his feet and, yes, "in the moment." Metaphors stolen from the spiritual East competed chaotically with those of guerrilla warfare, rock music, and pop psychology to suggest the necessary Zen-like reactivity, hit-and-run agility, hipster sensibility, and New Age sensitivity that the Market now demanded of the postmodern manager. Staying on top required "getting one's employees to think like 'barbarians not bureaucrats,'" Peters argued. One had to recognize that "today's economy [was] no Strauss waltz" but rather "break dancing accompanied by street rap," and that the "effective firm [was] more like a Carnival in Rio than a pyramid along the Nile." As if that role-model collage of Attila the Hun, Ice-T, and Carmen Miranda wasn't confusing enough, the new barbarian manager was also advised to become adept at forging relationships, especially those moist evocations of loyalty that would monogamously bind customer to product, inducing the client to love, honor, and obey the corporate brand for as long as they both shall live.[21]

Embracing the chaos of this new management style, Peters promised, would not only be "fun" (that most desirable of states in disneyfied America); it would also be democratizing and, yes, liberating. For only by surrendering to the whirlwind of change, Grasshopper, only by giving up the ghost of your faith in "right answers," could you empower yourself and your employees to be as free as you and they could be—that is, free of those chains that had once bound the self to the future good of colleague, clan, and community. Mammon's new and global Market was a jealous god indeed.

Street rap? Cannibalism? Perpetual revolution? The most successful of corporations proud to be cast in the moral image of William Burroughs? To postmodern management's multiform project of self-liberation, I can only respond by echoing their own classic caption of amazed admiration: you've come a long way, baby!

Or not. That in the real world such practices also seemed to involve liberating those same employees of their benefits and retirement plans; that the corporation's avid pursuit of consumer loyalty was coterminous with its organized campaigns of disloyalty to a work force which now could be downsized on a moment's notice; that the pitching of fun in the workplace and the injunction to foster client relationships seemed to require the forfeiture of both the time and the peace of mind to pursue fun and relationships anywhere else—these were observations about the new economy rarely acknowledged in the literature. They were not acknowledged because, as Frank exposes in hilarious detail, the overriding purpose of these books was to rationalize and even sanctify the antisocial agenda of Evangelical Mammonism, for whose actual activities, behind the mask of liberation, cannibalism was an all too apt description.

Although the new management theories were disingenuous in their attempts to turn materialist excess into moral progress, they were by no means divorced from the realities of the era whose degradations they aimed to justify. The authors were keenly aware of the anxieties of the managerial class that they were targeting, for along with the rest of the nation, corporate America itself was facing a rapidly destabilizing social environment—a killing of the covenants that had once civilized the commercial world. The sources of that demise, which is still ongoing, bear repeating here. With a parodic tip of the hat to the usual list-obsessed format of management theory, let's call them *The Four Agents of Destabilization*.

1. *Deregulation*: The triumph of corporate-supported, anti-regulatory politicians in the Anglo-American democracies—primarily Reagan and Margaret Thatcher, but also the so-called new Democrats and new Labor under Clinton and Tony Blair—led to a radical weakening of governmental control over economic policy. This new environment, however, not only proved hostile to labor, as jobs were turned into a sheer commodity to be traded to the lowest bidder in both national and international markets; it also threatened whole industries in the West and rendered day-to-day business operations

far less predictable. A multiplication of opportunities also magnified the dangers, and so promoted insecurity for managers and investors.

2. *Computerization*: Simultaneous to deregulation, the practical arrival of computer technology and its subsequent merging with the communications and entertainment industries opened up a whole new frontier of business activity, spawning a postindustrial revolution that would upset many of the old commercial presumptions and not a few of the corporations that had most profited from them. The once invincible IBM's egregious stumbling, start-up Microsoft's stunning surge to monopoly status, Apple's rapid rise, then fall, then rise again—these were the allegorical possibilities that both titillated and terrified corporate America, underlining the stark alternatives of riches and ruin that characterized the wild, wild West of high-tech enterprise.

Beyond the personal computer itself, the constant race for the next technological upgrade in nearly every industry kept commerce in a state of perpetual, often unpredictable change. The destabilizing impact on labor was just as great, for by automating knowledge assessment, the computer threatened even the educated white-collar worker with obsolescence. Of the four agents listed here, technological change was the most external to commerce's new ideological agenda, one that would have occurred without Reagan and Thatcher's political victories. But the disruptive social effects of computerization were much intensified by the libertarian campaign to delegitimize any governmental regulation of the marketplace.

3. *Marketization*: This relatively new term describes the final submission of the economy as a whole to the operative pace and speculative values of Wall Street. The key causative shift occurred in the eighties when corporate boards changed the way they paid their CEOs. As stock options took the place of salaries, upper management logically shifted its allegiance from the stakeholder's interest in the long-term health of the company to the stockholder's obsession with immediate share value. Once a community as well as a corporate leader, the CEO now assumed the role of a hired gun, and one whose primary objective was the rapid boosting of stock prices through strategies like radical downsizing. Few were immune to upper management's new *COOL!* and *CONTINUAL!* practice of cannibalizing the livelihoods of loyal employees, along with the stability of their local communities, for its own financial benefit.

Further, as more of American enterprise became marketized, sheer speculation began to replace careful analysis in the grading of stocks. Even as theorists of the Chicago school rhapsodized about a market economy run on the rational choices of democratic consumers, Wall Street was being infused with the delirious mood of a Vegas casino at 4 a.m. As the balloon of the dot-com boom rose on little more than the helium of hope, the distinction between the earnest practice of incorporation and the illicit progress of a pyramid scheme became less and less clear. Like some geek version of a conceptual artist, the new entrepreneur hung a two-page business plan on the wall, threw an opening party for his "initial offering," and then waited for rave reviews to arrive in the form of giddily inflated stock values. That particular fever eventually broke, only to be followed by similar cycles when electric utilities and then mortgage lending practices were marketized for commercial exploitation, leading eventually to the Enron scandal and the subprime fiasco.

The lesson by now ought to be clear: a fully marketized economy is far more susceptible to the irrational mood swings of speculation, and so, too, to scams that feast on the folly of golden-goose dreams. Likewise, the final severing of the profit motive from any calculation of social cost, which is also a legacy of our radically marketized economy, has proven to be one of the most destabilizing forces in the world today.

4. *Fashionization:* The increasing oddity of postmodern corporate practice seems to require as ballast a compensatory vocabulary of leadenly earnest nouns. "Fashionization" falls from the tongue like a truckload of gravel, but through it Tom Peters did correctly identify a crucial transformation in the standard operating procedures and accompanying values of American commerce. In the past, the fashion industry here had been little more than an exotic sideshow to the earnest practices of heavy manufacture. But as the logic of consumerism prevailed in the postwar years, it quickly became clear that, with its seasonal investment in planned obsolescence, fashion alone could generate the sort of unchecked sales that Evangelical Mammonism demanded. Soon, the whole consumer economy began to adopt the traditional strategy of women's haute couture, periodically restyling the old product line in a dozen new guises, and even macho sports teams were changing uniform designs every two or three seasons.[22]

More than any other trend, fashionization has generated the frantic shop-till-you-drop temper of postmodern life, and this change impacted the psychology of management no less than the mindscape of the fragile consumer who was dosing on Valium or Prozac to get through the day. Like the fifteen minutes of fame allotted to the pomo celebrity, even the most successful product line now had a May-fly shelf life, and who knew for sure whether one's next design would be as profitable?

With the broad adoption of fashionization, the moral logic of "canni-balizing oneself" was becoming the corporate norm. Peters' books were de-noting, then, a significant change in the corporate world's own moral field. In this dimension of virtue's demise, the "transfer of sovereignty" was from the old ethos of rational manufacturing (controlled, scientific, paternalistic, "immortal") to the new ethos of romantic marketing (fickle, artistic, trans-gressive, "suicidal"). Like "smart business person" Boss Laws, the consumer corporation had been born again after the image of the hip transgressor.

Insanity Defense

After we survey the impact of these four agents of destabilization, it isn't difficult to grasp why *crazy* was one of Tom Peters' favorite words. As with most of Virtual America's ironic utterances, we would do well to take that term literally instead. Once again, a Mammonite evangelist was "dissuad-ing pain" by spinning a harmful change into a plausible good. How should we adapt, then, to the Market's investment in craziness? Mimicking the hip photographer who cajoles his models into sex-kitten poses, Peters was advising his readers to "have fun with it." To have fun with this economy's insanity meant, first, to accept the logic that was both decimating whole communities for the benefit of large stockholders and defining William Burroughs as a moral hero. To the anxious managerial class who was his audience, the era's premier management theorist was offering the following advice: yours is not to reason why; yours is but to comply with the crazy agenda of the "permanently ephemeral" or be left behind.

In a crude sense, this advice proved correct because once the economy as a whole had been converted to such craziness, it became far more difficult for any individual corporation, much less single employee, to reject its logic by behaving sanely. As with all utopian propagandists—as with those who designed Stalin's show trials in the 1930s—it wasn't sufficient, however, for the gung-ho theorist to note the necessity of our submission to this new system; he also had to convince us of its inherent virtue: he wanted us to be-lieve, just believe, in its utopian promise. Borrowing again from the costume kit of heroic liberation, the Market propagandist was recasting the affliction of economic disempowerment into a fantasy of individualist triumph. Our reward for accepting these new and dehumanizing rules for economic pro-duction proved to be the same as the prize that we were offered earlier for accepting the logic of idealized consumption: we were designated as hip, as liberated, as rebels unbeholden to any cause beyond our own free agency. We were offered Virtual America's highest compliment by being defined as creative transgressors who were boldly committed to "taking risks" and "pushing the limits."

In return for our individual submission to the punitive fiats of Evangelical Mammonism, we got to wear jeans to the office on dress-down Fridays, play Metallica on our Walkmans, and ride, baby, ride our Harleys to work. In the place of democratic rights and economic self-control, we were offered a mass multiplication of "life-style" choices—Jeeps, ATVs, S&M games, body piercings, shock-talk radio, extreme sports, ultra-libertarian philosophies—all supposedly expressive of our rugged independence. In a kind of superstitious logic ironically reminiscent of the preliterate cannibal, we were asked to believe that our consumption of such products could magically transform an agenda of clueless conformity into an identity of potent liberation—that we had, once again, "come a long way, baby."

Against the moral logic of this economy, a few commonsense observations might be made, even at the risk of being labeled unhip. That, for example, cannibalism is not a credible sign of human progress. Or that a "barbarian management" is likely, in the end, to rule through violence. And, yes, the pursuit of the permanently ephemeral *is* crazy. It is a practice that will reliably produce both anomie and anarchy, widespread mental breakdowns and political chaos. Anyone who believes that such conditions are fun should visit an asylum or vacation in Rwanda.

It is no accident that Peters's theories were simultaneous to the NEA debates, for the bad faith evident in both was characteristic of an era whose real corruption lay not merely in allowing the selfish to rule but in the active sanctification of selfishness. These were the years when, under the aegis of Evangelical Mammonism, greed became good, our possessions holy; when the sacrifices of social service were transformed, in six steps, into the banal regimens of self-help and self-esteem. As the commandment to love our neighbor was replaced by the advice (usually dispensed by genial doctors of the social science type) that one should become one's own "best friend," self-promotion became equated with saintliness.

Within this new ethos, it began to make sense for entrepreneurs to expect that the government would insure their risks; for investors to expect both profit now and productivity later; for executives to expect golden parachutes for failing at their tasks; for research doctors to expect pay and perks from the same corporations whose drugs they were supposed to honestly assess—within such an ethos, it began to make sense that performance artists would come to expect that the public they taunted should gladly pay for its own humiliation. Despite all the concurrent "celebrations of diversity" that were occurring at that time, a distressing conformity was actively corrupting the many subsets of our complex nation. Converted to that genialized version of New World hope proclaimed by Delmore Schwartz's "true-blue American," we were staring into the future from our separate soda fountain booths, denying dilemma and demanding *both!*

This revision of the democratic citizen into the mindset of the spoiled child will not be easy to reverse, for as we shall see next, the masquerade of faux rebellion is but one feature of Virtual America's aggressive investment in prolonging adolescence.

7

The Iron Cage of Age Dissuasion

For there is many a small betrayal in the mind,
a shrug that lets the fragile sequence break
sending with shouts the errors of childhood
storming out to play through the broken dyke.[1]

—William Stafford

OFTEN IT IS ONLY by breaking our culture's tacit rules and drawing offended attention to ourselves that we can see with the stranger's clarified sight the matrix of meaning that has long surrounded us. As the whole of heaven can be found in Blake's wild flower, the faint smell of a faux pas, hounded back to its source, can signal sometimes the rotten state of our own divisive Denmark. So it seemed to me one day when, going about my business, I unknowingly spoke the unspeakable and profaned the current version of the American way more surely than if I had burned the flag or bad-mouthed mortgage interest tax deductions: while teaching a graduate seminar, I confessed parenthetically to the condition of being "middle-aged."

The impact of this mundane assertion was stunning to behold. As if I had sneezed and fifteen handkerchiefs, boxes of lozenges, and bowls of chicken soup had been produced simultaneously, all literary discussion ceased and I became the sudden subject of my students' tender and paradoxically parental concern. Surely, I was wrong. Surely, I could see that I was drastically misperceiving myself, for this was a matter, they seemed to presume, not of physical fact but of psychological self-image. Middle age was not a standard developmental stage in life, avoidable only via the mortician's table, but a kind of mood disease and hence curable—yet one more species of low self-esteem.

With kids at home, books in print, and a year or two from tenure, I was *mid* in every way then—mid-career, middle-class, middle-aged—and my students' denial of the obvious merely seemed amusing at first, the sort of classroom incident one likes to share for laughs with colleagues and friends. In this case, though, to retell the story only proved to reconfirm it. Each new audience, it seemed, would intervene exactly as my class had done, quick to deny that I, that *we*, could be classified fairly as middle-aged, and as the chorus of denial repeated itself, this collective flight from a mundane truth began to assume for me a more ominous air.

Admittedly, the desire to sustain one's youth is a universal longing, as perennial as nostalgia and, one could argue, not without its benefits. To aspire to stay young is to value hope, energy, resilience, creativity. Where is the real harm, then, in dressing to conceal one's age or in clinging years later to one's teenage slang and musical taste?

In proportion, there probably is no real harm, but ours is not an age, nor an economy, of proportionate behavior. As the pseudo-revolutionary Doctor in Josef Conrad's novel *The Secret Agent* predicted, we in the modern West, following the logic of our materialism, have come to worship our own bodies, heaven reduced to the here-and-now pursuit of physical health.[2] And where one worships, one does not laugh. The old irony implicit in Jack Benny's white lie about his age is lost on us now. The discrepancy between his actual appearance and his stated age would beckon forth today not laughs of painful recognition—*yes, we have to age; yes, we wish we didn't*—but earnest advice of the self-help sort: health club regimens, hair implant "systems," anti-aging vitamins, botox injections, inner-child therapies, a growing host of scalpel-sculpting surgeries and extreme cosmetic makeovers. The fountain of youth has been franchised now. Its fantastic themes unGrimm the screens in all our mainline movie houses as young and old alike drink in the dream of an idealized immaturity.

This cult of the adolescent is implicated in many of the disingenuous delusions that we have examined so far, including the masquerade of faux rebellion, the civic religion of Disneyism, and the demagogic appeal of Reagan's boyishness, still playing Mickey Rooney's upbeat "good teen" well into his seventies. Insomuch as maturity is inseparable from a recognition of suffering, the whole dubious project of "pain dissuasion" naturally includes a strong investment in "age dissuasion." Or, to phrase it differently, the "progress of genialization" is inseparable from (to coin another term in Melville's spirit) the *regress of juvenilization*: a regression grimly traced in the devolving phases of Michael Jackson's evermore juvenile, resculpted face.

When I entitled my first chapter "The Aging of Aquarius," I was aware of the irony haunting that selection, for one of the most conspicuous features of the sixty years under study here has been a reluctance to accept the realities and responsibilities of age. Like all generations, those in the postwar period have been presented with the chance to mature, but all too often it seems, to borrow from Bartleby again, we have preferred *not* to. To gauge a shift in character this sweeping, we need to examine not just egregious examples of juvenile decision-making but also the broader moral field that has been shaping our behavior, starting with a history of that field's construction.

I. A Social History of Age Dissuasion

Live long enough to be a burden on your children.

— bumper sticker popular in "adult communities"

Invasion of the Body Snatchers

The extension of American adolescence has been a privilege bestowed as well as a punishment inflicted. Raised by parents who suffered a decade of depression and a horrible world war—and who were deprived, therefore, of a childhood physically safe or economically secure—those of us born in the early postwar period collectively received, as a gift conceived out of their history's special hopes and fears, a *compensatory* upbringing. In the middle class, whose numbers ballooned until the seventies, never had childhood been so celebrated, so carefully insulated, so abundantly endowed with cultural support. Parks and camps, arts and crafts, lessons of every sort: education and recreation became our "work."

To be so safe, though, also meant to be isolated. Middle-class families were moving into separate enclaves, neither urban nor rural, new villages where their children were exiled not only from poverty's privations and potential violence but also from the rhythms of nature and the workplace realities of our expanding economy. There, the world's bad news, reduced to headlines, might stimulate discussion but couldn't bruise. There, one knew "of" but didn't really know—hadn't seen, heard, touched, or smelled. And for many this immunity would stretch beyond grade twelve. As college attendance surged, the exemption was extended from suburban park to campus green where quadrangle walls continued to hold the world apart.

And all along, whether at home or school, a trend in medicine years in the making enforced another sort of segregation. Birth, death, and all serious disease (including mental illness) were being taken from the home and placed in the realm of the treatment center. However well-intended or medically justified, these removals served to quarantine not just the danger of disease but the psychological reality of suffering itself. Severe pain had always suffused the human place, a dark hue in our native habitat, but now it was removed to small white rooms one visited briefly in afternoons, on schedules preset by administrators. Death—once the ultimate domestic reality, one's backyard the graveyard for those one loved—was now made distant and unreal: a rumor whose sanction one might appeal, a seedy address one's car might skirt on the beltways back to suburbia.

Through various advances in modern medicine, this dimension of our exile from those stages of life inevitably linked to the fate of the flesh was also extended. With our parents living longer, healthier lives, and with our own parenthood delayed through the freedom of choice the Pill provided, we remained both children and childless later into our lives than any generation preceding us. And in a sense, of course, even if our adolescence was unnaturally prolonged, who could wish otherwise? We *want* our parents to live; we *want* control over our reproductive lives. These feats are, we too easily forget, genuine gifts—luxuries that even the kingly once couldn't buy. To grow up middle-class in America in those postwar years was to lead a uniquely privileged life. Never had so many been so wealthy, so healthy, so free of pain and grief, so trained to escape the yoke of hard labor.

Yet to come of age, as so many of us did, without ever having witnessed a birth or a death was to suffer an impoverishment of the sort not tracked by economists, and to remain illiterate in ways unacknowledged by professional educators. In matters like these, to know "of" is simply not enough. Our privileged childhood left us as a group head-rich in such knowledge, aswim with bookish facts and TV's factoid pictures, but heart- and soul-poor. We emerged from college (those of us who escaped the Vietnam War) oddly imbalanced, socially urbane but metaphysically immature.

Both knowing and naive, worldly yet self-centered, made aware of many things but bereft of any scale to weigh their actual worth, ours was the very state of mind that the nation's marketeers had been relentlessly promoting. We were, in a sense, their ultimate product; our daily moods were schooled with attitudes conducive to boosting their profits—that "no request was too extreme" and that the rights of self were boundless, so long as we bought the right equipment. Each need, intensified, was then linked to a product line that the adman's client was ready to supply. Each new urge was quickly turned, through his commercials' dramaturgy, into a lesson whose one and only moral was ascension through possession. To be "somebody" meant to buy some thing.

In this sense, the great danger of our removal as a group from the realm of the real wasn't simply what we missed (the direct experience of life and death) but what took its place as well. Each step of our retreat—from working farm or city to suburban sanctuary; from outward-looking porch to air-conditioned den, with its prerecorded sounds and pictures cabled in—deepened our reliance on a flow of information. Unlike the experience it replaced, this form of information was always secondhand; more and more, the news we received was being composed to serve certain ends, the most common of which was salesmanship. What makes people of my approximate age unique is that we were the first to be raised in such an artificial place: the first suburban generation and, too, the first group of children that the adman could reach, and so teach, from cradle to grave through broadcast TV.

The advantage thus gained was more than incremental. Consumer advertising had been a significant force in American life since the 1920s at least, yet in the war to win our minds that little screen proved to be, like the longbow at Crécy, a decisive technological leap: the power of radio much multiplied through the simple addition of engaging the eye. As an ideological weapon, TV had both breadth and depth, stealth and force; one's message, cast "broad," could also literally pass through walls. Thus armed, the nation's salesmen no longer had to talk their way past our doors. In exchange for entertainment, people gladly turned them on, tuned them in. Their picture box became a high-tech Trojan horse from which the soldiers of salesmanship could routinely emerge every thirteen minutes.

For suburban parents then, TV must have seemed a welcome diversion, a cost-efficient compensation for the lack of nearby family and their exile from the city's many entertainments. For their children, however, it was something far more: our teacher, friend, and toy; that fond and doting nanny every family could afford, the one who baby-sat for free and at whose knobby knee we could see and hear our culture's current stories. What a bonanza we must have seemed to postwar marketeers: an entire generation, uprooted from family and from community traditions, planted there passively before their glowing screens, eyes wide and ears open, ever ready to receive. What a chance they had to intervene, to secretly usurp the role of instructor.

Viewed in this light, the political hysteria that characterized the fifties wasn't entirely misplaced. In a way, as Don Siegal's scary sci-fi movie savvily suggested, our bodies *were* being "snatched" while in our very homes, our allegiances transferred away from those we loved to alien and finally antihuman goals. In a way, as political pundits gravely warned then, our traditional values were being subverted. The real menacing source, though, wasn't Moscow's scheming Reds but the merchants of Main Street, our own purportedly *pro patria* Rotarian set. Despite its overt obsession with family values, mainstream commerce was covertly sponsoring a continuous assault on the family's prerogatives. This domestic subversion is never acknowledged by corporate leaders, who are quick to deny the propagandist power of their advertising even as they fund it exorbitantly, and who, while bemoaning the licentiousness of the poor and the corruption of family values by "liberal elites," loudly defend their own economic right to unchecked license and gladly rake in the dividends from policies that are clearly destructive to family life.

Those policies, it should be stressed, have a long tradition, dating back to the abuse of child labor in the ugly cradle of the Industrial Revolution. They can be viewed as but a logical expression of a commercial ethos highly specialized and profit-driven, an ethos less self-consciously anti-family than scientifically indifferent to social concerns. Corporate management's relentless downsizing, mandatory overtime, and exporting of jobs and pollution to the Third World poor; corporate finance's relentless dodging of taxes and egregious padding of executive salaries; corporate marketing's reckless boosting of transgression and addictive consumption: despite their deleterious impact on family, community, nation, and biosphere, all these now standard practices do make a kind of moral sense if one's conscience is commanded by postmodern Mammon's core belief that *more profit must equal better.*

For our purposes here, though, we need only note how the migrations that sent the rural poor to the cities and the middle class to the suburbs began a new round of indoctrination through alienation that is continuing still. This process proceeded through stages, each of which involved a dividing of the family's generations. The first stage, rapid and physical, was initiated by the move itself, often repeated when fathers changed jobs or whole industries moved. This "voting with one's feet," as President Reagan blithely called it, succeeded in severing the nuclear family from the guidance and care of the extended family and effectively removed grandparents from the governance of the home. The second stage, technologically based, was more subtle and psychological. In a metaphor appropriate to the atomic age, it split the nuclear family itself, diminishing the influence of parents by supplanting their instruction with the imagery and copy of commercial seduction. Thanks to the invasion of electronic information via radio and TV, most American children were hearing more words of advice from media copywriters than from the loving lips of their mothers or fathers.

That advice hasn't changed. The Siren song the adman sings, the one he beckons us to dance to, despite its new digital formats and multicultural accents, has remained the same. He still wants us to believe that the rights of self are boundless. He still wants us to presume that with the purchase of his goods, his latest service or advice, we are bound to become whatever we want to. The things we desire must change but not, ever, our desire for things. The market's outer flux, its bogus shifts of fashion and better-mouse-trap gadgets, require the cultivation of an unnatural inner stasis, a ceaseless state of craving ever fed by an oasis of immutable trust.

No, we mustn't change. Yes, like Peter Pan, we must continue to believe: in our "selves" and our ascension, the imminent arrival of our pixie-dust wings. Like Peter Pan, too, our self-image mustn't age. In the mirror, our mind's misty eye must continue to see that heroic teen-rebel who stopped the war machine, boldly flipping off the Captain Hooks of state, or who raged against the man by moshing in the pits of the punk-rock scene, or chanted the lyrics of gansta rap's CDs. That we were rising through the ranks toward tenured captaincy mustn't change the way we felt. We must progress but not mature; earn more but learn less; move up in the world and yet, in other ways, stay exactly where we were, moonwalking our way through life's usual phases.

This was no small task the nation's admen undertook. And yet their success, in contrast to their fellow propagandists in the East, arose precisely from refusing to think big. They had no grand schemes, no dialectic to direct their everyday tactics; instead, theirs was the genius, demented but effective, of the purely pragmatic. To get from there to here, they merely followed, step by dogged step, the narrow logic of self-interest. To make profits, they had to sell unnecessary products; to sell unnecessary products, they had to change the public's values; to change their values, they had to undermine those qualities of character that would inhibit self-indulgence. And those qualities, beginning with caution and ending with self-sacrifice, proved to be the ones traditionally ascribed to maturity: they were the virtues of middle age.

What the nation's marketeers discovered then was that we—the kids of Aquarius and all who came after us—must be made to resist the natural tutelage of age. They learned that maturity was their foe, and that their job, as is the job of every propagandist, was to make us believe that their enemy was our own.

A House and Self Divided

What happens when, minding this newly juvenilized moral field, an entire generation resists growing up? The results can be read in the public record of the last thirty years. They can be traced not only in the dissolution of the social contract between the classes, professions, and generations but also in the psychological demise of the democratic citizen. In its recrafting of the ideal American character—as promulgated by the unGrimmed fairy tale, the enclosed shopping mall, and the commercially sponsored radio and TV show—Evangelical Mammonism was demanding the formation of a single personality so inherently unstable, so at war with itself, that the pharmacy of pain dissuasion would have to be called in to help.

This, too, was predictable in a way. Living in an economy that had, at various times, divided the classes, the sexes, and the generations to increase efficiency and productivity on behalf of its own profitability, we shouldn't be shocked to find that even that most primary unit of democratic belief, the independent citizen, was eventually divided for exploitation. Our now all-enclosing economy was enforcing one set of ideal behaviors for behind the desk; another, and nearly opposite, for browsing in the mall. Each of us was supposed to labor like Sisyphus and consume like Falstaff, the sum of which (as calculated by the fuzzy moral math of free-market ideology) would also produce a naturally virtuous citizenry. Robotic efficiency plus sheer avidity would somehow engender not only personal happiness but civic righteousness.

The inner psychic tension implicit in this cohabitation of the efficient producer and the avid consumer did induce for a time a kind of frantic productivity. One wanted more and so worked more, wanted more still and so worked even harder. Yet to obey those mixed messages—to be both rationally self-disciplined and ravenously self-indulgent, working longer hours at unrewarding jobs so that one might sip the latest in-spot's sauce du jour—was both an exhausting and a confusing affair. The body longed for rest and the mind for simplicity, a single moral master to whom it could submit. *To want more / to work more / to get more / to want more*—what a tedious cycle. And, really, there *had* been a hierarchy all along, the efficient producer playing errand boy to the avid consumer's lavish list of wants. But, hey, if the real point was "to get," more than a few aging Aquarians began to ask, why not rebel against the puritanical notion of labor itself? Why slave to *earn* that which, as the adman preached daily, one innately *deserved*? If the real point was to profit and productivity only a means, why not find a shorter cut to the Elysian fields of the Treasury's green?

Such is the reasoning of adolescent self-esteem, and the results of its logic soon became clear with a host of dubious schemes: junk bonds, insider trading, the S&L scam, supply-side theory, lottery mania and casino construction, the dismantling of companies for instant profit, the egregious inflation of executive pay, the double-cooked books of WorldCom and Enron, the mass hallucinations of the dot-com craze and subprime fiasco, the giddy expansion of personal indebtedness, corporate welfare, and the federal deficit.[3] The urgency to "make it" had obscured and belittled the long-term and tedious requirements of *making*. To win, after all, was to have the most toys, the fattest or fastest-growing numbers on the board, and so the ownership of goods and not their actual creation became the dominant motivation.

The moral core of capitalist faith, its two most cherished claims—that rational self-interest is the greatest incentive to productivity and that, if left alone, the Market will always and justly regulate itself—had been compromised by the excesses of its own propaganda. Those young consumers that commerce had been indoctrinating since the fifties were now the economy's new movers and shakers, and there, in the corner offices of real authority, they proceeded to behave exactly as they had been trained for thirty or forty years, starting at age three while watching the ads between cartoons on morning TV: they esteemed their selves and, like transgressive teens, rebelled against the middle-aged regimens of service and savings.

The Demise of Civility

This destructive pattern was not limited to the economic sphere. In its implicit endorsement of a laissez-faire and ultimately lazy model for ethical behavior—because the Market as a whole justly (if invisibly) regulates our actions, we needn't really bother to regulate ourselves—the sanctification of adolescent behavior was suffusing every arena of American life. We saw it in the NEA controversy when the "free market" of expression (the artist's self-interest) was equated absolutely with the social good. We saw it, too, in public education where, for a time, the emphasis switched from instruction to facilitation, where much was "celebrated" but little required, students expected to teach themselves the skills and habits that any adult requires.

What these approaches shared was a dangerous naiveté about the nature and nurture of individual freedoms, a Pollyanna presumption that systems—whether free markets, open classrooms or, as in the case of Reagan's "mythic America," whole nation-states—are good in and of themselves. Humming the tune of the times, and one largely based on consumerist jingles, each approach tended to deify the individual. The single self (revolutionary artist, entrepreneur, preschool prodigy) was cast as a kind of protogod, a being whose native powers knew no bounds. But for all that pitching of its powers, this sovereign self proved to be a fragile bud, exquisitely sensitive to any slight or harm. And so when things went wrong, as they often do in the world outside the Magic Kingdom, each wounded party rushed to project an outer cause; each tended to presume that the fault had to lie in some external infringement on selfhood's sovereign rights—by government regulators, puritanical censors, or authoritarian teachers.

Such a temperament helps explain why, when disputes occurred and their will was crossed, these espousers of total freedom tended to become instant authoritarians. In their version of democracy, one writ by the ad-man and starring Narcissus, all professions but one's own must be brought in line, made to echo and endorse that sovereign self's designs, whether material or moral. Imagine a place with two hundred million such selves—so many divine-right consumers, each expecting (and pronto) not only pleasure, fame, and wealth but a general moral sanction for the triumph of its will—and one replays the cacophony of resentful self-interest that was dominating public discourse in the eighties and nineties. Like the temper of self-restraint that enforces it, the language of community, equality, and compromise didn't emerge naturally from those who had been raised on Mammon's glossy fantasies. The citizen's belief that we share a common fate was beyond the ken of the avid consumer and ruthless producer who were emerging then to take that citizen's place.

And so, in tallying the social costs of "age dissuasion," we can add to the widespread cultivation of economic fraud a loss of the civility that healthy democracies require. For when moderation can be enforced only by law, the spirit of liberty dies, and in the era's clamor to restrict speech and behavior—whether on the campus by the secular left or in the Congress by the religious right—one could hear the moans and whines of a society ill-fit for freedom. In the realm of rights as in the realm of riches, we were demanding the prize while disdaining the labor, just as we had been taught.

The Demise of Self-Mastery

Despite the illusion of individual sovereignty that was being pitched by both the privatization and self-liberation movements (the economic right and cultural left secretly allied in their narcissism), we couldn't insulate ourselves, our singular fates, from the corruption of our economy or the rancor of our political state. The outer commonwealth both reflected and affected the inner one; disharmony induced disharmony. So it was that the personal happiness, for whose sake and under whose banner so many bane-ful acts had been initiated, proved illusory as well. Despite two decades of "helping the self" under the therapeutic regimens of self-help and –esteem, and despite the pharmaceutical promise of becoming "better than well," Americans continued to feel the pathos of their own neediness. Rarely have so many well-fed people felt so righteous in complaint, so justified in pro-claiming their inner pain or rage. If, in Jefferson's words, happiness was a pursuit, then many believed that they were losing the race.

This, too, was a logical result of Virtual America's moral field. The evangelism of its Mammonism, always demanding a further expansion of profits, spurred the invention of a whole host of previously unacknowledged needs and the products to slake them. Marketeers would target some newly defined special interest group—the overweight, say, or, when trying to in-crease Paxil's customer base, the shy—whose members they would then sensitize, converting them to the calling of their own psychic pain. In this postindustrial phase, the consumer corporation was as much in the busi-ness of promoting *dis*-ease through its "awareness campaigns" as it was in the business of providing recovery. To sell its prescriptions for happiness, it first had to sell us on the intensity and diversity of our *un*happiness. And who could have guessed, before we had read online those six subtle symp-toms of our psychic distress, what pains such peas could cause, or how many of them lurked beneath our ego's cushy mattress?

One can see why, then, despite our obsessive pursuit of personal happi-ness—all that rigorous rowing on selfhood's behalf—bliss seemed to recede, like Gatsby's green light, into the realm of an unredeemable past. For the more we helped our selves then, the more help we found we needed. Rather than mastering our own psychic state, a condition that requires an accep-tance of pain, we had been trained to discern new causes for complaint. Under the aegis of Evangelical Mammonism, therapies, too— like donut flavors and athletic shoes—had to ramify and accessorize. They also had to follow Tom Peters's crazy prescription of "cannibalization" for "fashioniza-tion," surfing the fun wave of the "permanently ephemeral" product line. And with each new need rapidly begetting a network of further needs, our consumer economy's actual warranty belied the virtual one we still perpetu-ally read: here in Virtual America, in the malldom of our minds, *dis*satisfac-tion was now guaranteed.

Nowhere was this trap of self-fulfilling misery more clear than in our collective pursuit of "age dissuasion." Only a people trained to expect the li-cense of sheer fantasy could believe that extending adolescence into middle age could be a recipe for happiness. Sealed within our society's age-segre-gated spheres, we began to believe the glamorized revision of adolescent life that we saw on our screens: that sun-fun time among the dunes where busts always bulge in perfect proportion to fashion's decree, where skin always tans, nobody barfs, and nary a zit can be seen.

The Demise of Effective Parenting

The social garden, like the physical one, is built from a web of interdependencies that are balanced by a set of simple but immutable truths. Among those truths is this: society can only afford—economically, politically, psychologically—one generation of adolescents at a time. *Someone* must pay the bills, determine and enforce the fairest rules, plan for the future and exact its requirements in the here and now. Someone, in a word, must be prudent—a trait derided in a moral field inspired by Walt Disney, Ronald Reagan, Tom Peters, and William Burroughs—or the whole enterprise will derail.

That derailment came in 2008, and, without a significant change in the temper and telos of our everyday lives, it will occur again. To everything there *is* a season and by prolonging the season of our youth, we have been robbing our children of theirs—of their right to a phased graduation into the truths and obligations of the human condition, as refined by the virtues of democratic practice. Not only have we consumed through our indebtedness resources rightfully theirs to spend; we have usurped just as selfishly their rightful role as social rebels. By continuing to play at revolt ourselves, we have given them nothing substantial to revolt against, no firm ethical structures to test, resist, and finally renew. Deprived of those external systems, they have trouble constructing internal ones and so are all the more vulnerable to the manipulations of both the marketeer and the corner pusher.

Here, then, is the final debt to figure our sum. In listing the consequences that naturally accrue to a society which would deny the reality of consequences, this is the last and most telling result. Not only has age dissuasion helped to undermine our economy, taint our democracy, and promote a perpetual personal unhappiness; it also threatens to leave too many of our children unprepared for real life.

Our economy's much ballyhooed bottom-line accounting supplies the clearest sign of virtue's demise in this regard. If we really wish to gauge the values of the nation, as enacted and endorsed by the postwar generations, we need only to take note of the various rates that our free market bears. We need only compare the average weekly wage of those who service our cars with the income of those to whom we willingly entrust our youngest children's care.[4] The discrepancy defined (usually measured in multiples of two to three times) vividly graphs the economy we practice and clearly forecasts which of its "products," car or child, is likely to thrive.

Compare teachers to salesmen, or pediatricians to other physicians; graph the rapid real-dollar defunding of higher education in the public sphere in relation to increases in senior services; measure the hefty hike in payroll taxes (whose burden falls disproportionately on younger adults and the working poor) against the dramatic decreases in income and capital gains taxes (whose benefits disproportionately accrue to older adults and the speculative wealthy)—and the numbers will reflect the same flagrant bias. To borrow from Auden, "what instruments we have agree."[5] Our fantasies still flatter, but the facts are plain. Even before reaching retirement age, those of us in the so-called adult community have "live[d] long enough to be a burden on our children."

II. Specimens of Age Dissuasion

Entertainment Tonight

Nowhere was our economy's investment in the moonwalking regress of juvenilization made more symbolically vivid than on one of postwar TV's most popular game shows, *Let's Make a Deal*. Produced and hosted by the dapper Monty Hall, whose slick deportment and three-piece suits suggested a suburbanized carnival barker, the show had an extraordinarily long run, from 1963 to 1991, and some of its 4,500 shows can still be seen in the perpetual "ever after" of rerun heaven on cable TV. There, the once desirable prizes (Chevy Vegas, early video games, erstwhile stylish clothes) supply a kind of archeological display of our economy's "permanently ephemeral" product lines.

Like most game shows, *Let's Make a Deal* was an advertisement wrapped in a commercial enclosed in a promotion. The prizes to be won, and even the clothes that Monty wore, were as much the commercial message as the official sponsors' thirty-second slots. Unlike its close cousin, the quiz show, however, *Let's Make a Deal* didn't pretend to test its players' intelligence. Forgoing the winking pretense that some socially redeemable quality of mind earned one the right to acquire the prizes, the game focused instead on the emotional dynamics of purchase and possession. Every moment was framed as an anxious and exciting consumer decision: whether or not to "make a deal" in a world whose options had been radically reduced to cash or commodity.

To start, Monty would flash wads of crisp green cash, offering to purchase worthless items from selected members of his audience for ridiculous amounts—a hundred bucks, say, for a pack of gum or a person's shoe. But once so enriched, the player would then be tempted by the possibilities that lurked behind an array of three blank curtains: prizes that could range, depending on her luck and nerve, from the marvelous (a Caribbean cruise) to the humiliating (a year's supply of disposable diapers). Should the player keep her cash, or should she "make a deal" by purchasing whatever commodity lay hidden behind one of the curtains? And if the latter, which curtain should she choose? And once she had made that choice, should she stick with her selection if Monty offered her even more cash before she had a chance to look? And once she had a chance to look, should she swap the perhaps middling prize she had just won, the microwave or blender, for another chance at a grander one? Would she then win big or would her deal go bust?

By merging the avidity of consumption with the drama of gambling, the show reliably induced an emotional intensity, which was further magnified by the social pressure that naturally attends any spectator sport. During her hesitation over these grave decisions, the anxious player would be urged on by conflicting advice shouted from the in-studio audience, whose members were participating vicariously in the great expectations of the imminent deal. The game's already frenetic pace would then intensify at the end of the show when Monty would go berserk, making deals at an ever more rapid rate, offering to purchase mundane objects for absurd amounts.

The staging of consumer products as the idols of American desire; the deliberate reduction of all decision-making to deal-making, all value to cash value; the constant alternation of quackery and dupery (with its implicit message that someone is always being conned in the exchange); the clever manipulation of an emotional climate that played the avidity of hope against the fear of humiliation and that drew on the gambler's addiction to anticipation; the carefully engineered mass hysteria of the crowd; and the frantic shop-till-you-drop tempo throughout: for twenty-eight years, *Let's Make a Deal* projected the inherent decadence of modern consumerism in unembarrassed excess.

The show's allied investment in the juvenilization of the American character was most evident in the way its contestants were selected. Where other game shows picked their players ahead of time, *Let's Make a Deal* cleverly enfolded the process into the drama of the show itself. The front of the audience would be filled with adults (mostly women in the early years) who, as per instructions, had dressed themselves in silly costumes—as clowns or Raggedy Ann dolls, in bunny suits or Shirley Temple outfits. And when, at the start of the show, Monty would step into their midst, they would all beg on cue, jumping up and down around him, hands raised and waving, each pleading with the omnipotent show-biz personality *pick me! pick me!* A group of middle-aged adults, reduced to begging from their "host" while dressed in ridiculously juvenile outfits as if unruly first-graders vying for the right to pet a duckling on their visit to the zoo: even for postwar TV, which routinely undermined the dignity of the individual, this self-demeaning spectacle seemed extreme, the stuff of outrageous parody.

And yet the popularity of the show clearly wasn't based on the perception that it was camp. Few of its fans seemed to recognize how its format exposed the nudity of *our* emperor's new clothes. This was the show's underlying yet unacknowledged message: to enter consumer capitalism's new kingdom of heaven, we would have to become, under the guise of innocent fun, like little children again. The license to "make a deal," to be empowered with the chance to make a killing on TV's stage, required first this psychological regression: democracy's self-reliant citizen recast instead as a Raggedy Ann who has to plead with the grownups for a chance to play in their game.

The masquerade of Monty's game had three phases, and they were ones commonly favored by con men and cult leaders of every stripe. After initiating the players' juvenilization by forcing them to dress in silly costumes and plead with Dad for a chance to play, the game continued with the derationalization of their decision-making. For in contrast to other popular shows of the same era, such as *The Price Is Right* and *What's My Line?*, Monty had designed a game that supplied no logical basis for winning or losing. Memory, deduction, induction, savvy about human character or statistical probability: all varieties of effective reasoning had been rendered irrelevant. Even as the game highlighted the individual's freedom to decide—Hamlet's "to be or not to be" recast as Mammon's "to buy or not to buy"—it removed every rational basis for deciding. Instead, the players had to rely on a hunch or a superstitious faith in the coincidental alignment of numbers. To play the game was to return again to the Magic Kingdom, where the price of entry was a willingness to believe, just believe in the pixie-dust promise.

Temporarily stripped of both emotional maturity and analytical reason, the contestants then entered the third and final phase of their regression. The masquerade of sovereignty—that is, the way in which the freedom-to-choose was both accentuated and emasculated by the rules of the game—immediately flipped into a state of anxious passivity as the players awaited the results of their necessarily clueless choices. Forced to guess and so utterly dependent on lady luck, they then had to endure that either-or melodrama which is well-known to gamblers of every sort.

To win or to lose. To make a killing or purchase a lemon. The curtain she has chosen is about to rise and behind it awaits either immediate celebration (her dreams come true "out of the blue") or instant humiliation (getting "zonked," in the parlance of the show). The game's pace, intensity, and group-think cheering helped to distract the players from the realization that, in most instances, swapping reason for superstition and emotional maturity for childish hope are the predictable makings of a very bad deal.

Immaturity, Rash and Rational

While the popular game show was modeling why age dissuasion is a common tactic in the confidence game of salesmanship, headlines were spotlighting its disastrous impact on personal decision-making. I offer the following specimens as illustrative of the two distinct tempers that juvenilization still commonly assumes.

The first, which captured the attention of nightly newscasts all across the nation, related the story of a white, middle-class, Midwest couple, an engineer and a homemaker, who decided they needed a winter vacation and so flew south to warmer climes, leaving their two preteenage children behind for nine full days, including Christmas, unattended. When their daughters, ages four and nine, accidentally set off a smoke alarm in their suburban home, a neighbor notified the police who then arrested the parents when they finally deplaned from their Acapulco getaway.[6]

This so-called Home Alone case was especially troubling to the national conscience, I think, because it seemed to exhibit a purely hedonistic motivation for offensive behavior, absent any apparent pathological subtext such as drug addiction or mental illness. It was even more troubling, perhaps, in that all the various ways of categorizing the offending couple refuted our easiest, self-exculpatory presumptions about antisocial behavior: that the desertion of America's children is primarily a problem of single parent families, or of men, or of a mostly black and urban underclass, or of a corrupt cultural elite who have taken up residence on the two coasts.

The second example proves even stranger but no less troubling to our easy presumptions about the causes of immature behavior. Back in 1990, a terminally ill Californian was seeking a highly unusual form of legal redress. Credentialed in precisely those ways that we now soberly respect, this Silicon Valley computer consultant with a doctorate in mathematics from the University of Chicago wanted the court to force doctors to fulfill his final wish, which was, grotesque as it seems, to have his head cut off before his disease finally killed him. He wasn't pleading for some bizarre form of euthanasia (Dr. Kevorkian meets *Chain Saw Massacre*) but the opposite, really—he didn't want to die in peace so much as live forever. The plan was to have himself instantly frozen "alive" in hopes of being revived when the advances of science might cure his disease. And because he believed that his true self resided in his brain alone (recall his profession), and because the private companies that offer cryonic preservation charge far less for freezing a head than a whole human body (35,000 dollars versus 100,000 at that time), he was requesting decapitation so he could afford a procedure that he had come to believe might eventually save him.[7]

The great naturalist Louis Agassiz is said to have commanded a graduate student to study a single dead fish for weeks at a time to make him intimate with the form (and deformation) of animal anatomy.[8] This man's peculiar judicial request might serve as an equally instructive moribund specimen. If we think, and think hard, about a justice system that would entertain such a suit, about an economy that would spawn such a company, about the philosophy that predicated the man's reasoning, and about the ethical implications of investing one's resources in such a way, we might achieve an intimate comprehension of our culture's true anatomy, its current form and deformation.

Let it be noted first that this consultant's position was rooted in the basic premises of our prevailing practical philosophy, which is a marketized form of rational materialism largely stripped of Judeo-Christian values. Although his request may seem extreme to the point of absurdity, he was not being rash; his reasoning, to the contrary, was highly methodical, rational, and (some might even say) brave. After studying the evidence, he had accepted the terrible truth of a terminal diagnosis, researched his options, and made just the sort of cost-benefit analysis that those of the Chicago school like to imagine directs our economy more broadly. One could argue, in short, that this man was a good capitalist consumer, acting out of the sort of enlightened self-interest that is supposed to produce both material prosperity and social progress, and that he was a model democratic citizen, using the peaceful means of the law to pursue his constitutional right to direct his own destiny by purchasing a service that he could afford.

Is it fair to call such a request immature? If maturity can be defined as those traits necessary for the sustenance of a harmonious society, and if the sustaining of such a society depends on adults who have adapted to the realities of the human condition, including the reality of death, and who are willing, therefore, to bequeath both their wisdom and their wealth to the next generation—then, yes, I believe it is fair. Although opposite in temper, this rational request for decapitation is no less self-centered in its own way than the rash desertion of the vacationing couple and, as a model for adult decision-making, is no less destructive to our social compact.

But is it fair, then, to use two such extreme examples as representative? Society, after all, condemned the couple (they were pilloried in the press, convicted of neglect, and lost custody of their children), and the court finally refused the dying consultant's request. Yet, although these individuals did transgress the borders of the permissible, their ways of thinking were not *that* far removed from cultural norms that persist today. Middle-class children are left on their own every day in Virtual America, often by parents who are off satisfying their "own needs" as defined ever more expansively by our economy, and the denial of death has become a burgeoning industry here. Many millions of dollars are spent prolonging the lives of the mortally comatose and thousands of puffy words expended avoiding the one word sentence we all must share: i.e., death. Our movies may be notorious for their abundant body counts, but America's real-life relation to the fact of mortality is best captured by the octogenarian lady who, when informed that she was dying, responded plaintively: "Why me?"

Such childish expectations are not limited to the uneducated. Supposedly serious scientists, associated with prestigious institutions like M.I.T.'s Media Lab, have made claims that we can invent our way into an actual immortality.[9] Nor does political affiliation exempt one from the self-centered behavior of age dissuasion. Our liberal elite and Moral Majority alike invest in cosmetic surgery, throw adolescent road-rage fits, and flatter their "inner child," variously defined, to the detriment of their actual children. I offer this pair of incidents, then, because they illustrate my larger points: namely, that such juvenile behavior is very broadly based, and that it has been shaped by the moral field of our Mammonite economy.

As was noted earlier, the preferences of that moral field are themselves conflicted, reinforcing a pair of opposing moral temperaments, sibling rivals, one über-rational and the other super-rash, which our dying consultant and deserting parents illustrated in the extreme. While the ethos of rational production endorses rote obedience and mechanical efficiency, the ethos of romantic salesmanship pushes hedonistic impulsiveness and rebellion against authority. Although both clearly serve the corporation's bottom-line values, they model discordant identities. Even as management idealizes a coolly mechanical and narrowly accountable employee at work, marketing celebrates a hotly appetitive rebel at home and at play, and the former's Dr. Jekyll must somehow coincide with the latter's Mr. Hyde.

Because Hyde's dangers to the civic good are more flagrant, they naturally become the focus of public debate. In the gotcha game of the culture wars, each side cleverly "outs" the antisocial excesses of its opponent's rash behavior even as it ignores its own, for as the machinations of both wannabe gangsta Boss Laws and management guru Tom Peters demonstrated, the anarchy of Mr. Hyde is a "target of opportunity" for "the smart business person" of every stripe, left or right. Choosing to idealize ghetto cop-killing or corporate cannibalism may prove destructive to the social order, but insomuch as each can be used to boost one's own profits, both are deemed good by the conventional accounting of our current economy.

Postmodern Parenting: The Producer Model

As a final example of the insidious effects of these economically driven identities, I want to return to the problem of parenting and compare the rash model with a rational one. Let's imagine a slightly upscale and more admirably motivated version of the Home Alone family: a white, married, college-educated Midwestern couple with two preteenage children, Adam and Amy. Although both parents now work full-time, the mother gladly stayed home a full year after each child's birth and then relentlessly sought out the very best child care, regardless of price. In fact, committed to both gender equality and responsible parenthood, this couple had planned to alternate working part-time until Amy reached junior high. But when the father's company was downsized, he had to take on more work rather than less, and although the mother was still willing to sacrifice the career advantage of full employment, they found that, without the extra income, they couldn't afford a house in the community with the best public schools. So she extended her hours—as did the father, for his commute was lengthened an hour each day after the move.

Such sacrifices are characteristic of this couple. They have no desire to take impulsive vacations free of their children's company. To the contrary, their fondest fantasy, discussed over take-out dinners or whispered above the soundtrack of the children's Friday evening video, is to have a more relaxed and natural family life. But everything they read and their own employment experiences warn them that their children must be highly trained to survive the Darwinian reality of the new economy. So they take out a loan to buy the very best home computers and educational software, which they upgrade, then upgrade again. When Adam has trouble learning to read, they send him to a nationally franchised Sylvan Learning Center for after-school training and then hire a private tutor. When Amy shows ability in math, it only seems fair that they offer her tutoring as well, so they send her to a Kumon Math Center, and then they pay for her skating lessons to counterbalance Adam's soccer camp.

All of this, of course, means more expense and less time spent together, but they try to adjust by using cell phones and texts to stay in touch. Furthermore, Adam and Amy are guaranteed "quality time" on the weekend (there is a sign-up sheet over the microwave): four full hours when each gets to choose favorite activities and special foods, guaranteed the right then to be spoiled by the intensity of their parents' total attention. The couple also attends every conference, game, and performance they can. There, too, the intensity of their attention doesn't flag; there, as their children's passionate advocates, they work the system—lobby teachers, network neighbors, argue with refs—whatever it takes to wrest the best for Amy and Adam. Once, in fact, the mother refused to leave a principal's office until he agreed to transfer Amy out of a class where her gift for math was going unappreciated. She shocked herself then with the language she was willing to use on her daughter's behalf.

I could go on, but the portrait is complete enough and, perhaps, painfully familiar. What I find so insidious here is the extent to which the totality of domestic life is being shaped by economic models, motives, fears, and values: how much the grimly anxious pace of the postmodern workplace has come to command the domestic household. And, of course, for clarity's sake, I have removed all the potentially corrupting effects of contemporary consumerism, the hedonistic half of the mixed message the economy projects. Statistically speaking, this is a uniquely ascetic couple. Here we have no divorce, infidelity, rampant careerism; no alcoholism, drug addiction, compulsive shopping or gambling—none of the many forms of self-centered dysfunction that can tear apart a family. Here we have nothing so rash, just a perversely rational schedule of pervasive separation, a desertion of one's own children "on their behalf."

This household has been purged of sexist inequalities, but it has also been stripped of wonder, curiosity, improvisational play. Mother and father have merged into one cooperative, unisexual provider; the good parent has been reduced to the good producer whose job as parent is to supply society with the next generation of good producers—that is, with employees who are already accustomed to highly rationalized social environments and whose skills are upgraded to the ever-evolving specs of the time. This new parent doesn't teach by example; he-she hires various tutors, coaches, specialists in the field, renting the DVDs and heeding the schemes of commodified expertise. This new parent's role proves less to cherish and chasten than to outfit and facilitate; less to shape meaning than to make money, furnishing each child with all the materialist gear and rationalist techniques that the economy requires.

Even this household's happier moments have been reinvented according to the economy's preferred rhythms and terms. The notion of prescheduled "quality time," for example, converts parenting to corporate standards of executive efficiency. As in company headquarters, enhanced technique is supposed to reduce the need for management "face time," leading to the implicitly sad rationalization that the better we are as parents, the *less* time we will spend on our children's care. The parent as passionate advocate—the one lobbying hard on her child's behalf without broader concerns for truth, justice, or even common courtesy—also reenacts workplace roles and values, especially as defined by our ever-expanding service domain. Such behavior reflects the highly specialized code of conduct—the so-called professional ethics—of the lawyer, the therapist, the consultant, or the licensed accountant who does the books for both his own mega-church and an S&M supply house. Our job at home, like our job in the field, is not to reprimand but to represent. All clients are good clients. Our children have become our customers, and the customer is always right.

Specialists without Spirit, Sensualists without Heart

When our children become our clients, then even the family has ceased to be a possible sphere for moral instruction. When our domestic rituals are set to the beat and drawn toward the goals of our workaday schedules, then home itself ceases to be a sanctuary. Even at night we have no respite from the anxieties of a marketplace where the buyer must beware and only the fittest are supposed to survive; even in our living rooms we find no alternative to the economy's reductive yet contradictory commands to produce and consume, produce and consume.

In truth, the Mammonite economy that now pervades American life does not *want* people who are capable of creating and sustaining the rituals of domesticity. Calibrated by the dualism of its origins, it wants instead, and paradoxically, pure rationalists and pure materialists: efficient Dr. Jekylls and avid Mr. Hydes. And even if we could harmonize its demands for perfect efficiency and unending appetite, the merged model could only supply an impoverished version of human life. Acting out of that model, which reduces us to the mechanical by day and the animal at night, we still could not ripen into a fully competent, deeply caring, communally committed adulthood.

Maturity requires the acquisition of a broad, commonsense intelligence and a commitment to truth-telling. Evangelical Mammonism rewards instead both the narrow expertise of producership and the soft duplicities of salesmanship.

Maturity requires patience and emotional endurance. Evangelical Mammonism promotes the habit of complaining and impulsive behavior; it hypes the new injustice or psychic pain which then can be medicated, adjudicated, serviced for a fee.

Maturity teaches the selflessness of social commitment. Evangelical Mammonism promotes the selfishness of both self-liberation and deregulation (duty-free rights for the self and the corporation), and it boosts the value of sheer acquisition—that *more*, whether for me or the shareholders, *must equal better.*

Maturity depends on a steady transfer of traditional wisdoms between the generations through daily example. Evangelical Mammonism relentlessly eradicates traditional wisdoms through insisting that the new is always improved, and that youth is preferable to age. And it segregates the generations—into day-care, workplace, retirement communities—for more efficient service and marketing.

Maturity is grounded in a stoic acceptance of the human condition. It depends on acknowledging those facts that remain the same for every culture and generation, uniting the first with the last: that death is real; that our knowledge is limited; that, even in an age of technological advance, our rational control remains provisional—that "time and chance happen to us all."[10] Evangelical Mammonism promotes instead the fantasies of pain and age dissuasion, including a superstitious belief in the Magic Moment and a disingenuous faith in the Fable of Innocence.

Finally, while maturity directs the submission of physical desires and intellectual schemes to the discipline of higher meanings, Evangelical Mammonism co-opts and consumes—following the self-erasing schedules of the fashion cycle, it cannibalizes—all forms of higher meaningfulness. Its "fun" agenda relentlessly transforms quality into quantity, cultural diversity into commercial accessories, the organism of symbolism into the mechanism of market value. In a process that demeans not only what we want to buy but who we finally wish to be, this economy's bias toward "making a deal" is always working to transform the community-saving hero into the commodity-sponsoring star.

At the end of *The Protestant Ethic and the Spirit of Capitalism*, Max Weber emerged from his sober and objective analysis to speculate on the future character of what he famously called the West's "iron cage" of capitalist endeavor. "No one knows," he wrote:

> who will live in this cage in the future, or whether at the end of this tremendous development entirely new prophets will arise, or whether there will be a great rebirth of old ideas and ideals, or, if neither, mechanized petrification, embellished with a

sort of convulsive self-importance. For of the last stage of this cultural development, it might truly be said: Specialists without spirit, sensualists without heart; this nullity imagines that it has attained a level of civilization never before achieved.[11]

It wasn't long ago that, with what sometimes seemed "convulsive self-importance," we were proclaiming the global triumph of our way of life. Now, after the fiasco in Iraq and our financial collapse, we might wonder at the extent to which we have achieved instead just such a "nullity": a civilization whose vanity has been based on the fantasies of age dissuasion; a claustrophobic place whose all-enclosing cage *prefers* (and so produces) "specialists without spirit, sensualists without heart."

8

Auguries of Decadence

. . . . human kind
Cannot bear too much reality.[1]

—T. S. Eliot

In March of 2003, as American troops gathered in Kuwait, just days away from invading Iraq, and Fannie Mae and Freddie Mac were about to buy eighty-one billion dollars of subprime mortgage securities from Wall Street's quacks, Monty Hall's *Let's Make a Deal* had a brief revival. And although this born-again production was quickly cancelled, the nature of the competition it faced, along with the transformation of its own format within that context, demonstrated all too clearly the downward slope of TV programming. Season after season, the industry had been slip-sliding its way into tabloid pandering via a delirious and dollar-greased pursuit of ratings, but these reinventions of the old game show marked a new phase in that shameless descent. Dubbed "reality television," the revised shows painfully exposed the actual character being shaped by our pervasive economy's Invisible Hand—a character whose addiction to magical thinking was now even directing, it seemed, the conduct of fateful public policies.

As it so happened, I was watching a lot of broadcast TV during the period in question. Coincidental to the Iraq crisis and the inflation of the housing bubble, I had assigned myself the task of studying the new programming, and the intensely ironic interplay then between reality as conveyed by the day's grave news and "reality" as framed by the evening's entertainments made for a dizzying spectacle of pain and folly. Awful archival pictures of wailing Kurdish women widowed by Saddam Hussein's chemical weapons cohabited in the mind's eye with the puffily bruised and cross-stitched faces of would-be Cinderellas, who had won the chance to be born again via cosmetic surgery on *Extreme Makeover*. The martial bluster of talking-head TV's many arm-chair patriots, who were predicting what "we" would surely do to Iraq's Republican Guard, eerily echoed the macho posturing of contestants on *Fear Factor* prior to their submergence into a tank of writhing snakes—which was, after all, not a bad metaphor for our plans to invade and righteously school a venomously factional Middle East.

"Elimination" had distinctly different emotional resonances then, depending on whether the threatening vehicle was an Iraqi nuclear missile[2] or the vote of a game show's "tribal council," yet the overall shape of these suspenseful narratives proved much the same. Each adhered to that "common dream" long conveyed on our silver screens. One way or another, each story would climax as-we-like-it (*as-we-like-it . . .*). Our victorious soldiers would soon be showered with kisses and flowers on Baghdad's streets,[3] and someone—another real person just like you and me—would win a mogul's mansion or a starlet's stunning breast-line, the true love of their life or the recording contract that had always been their dream. *Do you believe in miracles?*

Alas, as the impresarios of both sorts of show knew all too well, we do.

I. Reality Television in the Age of Empire

Fame Game: Simulating "Real" Celebrity

Asked if he could insult the contestants the way modern game-show hosts do, Hall said, "I can't. I don't like it. It's an anathema to me." [4]

—an interview with Monty Hall

Although, as we saw last chapter, *Let's Make a Deal* did juvenilize its participants, Monty was sincere in a way when he expressed his revulsion at the newer shows' tactical investment in insulting their guests: *Let's Make a Deal* had never been that direct. *Its* demeaning of their dignity had always been masked by an aura of beneficent paternalism. The show had debuted in 1963, after all, when the nation's self-conception was still basking in the glow of family shows like *Leave It to Beaver*, and in designing his game Monty had been careful to honor the era's preferred pretense of innocent fun: rather berate his guests, he had gifted them with cash. But the revival of his program came in an era when many women had careers and when one out of every two marriages ended in divorce (often leaving a caretaking mom with kids to support on insufficient alimony), the sight of adult women pleading for cash from a dapper male host risked appearing either ludicrously archaic or painfully offensive.

Much else had changed in the cultural context as well. After four decades of "defining deviancy downward,"[5] the American masquerade of innocent fun had become much harder to sustain. For an audience accustomed to tabloid talk shows, pornographic cable channels, and slandering websites—an audience intimate with the reproductive failures, dysfunctional relationships, and substance abuse problems of its actors, athletes, and politicians—sublimation and discretion no longer proved effective. By 2003, "transparency" had become the reigning imperative. Opening up was the unavoidable admission price to public life: no zipper left unzipped, no secret habit unconfessed, no closet contents unexamined by Geraldo's leering camera.

The beast of Virtual America's publicity machine not only haphazardly feasted on such scandals; it demanded them. And for both the average Joe who longed to escape his anonymity and the aging star who had gone out of fashion, this new media market's blood lust for gossip supplied the easiest route to claim or reclaim their fifteen minutes of televisual fame. In a ruling value system where *more attention* (in the form of ratings) *must equal better*, the scandalous life could be as "good" as, and sometimes better than, the traditionally virtuous one. Sometimes—as we saw with Boss Laws, the fraternity sweetheart who had pitched herself instead as a cop-killing gangsta—that might even lead to confessing to sins one hadn't committed.

All these changes had an inevitable impact on the game-show format. By 2003, at the height of its revival, a paparazzi-style insistence on full exposure had been built into many of the new programs. Now, in the midst of the ten-week long game, the audience at home could overhear the scantily clad players confess their secret lusts and loathings, and could participate vicariously in their Machiavellian plots, the whispered hatching of the latest betrayal. Later, in a staged reunion, the former competitors might watch together taped excerpts from the show. Waxing nostalgic with laughter and tears, they would then submit to a group interview, during which (just like Julia Roberts before Barbara Walters) they would open up about their feelings and philosophize retrospectively about the "meaning of the game."

But whatever the intricacies of the specific game in question or the profundity of the meaning that a player milked from its passage, a once tacit truth about the game-show format had now become transparently obvious. The ultimate prize, the allure that transcended the Caribbean cruise or even the jackpot million, was the dramatic transformation of one's social status.

Stronger even than the desire for commodities was the lust to be noticed, to be known, the sheer craving for notoriety. Every game was, at heart, a simulation of the media's own fame game. Each program granted the average Joe or Joelene the right to cross over to the other side of the camera's avid eye and assume, however briefly, the cherished status of a celebrity. After a lifetime of admiring and applauding from afar, just one of two-hundred million anonymous Echos, each contestant had a chance to play Narcissus for a day.

The revival of the prime-time game show had been dependent, in large part, on updating the techniques of simulation for that game-behind-the-game. Just as the same special effects that had sold a sixties action film couldn't draw a mass audience in 2000 because they no longer passed for real, the old game-show formats had lost the authority of semblance—they didn't seem sufficiently like the media fame game as it was currently being played in Virtual America. And so, to enhance the appearance of reality, the new generation of shows added both breadth and depth to their simulations.

Breadth—the democratization of desire in pursuit of market share— had been a standard approach for all forms of marketing for a hundred years. 2003's most popular quiz show *Who Wants to Be a Millionaire?* supplied an obvious example of its strategic application, for although one's actual chances of appearing on the program were nearly infinitesimal, the decision to dumb down both the questions themselves and the format for answering them had created an effective simulation of accessibility. True or not, it did *seem* now like you could be the one sitting in the spotlight across from host Regis Philbin—that regular gal or guy, who, with a little help from phone-linked friends or the studio audience, could nail that final answer and ascend to the status of a millionaire.

In fact, the literal use of spotlighting was a shameless feature of that game's simulation. After a finalist won a chance to play, he would first submit to some personal questioning by the affable host, just like one of the real celebrities on Regis's morning talk show. Then the set would go dark, ceiling lights would swirl and, with a flourish of melodramatic music, a bright funnel of light would suddenly illuminate the lucky player. The symbol of passage couldn't have been clearer: this chance to play the game also afforded one the even dearer right to participate in the game-behind-the-game. As the colonial Pilgrim had once been struck by the saving light of grace, the pomo American had been selected for celebrity by the day's omnipotent publicity machine. Disney's fabled Magic Moment had been revived. Regis's guest had been allowed to cross over to the other side, stepping onto the set of fame's virtual kingdom.

While the breadth added to that simulation of celebrity had been achieved through a clever tweaking of the traditional format, the new depth was more an artifact of the surrounding media-mad culture. Although there were some notable exceptions, the fame of the old game-show contestants had tended to evaporate quickly. But in an era when even the serious news weeklies dished and local news shows shamelessly flogged their network's stars in hopes of boosting their ratings, a prime-time contestant's adventure in celebrity could easily be extended. Even this week's loser on *Survivor* got his interview with Bryant Gumbel on *The Early Morning Show*, and in a time slot equal to and interchangeable with an actual movie star or prominent politician. Even that runner-up on *Bachelor*, whose hopes for a hunky hubby had been dashed, might win an agent, publicist, and modeling contract, or a chance to star in the spin-off series, *Bachelorette*. Mammon's media beast needed to be fed. As industrial America had once mass-produced widgets and washers, Virtual America now manufactured its seasonal celebrities, ever ready to imagineer yesterday's nonentity into today's hot property.

Within this cultural context, the enhanced special effects of the new game show seemed especially convincing. Just as the choreography of the old cinematic cowboy fight now seemed comically fake while the day's martial combat, as staged by Ang Lee, could pass as breathtakingly real, the new-and-improved format *appeared* authentic. Watching its Joes and Joelenes being magnified by the prime-time spotlight, and then following them as they were being interviewed by David Letterman and gossiped about on celebrity websites, the audience at home found it easy to believe that you or I, or even that shy co-worker two cubicles over, could become a real star.

Dumb and Dumber:
The Demise of Dignity in the Guise of Celebrity

But like the jealous Jehovah of old, Mammon's fickle publicity machine now demanded of those it elected the harsh transparency of full disclosure. To audition for celebrity required playing by the new rules of the fame game as they had been established by tabloid moralists like Fox's Rupert Murdoch. Any effective simulation would also require *this* dimension of the "star treatment"—that Joe would have to undergo the same proctological examine as Rob Lowe, Joelene the same invasion of privacy suffered (and sought) by Britney Spears. In the new shows, where one was asked to eat a plate of worms or meekly bear the gratuitous insults of scornful judges, the real test of character had now been exposed: how demeaned was each contestant willing to be for a chance at instant fame and mucho money? In TV's revision of Hollywood's star machine, this was the psyche's version of the body's casting couch, the new submission required to become a player in the game.

To Monty Hall's dismay, the once tacit humiliation of the guest had now become a frank and foregrounded feature of the shows. Sometimes, as in the case of *America's Funniest Home Videos*, it constituted the show's sole content. Given that, unlike *Temptation Island* or the bachelor programs, *Funniest Home Videos* still clung to Monty's masquerade of innocent fun, it might seem an odd show to examine next. Yet the very fact that it was so broadly accepted—its contents, like Disney's, presumed to be "good for the kids"—marks it as representative of Main Street values.

Financially, the show's concept was savvy, establishing what surely must have been one of the cheapest productions on prime-time television. Exploiting the fact that most middle-class families were already playing paparazzi to their own domestic lives, the producers simply asked the public to comb their video cams' archival footage for the "funniest" moments: accidental collisions, wedding-toast malapropisms, all those literal or figurative wreckages that transform the average guy's would-be swan dive into a gut-busting belly flop. Flooded with submissions, the producers selected the best of those personally worst moments, and then invited the finalist families onto the show, where their past follies would then be replayed to much laughter before a live audience.

But this was still a *game* show, after all—a competition that required the selection of a winner. All cultures play games, and to win at a popular one normally signals a specific mastery highly valued by the community at large, skills that can vary from jousting in medieval Europe to chess-playing in postwar Russia. But in an hyper-extension of democracy's traditional aversion to the uppity individual, winning in Virtual America now meant gladly exposing one's most embarrassing moments. Both the show's popularity and its G-rating suggested the degree to which the willing humiliation of the individual before the group had become a conventional virtue.

The moral supremacy of group conformity over individual dignity was further reinforced by the judging which, rather than being assigned to a panel of "experts in the field"—professional comedians, say—was the responsibility of the audience itself. At the end of each show, those in the studio were asked to rate the tapes against each other and submit their electronic vote. Which of the three had been the funniest home moment: Dad falling off the roof in his Santa suit? Mom's flambé dessert setting the dinner party's table cloth on fire? or little Jason being nailed in the 'nads by a wiffle ball and keeling over in pain and humiliation before his guffawing pals? As the talent search for *Gone with the Wind*'s Scarlett O'Hara role had shown, Americans had long yearned for the spotlight, but something had changed in the ensuing sixty years. This wasn't the glamorous chance for a torrid kiss with a highly desirable leading man in the era's most anticipated film. The families of today's Living's Town were now competing instead for bit parts in the latest sequel to *Dumb and Dumber*. And who knew, *really*, whether the winning entry (that is, the democratically assessed dumbest activity) was itself real? In an era when transgression was routinely faked to capture the spotlight, why not innocent ineptitude as well? And indeed the producers of the show were routinely finding phony submissions among the 1500 they received each week.

Nathaniel Hawthorne had been one of the earliest to caution America about the demise of the Protestant self—a loss that was being driven, he thought, by a flight from public and private truthfulness. By 1850, he was urging his readers to "show freely to the world, if not [their] worst, yet some trait whereby the worst may be inferred."[6] But in the fun-house mirror of TV's simulacrum in 2003, best and worst had been inverted. False propriety was hardly a pressing problem in a conventional economy increasingly dependent on notoriety instead. It took the full length of *The Scarlett Letter* for Hawthorne's secret adulterer, the Rev. Dimmesdale, to drag himself into the public square to admit his sin, after which he literally died from the agony of his self-exposure. But in Virtual America, where one went to the bank rather than the grave on the wages of sin, thousands of Dimmesdales were fighting for a chance to expose themselves on TV's talk shows, eager to clutch the soggy Kleenex of confession for the sisterly Diane Sawyer or to toss on cue the furniture of their rage for a winking Jerry Springer.

The inner muddle of motivations that so obsessed Hawthorne had been projected outward to become a very public babble, and who could tell the difference, really, between the true confession and the staged, between a genuine threat to national security and the mushroom-cloud rhetoric penned and polled by the political consultants at Jargonese & Jade?

Fast-Forward Decadence

In "Auguries of Innocence," William Blake had written that all the motions of eternity might be spied in the compression of an hour. On a smaller scale, in a kind of fast-forward version of "defining deviancy downward," the entire cynical cycle of truth's befuddlement could be discerned during the game-show revival, a summary of whose competitive one-upmanship might be aptly entitled, Auguries of Decadence.

In Fox's *Who Wants to Marry a Multi-Millionaire?*, the first of America's bachelor shows, the prospective brides mustered the masquerade of their love for the eligible Rick Rockwell while everyone knew, without saying so, that their tacit motives were immediate fame and serious money.

Just like real celebrities then, the multimillionaire and his instant spouse, Darva Conger, were investigated by the nation's army of tabloid journalists and quickly found to be scandalously wanting. The groom, it turned out, had been accused of physical abuse by an ex-fiancée[7] while the bride had plumped her application with a bogus claim to being a Gulf War veteran.[8] Winning a quickie annulment, partially on the grounds that she had refused to consummate the marriage, Conger then promptly exposed to the nation what she had refused to surrender to her would-be mate, baring all in *Playboy* for a reported half million. Meanwhile, after touring the talk-show circuit with the sad tale of his broken heart, the jilted Rockwell tried to jump-start his second career as a stand-up comedian.

In the initial aftermath of the scandal, it appeared that the new bachelor game show was dead on arrival. Even the shameless Fox was momentarily embarrassed, the chairman of its entertainment division insisting that the one-time special was "hardly reflective of what we hope to accomplish" and publicly pledging that such shows were finished.[9] But what really bothered TV's mood merchants was the realization that the contestants had proven to be as fraudulent as their own production teams—a flaw easily amended with better pre-show research. And if the post-game publicity had been bad, the all-important numbers had been outstanding. An estimated twenty-two million had tuned in to watch the couple exchange their hasty vows, nearly double the ratings that Fox had scored in the same time slot the week before with its highbrow concept, *The World's Sexiest Commercials*.[10] And since, in fact, such numbers are exactly "reflective of what [commercial networks] hope to accomplish," this decadent extension of *The Dating Game* concept was cleverly retooled for a quick revival.

By extending the length of the pseudo-wooing from a two-hour special to a full series, ABC's *The Bachelor* allowed its overwhelmingly female audience sufficient time both to bond with the eligible hunk and to select their favorites among the competing women. Now the producers could prolong the drama of public humiliation via romantic rejection. They also had time to supply up-close-and-personal interviews, a kind of video diary revealing the contestants' "feminine wiles" and hidden feuds, and offering you-were-there peeks at evening dates, which, just like those of the real stars, always took place in glamorous locales, and where the bachelor and his try-out spouse would open up about their feelings over bubbling champagne in a frothing hot tub. This was bread and circus, American-style. ABC was pandering a gladiatorial voyeurism for the chick-flick set, with the same "due prurient insincerity" as its masculine equivalent (also recently revived for prime-time viewing): professional wrestling.

How could one possibly top such an exercise in omnidirectional cynicism? Leave it to Fox to find a solution, and one truly reflective of its primary accomplishments as our "conservative" network. Just as the women had mustered their seductive facades, cosmetic and emotional, to seduce the wealthy bachelor, *Joe Millionaire* now staged a tit-for-tat masquerade on them. For despite a castle-sized mansion whose pretensions would make Jay Gatsby proud, the eligible guy this time wasn't the wealthy heir whom the producers had promised to the contestants. Off-camera in real life, he was instead (get it?) just your average Joe, a blue-collar worker with zero status and minimal dough. The audience at home had been let in on the cruel joke so that they could savor the piquant irony throughout. All that anxious strategizing, all those weeks of submitting to the prying camera with the strong likelihood of being publicly humiliated, and the sole survivor, the so-called winner, would have the royal red carpet pulled out from under her at the very moment of her apparent triumph, at which point she would have to face yet another test of character. Would her love remain true when confronted with the revelation that *her* Joe wasn't a millionaire, after all? Would she still stand by her man when she learned that he was, *really*, just a carpenter?. . .

But as it turned out, the joke was on the viewing audience as well, for thanks again to the intrepid legwork of tabloid America's investigative journalists, we soon learned that, despite the network's promises, Joe wasn't *just* a carpenter either. Rather, just like Rick Rockwell, Fox's first bachelor millionaire, he was also a show-biz aspirant: someone who, contrary to the profile of your average construction worker, had once modeled men's underwear.[11]

Lies within lies, winking pretense allied with disingenuous credulity, avid cynicism staging deliquescent sentimentality by (and for) the numbers: *this* Plato's cave of shadowy representations was not Hawthorne's native terrain. To get an early gauge on deception this complete, we have to move from the settled townships of Massachusetts back to Melville's steamer on the Mississippi where the marginal commerce of the confidence man prophetically suffuses every conversation. There, in the climactic chapter, the next generation of American Quack offers his Dupe, as a bonus gift, "the Counterfeit Detector," with which, he promises, one can reliably separate all the real dollars in circulation from the fake. But, of course, this free Detector is itself a fake, yet another dimension in the shadowy play of seductive simulation.[12]

It is in this meta-level of cynical deception (the falsification of the very instruments of truth detection) that we can find the successful strategy behind Virtual America's new game-show productions. The bouncy immediacy of the mobile camera, the sisterly intimacy of the whispered confession, the casting of real people rather than studio actors in what nevertheless proved to be reenactments of old soap opera plots: using the latest techniques and technologies, the shows had acquired the look-feel of the documentary. As with Ang Lee's updated version of cinematic combat, their simulations were sufficiently adept to let the audience believe once again in the reality of the Magic.

⇌

For reasons that ought to be obvious now, all these changes presented major challenges to Monty Hall's new production team. Given that 2003 was the fortieth anniversary of the show's debut, they had hoped to ride a wave of nostalgia, but the translation between eras was proving difficult. How were they to restage an arresting spectacle of degradation within and against this new field of "reality television" while still holding true to the show's founding format, including Monty's principled prohibition against overt insults? Dressing up as a turnip while pleading like a toddler for a chance to play the game seemed pretty tame compared to eating sun-warmed cow brains flecked with flies (*Survivor*) or submerging oneself in a tank of dead squid (*Fear Factor*). Getting zonked by curtain #2's disposable diapers paled in comparison to being romantically dumped before an audience of millions or having a B-list celebrity judge publicly scorn your performance on the latest amateur star search.

If we need a vivid benchmark for the nation's "defining deviancy downward," this will surely do: by 2003, Monty Hall's original concept was too principled to succeed in TV's current marketplace. Even updated, his revival of *Let's Make a Deal* failed to take off—although in their attempt to attract an audience, Monty's team did display the sort of shameless hustle that might have merited applause from the new vulgarians at ABC or Fox. In one segment of the reinvented show, the producers replaced the old boring curtains with three very buff young men, all dressed in tartan kilts, and shortish ones at that. To find out what they had won, the contestants, all female, had to pick a laddie and then reach up under his kilt to receive their prize. Here we have a handy mapping of the human progress which, we are told by earnest advocates of the Chicago school, necessarily follows the Market's brave and restless search for profits: the cash that had once emerged from a pocket of Monty's stylish suit was now attached to a faux-Scottish studmuffin's bare upper thigh.

This, on NBC (the nation's oldest network), at eight p.m. (still a so-called family viewing hour), and hosted by the glib and chipper Billy Bush (former co-anchor of the tabloid news show, *Access Hollywood*). During the week of the show's debut, the most popular program on each of the four main networks was "reality-based," lottery ticket sales nationwide were about 850 million dollars,[13] and the *New York Times* cited recent Gallup polls which had found that 48 percent of Americans believed in creationism.[14] After only three airings, the network abruptly canceled Monty's new production—*its* deal got zonked. The bad news was announced on March 19, 2003. Late that same evening, Billy Bush's cousin, exuding self-confidence in a white shirt and red tie from the Oval Office, interrupted the networks' regularly scheduled programming to address the nation. *Operation Iraqi Freedom*, the pilot series for the new and enlightened American imperialism, had just been launched.

II. Educational Television in the Age of Empire

"How to Get What You Really, Really, Really, Really Want"
—title of a PBS lecture by Wayne W. Dyer, Ph.D.

Money Note: The Juvenilization of the Audubon Set

A parallel downslide was taking place on PBS. Republicans had succeeded in cutting the network's federal budget, with the intention of forcing its managers to submit to the great moral discipline of the marketplace, and as a consequence of that trip to the libertarian woodshed, PBS programming, once the proudly prim site of anglophile entertainment, began to descend into one long fundraising infomercial, targeting the managerial classes. How to filigree period molding, or make four-star mozzarella, or cure oneself of the incurable through the latest spiritual regimen or herbal remedy: each of these self-help sermonettes would be interrupted by a seemingly endless phonathon, the station's assistant manager pleading for donations in exchange for a DVD of this evening's show or the entire collected works of its expert host—who might even be there, in front of the phone bank, to take viewer questions, her every helpful answer a chance to pitch the full product line of her commodified wisdom. This was the public domain's pathetic version of corporate "synergy," charitable donation shamelessly cohabiting with commercial self-promotion of the mind-cure sort.

Still, the look-feel of the programming retained a semblance at least of its old identity. Although Evangelical Mammonism had fully saturated the nation's mindscape, its ethos was inflected differently within our various classes and professions, assuming in each case the specific guise of the local traditions preceding its triumph. As the audience demographics of Fox and PBS differed dramatically, so too, then, did those networks' characteristic compliance to the new Mammonite value system. Insomuch as this system was tacitly revising our ultimate beliefs without requiring a shift in our nominal religious affiliations, a relevant comparison would be the dramatic differences between evangelical and mainstream Protestantism.

Like the former's church services, the commercial game show, reinvented as "reality television," preferred the masquerade of born-again enthusiasm. It stoked and even faked an effusion of emotions and shocking confessions, favoring the sheer spectacle of shame and redemption before a congregation now millions in number. But the target audience for PBS was an upper middle class whose members might happily go to the bank on the sale of such cheesy infoproducts but who, still uneasy with the prospect of "opening up" themselves, preferred to maintain a semblance of decorum. No weeping, no shrieking, no speaking in tongues in the pews on *this* set. No chowing down on cow brains either . . . unless they were lightly sautéed with wine-infused truffles by a lecturing chef. This was still *educational* television.

Of the three psychological phases common to many con games and cleverly built into Monty Hall's original show—emotional juvenilization, followed by intellectual derationalization, leading to a passive submission to superstitious thinking—the appearance of the second phase was especially unacceptable for PBS, whose original mission, after all, had been the sober transmission of bookish knowledge. But if PBS now had to submit to the so-called moral discipline of the marketplace, and if, in ways I have detailed throughout this book, that marketplace was itself increasingly dependent on stoking irrational motives to boost its sales, then those irrational appeals would have to assume the guise of their virtual opposite. On educational TV, our economy's true dependence on pixie-dust dreams would have to wear the mask of rationalist expertise.

That masquerade was evident on one of PBS's most popular series, *Antiques Road Show*, whose episodes were endlessly repeated during this same period. Just like the commercial game shows—whose temper, however, it thoroughly shunned—the program exploited that commonly held hope for the strike-it-rich moment. In this case, though, the secret pot o' gold lay concealed behind the dusty facade of the quaint collectible: that Cinderella object which, with but an approving nod from the properly discerning prince, might instantly ascend to royal value. To democratize its appeal, the program went on the road, inviting residents in each new locale to bring out their yard-sale specials and attic effluvia—that chamber pot bought on a whim in 'forty-six, that painting purchased for a pittance by bohemian Aunt Milly on her trip to Paris. The owners would then gather in long lines in a rented exposition hall, waiting there to have their umbrella stand, rococo clock, or toy soldier set assessed by one of the many specialists the producers had assembled.

The show itself would focus on the interesting finds, at which point it would slip, in true PBS fashion, into an educational mode. After acquiring some background information about where and how the object had been acquired, the relevant expert would supply a little lecture—about, say, the life of the craftsman who had carved the wooden box or the glazing technique applied to the Asian tea cup—indicating along the way the finer points and detracting qualities of the piece in question.

Having tipped its hat to the station's traditional educational mission, the segment would then turn to its actual raison d'etre by supplying an answer to the one pressing question that had drawn the long lines in the first place and held the attention of the TV audience. Although the objects themselves varied greatly, each still had to submit to the same final evaluation, which also proved to be the emotional climax of the segment itself. All that sober analysis had to lead to this peak moment: a ritual exchange which, in its rigidly formulaic approach, resembled what music producers like to call "the money note" and pornographers, more grossly, "the money shot."

First came the build-up in the form of two questions that, almost without fail and in the same sequence, each expert would ask of the owner before him. "How much did you originally pay for this piece?" followed by "Do you have any idea of how much it is currently worth?" Only then, with the original investment specified and the owner's ignorance of its current value confessed, would the expert pronounce his summary judgment: "In today's market, your feathered boa would likely bring . . ."

This robotically staged "money note," with its epiphany of final value, was inherently dramatic for viewers like myself for two fundamental reasons. First, and most obviously, we were not likely to be experts in hardwood inlay or pottery glazing and so were unable to discern subtle differences in quality. Just as importantly, however, the judgments of "today's market" were themselves only haphazardly linked to qualitative evaluations. Although the show did a fine job of presenting the look-feel of rationalist evaluation, the "money note" itself sang a different lyric. After watching a few of these evaluations, one quickly got the message that the aptly named

Invisible Hand could be as ineffable and volatile, as potentially *ir*rational, as the jealous Jehovah It had replaced.

Neither beauty nor craftsmanship, nor dutiful custodial care could guarantee the bounty of the Market's favor. An old cherry secretary might be exquisitely refinished only to have its value diminished because the authentic dings and scratches of its domestic history had been removed. The afterthought of storing an old toy in its box (a sign, perhaps, of its failure to amuse) might actually serve to double its return on the auctioneer's block. And as is the case with all market-based evaluations, each collectible was subject to the sort of mania which, in seventeenth-century Holland, had once assessed a single tulip bulb as more valuable than a merchant's mansion.

So apparently sedate and educational, the *Road Show* was at its core, then, a lot closer to *Let's Make a Deal* than either its producers or its audience would have cared to admit. The show's rationalist evaluation was but another form of Monty's curtained carnival of deal-making magic—were you about to score big or about to get zonked?—as transcribed and restaged for the Audubon set. The commodity may have been upgraded from a monster pick-up to period porcelain and the host socially elevated from a vulgar barker to an effete appraiser, the premise may have shifted from entertainment to education, but the ultimate message was still the same. Both programs were, in fact, instructional and their shared lesson was this: that all forms of human value, whether sentimental, political, religious, or aesthetic, had to be converted to their market value. The rich and the poor, the tasteful and the vulgar were to be judged alike by Evangelical Mammonism's final calibration of the good and the true. *More* was always better, and money was always *more's* ultimate measure.

Beyond the masquerade of rationalist rigor, what I found most striking about *Antiques Road Show* was the passivity of its guests, the implicit pathos of those long lines of presumably intelligent Americans wanting to be told what their own heirlooms were worth. This too, though, reflected a common experience in our marketplace economy. To buy even a pair of athletic shoes these days is to confront a mind-boggling array of models and brands, each cloaked in an obtuse terminology of expertise cleverly pitched by their marketeers, leading the consumer to feel like an illiterate serf begging for answers from his Latin-chanting priest. Having been there myself, I sympathized, then, with the guests' passive obeisance before the appraisers, and that led me to recognize a further similarity to *Let's Make a Deal*. Not only did the *Road Show's* display of rationalist rigor finally bend to serve the same marketplace magic; it also modeled its own brand of juvenilization.

This was a very different child-like role, to be sure, mainstream and rationalist rather than evangelical and romantic. The site of *Masterpiece Theater,* after all, couldn't adopt the faux rebel-teen of MTV. If PBS was going to convert us to the cause of immaturity, the role preferred would have to be that of the teenage rebel's old high-school foe. This would be the safe-and-sane version of age dissuasion, the adult professional expected to regress to her former self, the over-achieving A-student.

Cosmeceutical Transactions: Pitching the Magic on PBS

The promotion of the over-achiever role was especially apparent in the guru fundraisers that the public stations were staging to plug those gaping holes in their now privatized dikes. One sign that the stations' managers had learned their lesson from this involuntary trip to the libertarian woodshed was their conversion to the soft duplicities of salesmanship, especially to the bloviated terminology of high-tech progress. While the hawking of aerobic tapes, ·ab machines, and miraculous meat roasters on commercial TV had been tagged with the odious but accurate term infomercial, the parallel pitching of financial wizardry, naturopathic remedies, geriatric sex advice, and New Age spirituality on PBS had been upgraded by the system's PR team into something called "transactional programming." The term appeared to refer to Transactional Analysis, among the most upbeat of psychotherapies,[15] and the promotional strategy was clear. This was the same mind-cure marketplace that we examined last chapter: that strategy of "fashionization" which, in order to sell its serial regimens of recovery, first had to pitch a whole new zoo of psychic diseases.

You won't be surprised to learn that getting your whole self righteously cured on PBS proved even more complex than getting your game-day feet properly shod. This I discovered when I tuned into a Dr. Nicholas Perricone's transactional program one bewildering evening. I had missed the start of the show and so, too, the biographical frame that might have clarified the whole. The energetic Perricone was lecturing like mad, with charts and graphs and a virtual bombardment of gravid physiological terms: alpha lipoic acid, NTP complex, dual solubility. There were repeated references to "the transcription factor" and, more ominously once, to something called "nuclear factor kappa-B"—which, in an earlier phase of my life, I might have presumed to be a killer cocktail at a fraternity party, as wryly named after the very worst line in a sci-fi film.

Clearly no sardonic undergrad humor was permissible here, however. The doctor's tone was earnestly urgent and occasionally even grim, with references to the serious consequences of our irresponsible living: dietary addictions and life-style habits that studies had shown to be "associated with" insomnia, memory loss, depression, and cancer. (Not to worry, though; good news was in the offing—this was, after all, mind-*cure* television.) Some of the members of the small in-studio audience, I noticed nervously in my initial befuddlement, were taking notes, and suddenly I felt nineteen again, behind in my reading and late to class: habits associated, studies have shown, with a fondness for killer cocktails and late-night movies. Soon enough, however, I began to discern a revealing pattern within the obtuse rhetoric. Just as when Iago seduced Roderigo into joining his conspiracy against Othello by interweaving his argument with variations on the tempting refrain *put money in thy purse*,[16] Dr. Perricone kept larding his lecture with references to skin care—memory loss *and* wrinkles; dietary savvy *and* silk-smooth skin; actuarial longevity *and* dermatological suppleness.

I shouldn't have been shocked but was, momentarily balking at the conclusion I had drawn: *this* was what all the science was about, the lecture finally for? Could this really be the old proletarian "school of cosmetology" recast as a course in biochemistry for Vassar graduates? Vidal Sassoon cross-dressing in the lab coat of Louis Pasteur? But how was I—the clueless non-scientist, the illiterate serf who couldn't tell the formula of lipoic acid from that of lysergic acid—to judge for sure?

Any doubts I had were soon resolved, however. And for further confirmation, I turned to Dr. Perricone's website, which identified him as the author of the *New York Times* bestseller *The Wrinkle Cure*, now available (*put money in my purse*) with but a click of one's mouse. It also highlighted his credentials as an "anti-aging expert" and "a pioneer in the field of appearances." The good doctor, it turned out, had also pioneered his own line of skin-care products, the old cosmetics now transactionally rescripted into something called "cosmeceuticals," and he was generously offering to save the day for American women by offering for sale (*fill my purse with money*) this new pharmacy of age dissuasion.[17]

But Perricone wasn't the most irritating burr under my psychic saddle during this period when I assigned myself the task of keeping track of PBS's transactional programming. Nor was Suze Orman, whose tough-love financial advice tended to make sense, although often of the most obvious sort. No, my special irritant was someone called Wayne W. Dyer, Ph.D., whose bald pate and palely pious face seemed to permanently occupy the PBS screen during this period.[18]

Full disclosure: I instantly loathed Dr. Dyer. The basis of my bias was rooted more in the nature of his specialty than in his version of the guru personality, which, when judged against the field, proved surprisingly bland. Perricone and Orman were also in it for the money, and the former did appear, to this layman anyway, to be prostituting science, pandering an age-old vanity under the guise of medical therapy. But at least their specialties, finance and "the field of appearances," were Mammon's native territories. Dyer, however, was the supposed anti-materialist, pitching the balm of a New Age soulfulness. His was the latest boutique chain in a mind-cure nation where salvation is routinely marketized into salable therapies and where the sovereign self, mysteriously unhappy despite its divine-right status, suddenly learns to heal itself . . . with just a little help from a fully accessorized line of books, DVDs, "inner peace cards," and daily online messages.

Like Perricone, Dyer drew on a vaguely familiar vocabulary of expertise—in his case, the spiritual wisdom of the East—paying homage to themes such as love and forgiveness. But the true end that all this sacred rhetoric had been co-opted to serve was clearly revealed in the title of his talk, repeatedly rebroadcast for fundraising purposes: "How to Get What You Really, Really, Really, Really Want." (There really are four *reallys*—I went back and counted.) Just as the rationalist rigor of *Antiques Road Show* had actually served to confirm the *ir*rational magic of "market value," Dyer's spiritual wisdom had been mustered to pitch *its* virtual opposite, that narcissistic wishfulness long-preached by the civic religion of Disneyism.

In a marketeering culture whose favorite lie is that the customer is always right, each sales pitch must adjust itself to the special biases of its target audience, and so here on PBS, the magic was made to seem real—*Real Magic* was the title of one of Dyer's early books—*because* it assumed the opposite guise, that of the scholarly or spiritually wise. The promise was finally the same as Disney's—that "anything your heart desires / will come to you"—but the means had changed from lady luck to earnest education. Not only was the perfection of one's romantic-economic-religious life imminent; the process of its achievement could be broken down, just as Descartes had promised, into progressive and neatly numbered steps. For the A-student who could master those steps, the perfect score awaited in the form of the ageless face, the endless orgasm, or (in Dr. Dyer's case) a spiritual bliss where getting the goods was exactly equivalent to heeding the Good.

The cult of the adolescent had prevailed here, too, but now the metaphor had shifted from the high-school pep rally to an SAT preparation class. Dyer may have modeled his demeanor more after the students' favorite guidance counselor than a sideshow's carnie, but the title of his talk still radiated the come-on of a classic con. Who wants to get what they really, really, really, really want?. . . Like the old would-be contestants before Monty Hall, the transactional audience was also answering, if more mutely and discreetly: *me, me, me, me . . . please, please, please, please . . .*

III. Evangelical Television in the Age of Empire

*Under this anointing, the words I speak cannot fall to the
ground. Under this anointing, everything I say, happens.*[19]

—televangelist Benny Hinn

Tongues of Fire on the Tigris

In truth, I found Perricone's "cosmeceutical" lectures and Dyer's banal exposition on visualizing one's dreams and going "the extra mile" so irritating that I couldn't bear to watch for long. The remote control too close a temptation, I dodged my self-assigned role as cultural critic and began to channel-surf instead. Eventually, though, even this exercise in evasion became a structured lesson as, flipping back and forth between PBS and TBN, I began to "compare and contrast" their spiritual messages.

For those who do not know, TBN is the Trinity Broadcasting Network, a California-based media megaphone for the Father, Son, and Holy Ghost, on whose sets the big-haired revivalists, like so many Jaggers stoned on lyrics as penned by St. Paul, still jut-strut their godstuff. There, in hopes of relating to today's youth, buff evangelists pump awesome quantities of iron for Christ their Lord, and there, too, prophets reveal the miraculous concurrence between the ancient scriptures and the nightly news. An earthquake in Peru, a plague in China, a rumored coup in Iran, the nineteenth collapse of the Middle East "peace process"—each and all had been prefigured; each confirmed the Plan, chapter and verse, as decoded and declaimed by the telepreacher.

My great discovery during these flights from the likes of Wayne W. Dyer and Nicholas Perricone was the charismatic televangelist Benny Hinn, who occupied TBN's screen then with a frequency that seemed to match all the transactional gurus combined. How I had missed him until then was something of mystery, for he proved to be, I quickly discovered, both a celebrity within the field and a figure of abiding controversy. A web search on his name called up thousands of sites, most of them run by other evangelicals who were accusing Hinn of various forms of heresy.

Given the schismatic-to-the-point-of-anarchic character of evangelical Protestantism, the presence of these spiritual vigilantes was hardly surprising, and surely the green-eyed monster was also fueling their scrutinizing zeal. For say what you will about the falsity or folly of Benny Hinn's doctrine, the man knew how to bring in the numbers. The market's Invisible Hand, if not the Mosaic one, had led him into the land of milk and money. Hinn's TV show *This Is Your Day* was broadcast daily on some 500 channels worldwide, and his 1990 book *Good Morning, Holy Spirit* had been one of that decade's most popular Christian offerings. Hinn's refusal to join the Evangelical Council for Financial Accountability had cloaked his books in mystery. But estimates of his ministry's annual income ranged from sixty to a hundred million dollars, and an article in the *Dallas Morning News* revealed that Hinn had raised some thirty million for a proposed Healing Center that, money in hand, he had never bothered to build—a delay he then claimed to be as divinely inspired as the initial project itself.[20]

Who was this star of the charismatic set and what were the sources of his allure? Born in Palestine in 1953 to an Armenian mother and a Greek father, Benedictus Hinn had arrived in America via Canada, just like Monty Hall. His family had been Greek Orthodox (another "false religion" according to one of the vigilante websites), but he had reportedly been born again as a young man and then deeply affected by a service conducted by the faith-healer Kathryn Kuhlmann. Hinn began preaching in the early seventies, but his ministry took off, appropriately enough, in central Florida—home to Disney's Magic Kingdom—when he founded the Orlando Christian Center in 1983. Eventually, however, no single congregation could contain the appeal of his message, and so Hinn resigned his pastorate in 1999, moving his ministry to Dallas with the intention of concentrating on his worldwide crusades and TV broadcasts.[21]

Some critics within the feuding family of evangelicals like to claim that Hinn stole most of his preacherly presentation from the now deceased Kuhlmann, including the startling habit of dressing in an all-white suit—which was as well, I couldn't help but recall, a favorite of Elvis's, the costume of choice during his Vegas phase. But whether this charge of plagiarism was true or not, I also suspected that Hinn had brought something new to the act by the simple fact of his ethnicity. With his darker skin and exotic accent, he was offering a subtly different medium for the old faith-healing message, and one better attuned to a multicultural America.

Both the medium and the message were accessible every day. His TBN show typically broadcast excerpts from one of his crusades where the old revivalist tricks, once native to rural Southern tents, were now being staged in major urban convention centers. The temper of these evangelizing performances was updated as well—which is to say that accusatory hellfire had largely given way to mood-enhancing hopefulness. Despite occasional warnings about the Devil, Benny Hinn's demeanor, like Ronald Reagan's, was perpetually "up". His was the bible of confidence, of metaphysical trust. As a true vehicle of God, he was the direct recipient of "revelation knowledge," and the news beaming in from the other side of the man-God divide, he was glad to report, was mostly good. The Lord's blessing, like retirement lots in Arizona's desert, was now available to all (*put money in my purse*) for just a small down payment.

Hinn's delivery was often over-the-top, but that, too, of course, was part of the tradition. Sometimes, as if the very bellows for the Breath of Life, he would literally blow the Holy Spirit into the convention center, awe-chilling the audience with its electric flow. Sometimes he would throw it like an invisible ball, a full-court pass on the Lord's fastbreak. Nor was he averse to removing his white, white jacket and swinging it out toward a swooning section of the crowd—a stripper's teasing gesture that also evoked the seductive ghost of many a rock star. But these were merely the warm-up drills, the frills not the fundament of Benny Hinn's game. The name of the tour whose excerpts were being shown was, after all, the *Miracles Crusade*. No pussyfooting around here, no distant promises or delicate discourses on the Kingdom of Heaven as metaphor. This was the man, it was said, who had healed the ailing heart of heavyweight champ, Evander Holyfield, and he brought the same game-day magic to every broadcast.

During the dramatic climax of these revival meetings, the immaculate Hinn would call forth the diseased, and there on stage, his white-sheathed arm a lightning rod for grace, he would "rebuke" the cancerous growth or shriveled limb in the name of the Lord. This was hands-on healing, the transfer of spirit to irresistible effect. Some forces are stronger than the muscled will of man or the errors of Nature, and the ailing, once touched, would collapse in a shudder, one after the other, like so many stun-gunned steers, only to be caught and cushioned from accidental harm by a group of strategically placed young men, spotters for God's gym, who were also part of Benny's team.

The excerpt from the tour might continue with some testimony about past healings. Then, turning back to the studio, Benny would address the camera directly, suggesting that the audience at home draw closer to the set. It didn't matter that we weren't there with him in the flesh. It didn't matter that Benny wasn't wearing his white suit, nor that he was now reduced to a mere talking head. This was still your day and mine, time for our own miracle. Freed of the limits of physical causality, Benny could beam his rebukes of disease, despair, and deviant dissolution directly through our sets. According to *his* cross-promotional covenant, the healing powers could be televisually conveyed without the usual laying on of hands. Under this anointing, the words he spoke could not fall to the ground. Under this anointing, everything he said *would* happen. A man was being healed of diabetes, Benny would intone into the camera. A kidney was made whole, even as he spoke, in the name of the Lord.

Given the scope of these performances, I shouldn't have been shocked but was when, flipping to TBN one day, I found Benny on his knees, hands raised, slain in the spirit and speaking in tongues. *Glossolalia!* For a lapsed mainstream Protestant and PBS viewer like myself, this was exotic stuff and, truth be known, powerfully alluring. As the prim Victorian was drawn shamefully, secretly toward the cockney whore; as today's multitasking, shop-till-you-drop Seattleite might view the lolling bum in Pioneer Square with a queasy fascination, forced to resist the sudden itch of a voice that keeps insisting, *you could do that, you could just up and quit*—so, too, I was drawn to this appalling yet appealing spectacle before me.

For someone who had labored on language seven days a week for nearly thirty years; someone who weighed every word, struggling to match sound with sense, patching errors and quilting meaning, Benny Hinn's tongue-of-fire babble was the molten golden calf stamped with my soul's name. Here was my own feast of the forbidden: a divine endorsement of the utterly inarticulate. Here was the rapture of utterance purged of the dross of mundane meaning, a language fully liberated from all the tedious trials of accuracy, the picayune parsings of syntax or semblance.

Wasn't this the hope of every poet: words surging above the-failure-of-all-words into the current of purest feeling? Wasn't this the radical core of the Protestant promise redeemed at last: the single soul (freed of the priest, the robe, and the ritual railing) made at one with the Spirit? Here was American individualism at its spiritual zenith, each single soul made into his own tribal Moses . . . but better this time, new-and-improved. More than simply see and hear the sacred signs when brought to the holy mountain top, each might *become* the burning bush: our mouth the course for God's own voice, our body the torch for His holy fire, ablaze with those flames which, even as they illuminate, do not consume. Here was that mysteriously missing joy in life, not only reborn but compressed, condensed. This was "up" to the tenth, and who wouldn't want to touch . . . to *hug* the third rail of such a power?

Of course, I knew that the event was being staged, just as I knew, when watching a stripper, that her come-hither look wasn't really meant for me. But such knowledge didn't prevent my buttons from being pushed; nor did it stop me, despite my better judgment, from heeding Benny's previous invitations to draw closer to my set. And what was the triggering occasion for this, his sudden release into spiritual fluency? . . . I shouldn't have been shocked but was when, finally rising from his knees and returning to that fallible language shared by you and me, Benny explained the source of his joy. America's army had just invaded Iraq, and the Lord had told him (*have you heard the news, Brother?*) that many Muslims were on the verge of converting to the Cross.

Lazarus, Rising

Although a dominant star in the charismatic firmament, Benny Hinn was not alone then pitching the Magic in its Christian accent on TBN, and when I wasn't being seduced by glossolalia, I went about my self-assigned business as cultural critic—I "compared and contrasted" as an A-student should. The formalist in me quickly noted how the format of these programs tended to mimic that of the secular talk show. Each had a host or set of co-hosts (Katie Couric and Matt Lauer on NBC, Paul and Jan Crouch on TBN); each invited famous guests in their field to perform for the audience (to sing or joke on Letterman's show, preach the Word on *Praise the Lord*) who would then be invited to chat with the hosts. In each case, too, the folks at home were being offered the same titillation of transparency, another delicious chance to see what the celebrity, whether secular or sacred, was really like.

Meanwhile, beneath the masquerade of their bonhomie, the guests on both shows were pursuing other motives. Each was there to pitch his own cause: that coming crusade or concert date, that tell-all book or movie release. The relevant titles and dates would flash on the screen for all to read, and the quality of the goods would then be endorsed by their compliant hosts. The hosts, too, had their "money moment"—or rather many such moments—but here the evangelizing programs more resembled the guru phonathons on PBS. As with Letterman or Regis, the prevailing telos on TBN was still salesmanship, but the hosts were the sponsors of their own shows now, the commercial ad righteously reborn as a donation to the evangelizing cause. Someone had to keep the agents of the Lord in hair spray and make-up so they could better spread the Word to the orphans in Sri Lanka. Someone had to fund those Healing Centers that the Lord giveth and then taketh away.

Appealing for a "love offering," the host would cite biblical proofs that a little earthly generosity would reliably purchase divine intervention. No pussyfooting around on these shows either. Here was the old charismatic's quid pro quo, where the logic of salesmanship met the magic of superstition under the thinnest guise of righteous giving. Money for me, miracles for you, that was the underlying message—yet one more echo of the perennial transaction between Quack and Dupe. I was witnessing, it seemed, the final corruption of American exceptionalism: the rot of the Protestant soul on its sugary diet of sovereign hopes and pixie-dust dreams. Here was the evangelical's version of the papal indulgence. Pay now, disciple, and your words, your wishes won't fall to the ground. Pay now, Lazarus, and rise later from the cold sleep of the dead.

And, no, I am not indulging in hyperbole here. A little online research uncovered the following transcript of an earlier broadcast of *Praise the Lord*. Benny Hinn was the featured guest, and, as the cofounders of TBN, Paul and Jan Crouch were Benny's broadcasters as well as the show's hosts.[22] Hear his anointed words then, hear what Benny had to say about those who were so ably helping him grow his ministry.

> Benny Hinn: *But here's first what I see for TBN. You're going to have people raised from the dead watching this network. . . . people around the world who will lose loved ones, will say to undertakers: "Not yet. I want to take my dead loved one and place him in front of the TV set for 24 hours."*
>
> Paul Crouch: *Benny Hinn! Jesus!*
>
> Benny Hinn: *I'm telling you. People will be—people—I'm telling you, I feel the anointing talking here. People are going to be canceling funeral services and bringing the dead in their caskets, placing them—my God! I'm feeling the anointing here—placing them before a television set . . . they will be raised from the dead and they will be raised by the thousands. . . .*[23]

Talk about logrolling! And I thought blurbing in the book business was bad.

But when I flipped back to channel 9, only to confront one of its guru advisers, or to channel 5's nightly news, where self-confident members of the administration were promising instant enlightenment on the shores of the Tigris, from tyranny to democracy with but a wave of their wands, the outrageous Benny Hinn began to seem mainstream, after all. My exercise in evasion suddenly gave way to a sense of entrapment. There could be no escape, it seemed, in Virtual America. From blue-collar to blue blood, from entertainment to education, from objective NBC to evangelical TBN to transactional PBS—wherever I turned, it was "deja vu all over again."

The satellite photos *proving* Saddam's possession of mobile weapons labs; the telepreacher's list of biblical citations *proving* the imminent arrival of the righteous Rapture; Dr. Perricone's charts *proving* that *his* truth would equal beauty, his beauty a better life: as each Counterfeit Detector only served to reinvent the original con, each apparent exit quickly looped back to the center of the mall. "Empowered" by my remote, I could change the channel but not the underlying message. Wherever I landed, I was assailed by the same aggressive unGrimming of the human condition: the Cinderella magic of *Extreme Makeover* in all its various and now global editions.

Even the blandest salesman, it seemed, was working some version of the same outrageous pitch. Although he lacked the Country Western pompadour, spangled couture, and over-the-top effusions—although he appeared instead to have been cross-promotionally dressed by the folks at Land's End and teleported directly from the Microsoft campus—Dr. Dyer, too, was hawking miracles for cash. The accent was very different, but he still spoke a language of righteous exemption akin to Benny Hinn's. Although targeting different classes, each was singing a version of Jiminy's old song where no dream is too extreme and hopes come true out of the blue. Appealing to that Mouseketeer child who had fathered America's Peter Pan adult, each was reassuring us that we should love the world because we could trust it—trust it to fulfill our wildest wishes. Each was offering us a key to the Magic Kingdom, and all we had to do to was to go that "extra mile," reach that next level of contribution to the cause. All we had to do was send in our dues, just a dollar a day, and each of us could join the Miracles Crusade.

This, then, too, was part of the picture, the "spiritual" complement to "reality television" at the dawn of the empire in 2003. These were the messages that brought in the numbers, and so were reflective of what we hoped to accomplish in those same heady days when our born-again Emperor, newly clothed in the chaps of cowboy bravado, dared the Devil to "bring 'em on,"[24] proclaiming from his throne our nation's readiness to save (*fill our banks with money!*) a sinful but soon to be grateful world.

"I know where I am," Bartleby said. Something further may follow from this Masquerade.

9

Truth or Consequences

We must prefer real hell to an imaginary paradise.[1]

—Simone Weil

IN DEMOCRACIES, THE VALUES implicit in the most popular games do predict something of the character of those who win higher office, and given that the sampling of TV shows captured last chapter happened to coincide with a pivotal period in American history, their common flight from truthfulness into fantasy did suggest the quality of the governance that was addressing the serial crises of the day. As we saw in Reagan's "role of a lifetime" presidency, the nation's postwar leaders had long been mimicking the tactics of its TV producers, both groups adept at staging reality "as we like it" for the self-centered motives of power and profit, and when analyzed in retrospect, the nominal opposition that followed Reagan's rule made only a marginal difference. With its hyper hopes for a globalized marketplace, Clinton's "third way" did more to justify the avid ethos of privatization than it did to check the system's Mammonite excesses.

So it was that by 2003 the Pollyanna promises of free-market ideology, broadly endorsed by both parties, were routinely covering for the quid pro quo of the crony payoff. In a process lubricated by the nation's army of revolving-door lobbyists,[2] a "love offering" in the form of a campaign donation activated one's eventual passage to a no-bid federal contract or the right to rewrite crucial legislation. Corruption mirroring corruption at home and abroad, the government's programs, like our televised ones, were now being "brought to us by" their corporate sponsors. And just as Melville predicted, something further did follow from this phase of the Masquerade: there were real-world consequences to our collective conversion to its magical thinking. Soon, that triumphant "end of history" predicted after the Soviet collapse was ironically assuming an apocalyptic cast as we suffered a string of self-induced calamities with multiple repercussions but two main acts: the second on Wall Street, the first in Iraq.

I. American Raj as Desert Mirage

Afghanistan and other troubled countries cry out for the sort of enlightened foreign administration once provided by self-confident Englishmen in jodhpurs and pith helmets. . . . To turn Iraq into a beacon of hope for the oppressed peoples of the Middle East: Now that would be a historic war aim.[3]

—Max Boot, *Weekly Standard*

On the foreign policy front, neoconservative ideologues like Max Boot emerged from their influential think tanks after 9/11 to cynically pitch (while sentimentally half-believing) Hollywood's version of colonial history. Despite the promises made and many millions spent by their hero Ronald Reagan some twenty years before, SDI's magical missile-shielding roof had never materialized, leaving us vulnerable, they warned, to Saddam Hussein's secret cache of nuclear arms. And because Saddam was an indisputably murderous tyrant, not only would an American invasion of Iraq be justified as a preemptory act of self-defense; it would also supply "a beacon of hope for the oppressed peoples" of the region.

Framed by fond memories of Cary Grant in jodhpurs riding to the rescue of the British Raj, the new American imperialism was genially projected by Boot and others as a heady mix of fun adventure and heroic moral mission. As that story line required, the Iraqi people were recast as would-be Gunga Dins, so grateful to their invaders that they would risk their own lives to blow the bugle of freedom in an American key. And while Benny Hinn and other administration allies on the religious right entertained the fantasy of heathen Muslims converting en masse to the Christian cross, the policy hounds really running the show emphasized a different version of the white man's burden. Under their charge, radical capitalism would save the day, the many bibles sent over by the Rev. Franklin Graham mere supplements to the gospel according to Milton Friedman.

Either brand of conversion required, of course, that the war be won, and, nearly radioactive with technocratic hubris, the nation's Secretary of Defense patiently explained to its hapless journalists how our reinvented military could do a quick and painless conquest. As waged by our smart weaponry and the Secretary's own new-and-improved tactics, the old imperialist project of civilizing the barbaric outpost could be now completed in about six months' time—a calendar whose exquisitely technical calculations just happened to coincide with the presidential election cycle. With but a wave of our laser-guided wand, the administration's many minions assured, the mission would be accomplished. After being greeted with flowers, the bulk of our army would soon ride out of Baghdad, as the Lone Ranger always had, to the tearful goodbyes of a grateful townsfolk, and a region writhing with hostilities centuries in the making would soon be reborn after the image of today's Palo Alto, complete with Wi-Fi cafes and Wikipedia whiz kids trading IPOs over double mocha lattes.

Once again, the bogus expertise of utopian materialism was masking the narrative logic of a dream-machine product—this time the plot of the action-adventure blockbuster as produced by Jerry Bruckheimer and starring Tom Cruise. But when you attempt to transplant *Mission Impossible* from the cinema's screen into the realm of real acts, the pixie dust wears off quickly, and that mission is shown to be what it always had been and always will be—impossible. And as the people in Iraq behaved like real people rather than staying in character as required by the script, "mere anarchy was loosed upon the world" once again.[4] The cinematic images of instant victory soon gave way to a nightly cascade of mayhem and murder. After the cheers accompanying the staged toppling of the tyrant's statue came the cheers accompanying the desecration of American corpses: the chilling ululation of tribal loathing turned to gloating over flame-charred bodies.[5] This was the *real* "reality television," in which sugar-plum visions of IPOs and of the sentimental self-sacrifice of loyal Gunga Dins were ruthlessly supplanted by the instant amputations of IEDs and the self-obliterating rage of suicide bombers.

Along with the abject failure of the Magic Moment's promised transformation came the multifaceted collapse of the phony Fable of Innocence that had justified its faith-based mission in the first place. Despite the mushroom-cloud rhetoric, there were no weapons of mass destruction after all. No anti-American conspiracy, it seemed, between al-Qaeda terrorists and the Baathist regime—hardly a shocking fact given that religious fundamentalists and Stalinist-style secular tyrants don't occupy the same mental universe. With the faux emergency provoking the heroic intervention revealed as just that, the Fable of Innocence now had to rest alone on the good intentions of the white man's burden. The claim to be bringing the rule of law to a truly despotic land was undermined, however, by the inconvenient fact that our invasion itself broke international law by asserting the license of "preventive warfare."

And all that preaching about universal rights couldn't quite square with the despicable images from Abu Ghraib, the reports of programmatic abuse from Guantanamo Bay, or the leaked stories about secret interrogation camps strategically placed in former outposts of the Evil Empire. The president's inspiring speeches about the manifest destiny of democratic civilization serenely floated over his minions' scornful dismissal of the Geneva Conventions, one of the political world's few civilized achievements in an otherwise barbaric century. A nation recently shamed by lawyerly debates about which orifice receiving the presidential phallus constituted "sexual relations," now learned of scholastic determinations as to how many seconds a shackled prisoner's face could be smothered with water-weighted cellophane before such an "enhanced interrogation technique" could properly be deemed torture.[6]

This was *America*, mind you, whose first military leader refused, among many acts of exemplary self-discipline, to endorse the abuse of British prisoners, even as his own captured soldiers were being summarily executed as traitors to the crown.[7] But the administration and its allies had their own vision of ideal leadership, and following the moral logic that characterized most of their policies, they selected the exiled businessman Ahmad Chalabi as the Iraqi incarnation of George Washington. Adding a holster to his designer suits, however, couldn't quite conceal that the man who had so charmed the warmongering neocons with his statesmanlike qualities was a fugitive wanted for bank fraud by our closest Arab ally. That in their minds' pixie-dust theater the bully-tyrant Saddam should be replaced by the corporate huckster Chalabi only demonstrated how closely the folly plotted out in Melville's final novel was now being followed: on this voyage of virtuality, too, the cosmopolitan con man would close the sale on the American dupe.

As for the occupation itself, forget about the gospel according to Milton Friedman. Scratch the thin surface of the libertarian rhetoric about the entrepreneurial creativity of radical capitalism, and one found the racing engine of sheer acquisitiveness fleeing the free market for the sure bet of the no-bid federal contract, as secured by crony contacts[8] and protected by supervisory agencies which, like the monkeys three, neither saw, nor heard, nor spoke of any evil. Big Government wasn't so bad, after all, when one could feast on its revenues. Like most every other practice in postmillennial America, the waging of war was now being aggressively privatized, which in practical effect meant this: while a limited number of soldiers were recycled again and again to risk life and limb for minimal pay, many politically connected private contractors were getting rich for servicing the occupation.[9] For some, love of country would prove lethal; for others, all too lucrative.

Once again, the sentimental trope masked the cynical motive. Even as the political rhetoric of the day extolled the soldier-patriot, the actual policies in place were rewarding the corporate mercenary instead.

Eventually, these real-world consequences compelled our leaders to adopt a radically diminished definition of success. The mirage of an Iraqi Palo Alto gave way to the glacial retreat of an "exit strategy" that might save a little face—though not the lives of the over 4,000 American servicemen and 100,000 Iraqis, all of whom died under the "self-confident" aegis of our "enlightened foreign administration."

II. The Science of Self-Deception, Subprime Division

"It's laissez faire until you get in deep shit."[10]

— John Gutfreund, former Wall Street CEO

Evangelical Economics

Yet, even as the "imaginary paradise" of an Americanized Middle East was being decimated by a real-world explosion of anti-imperialist rage and sectarian slaughter, a delusionary faith in the wonder-working genius of radical capitalism was surging forth on the home front, undeterred. Both the mystical math of our high-tech economists and the mythic images projected by the nation's marketeers were predicting a Mammonite rapture for you and me. The mega lottery, online poker, the televised audition into instant stardom, the born-again magic of the extreme makeover, the license to win or wed a millionaire's estate: how-to and can-do *would* do, and soon. With a little help from a personal coach or one of Big Pharm's transformational pills, each of us could get what we really[4] wanted, each of us could become "better than well."

Even the practitioners of the once dismal science had assumed this evangelical air. Just as we had recently been promised the "end of history" through the global triumph of our political system, our economists were announcing an absolute end to calamitous risk. In 2003, during his keynote address to the American Economic Association, Nobel Prize-winner Robert E. Lucas insisted that "the central problem of depression-prevention [had] been solved."[11] Such a feat was possible because, in the earlier words of perennial Democratic adviser, Larry Summers, "the laws of economics [were] like the laws of engineering"[12]: universal, exact, and, if properly applied, infallible. According to Republican favorite, Alan Greenspan, an acolyte of

Ayn Rand who led the Federal Reserve for twenty years, and whose speeches were parsed by Wall Street and Congress as if he were Adam Smith himself, the Market was inherently self-correcting. The cleansing agency of unfettered competition would purge the system not only of inefficiency but also immorality. As hastened and chastened by the Invisible Hand, avaricious self-interest would, inevitably, emerge "enlightened." Our great mistake, Greenspan preached, lay in trying to direct that Hand, for once freed of our regulatory chains, It would lift us all into a realm whose superabundance was also the work of meritocratic justice, the goods and the Good wrapped in one. From his Delphic seat in the nation's capital, our Oracle of the Numbers was, in effect, reaffirming for us the same Fable of Innocence pitched by Disney. Like that little boy prophet and "true-blue American," Jeremiah Dickson, he fully expected the bounty of *both!*

On June 3, 2003, six months after Lucas's address and just a month after the president proclaimed that our mission in Iraq had been "accomplished," the privatization movement reached its apogee of official acceptance. In a photo op, representatives of four of the five federal agencies most responsible for overseeing the nation's financial industries posed with tree shears and a chainsaw as they publicly endorsed an initiative that would slash the government's right to rein in banking practices.[13] The fervor of liberation was in the air, and like palace guards choosing to join the revolution's storming mob, these regulators were hastening the demise of their own authority. Mammon was leading them on, pied-piping the promises of his utopian doctrine. As fueled by the antigravity mojo of our technocratic expertise—whose math few understood but whose magical promises most everyone believed—stocks would rise forever, home equity inflate faster than credit-card debt, and financial instruments evolve so that even the poor could own a faux chateaux on tropical sands.

The results of *these* "laws of engineering" were astonishing to behold. From the early 1980s, when the privatization movement was first introduced, to 2008, when the market crashed, the average pay differential between an American CEO and his worker leapt by a factor of nine to stand at 360 to 1.[14] In late 2007, the Dow Jones Industrial Average soared above 14,000 points, and, engorged on profits the year before, Lehman Brothers, one of the nation's five major investment houses, had doled out 5.7 billion dollars in bonuses while rewarding CEO Richard Fuld with over 122 million in total compensation—an impressive yearly sum, to be sure, but one that placed him only fifth on *Forbes's* prestigious list of the highest paid executives.[15] Not to worry, though: the Magic Moment of the "money note," as triggered this time by the enlightened avarice of the housing market, was now democratically accessible to all. Joe and Joelene could buy into the dream as well as Buffy and Skip.

With house values rising at 8 percent per year (faster in hot spots like Vegas and Florida), going "all in" seemed to make sense. Scouting real estate listings, budding entrepreneurs flipped investment properties as easily as free-range burgers on their backyard grills while others refinanced their homes, using the extra cash from their inflated equity to purchase more products—most of which had been made in China. Thanks to the liberation from federal oversight, as brought to us by both the Clinton and Bush administrations, the number of subprime loans exploded, and now even a nanny could become a real estate mogul, owning multiple condos with no money down.

Every day had its Cinderella moment, the royal castle (if not its prince) made suddenly available to the weary working poor. In comparison to the wonder works of the Invisible Hand, even Oprah's generosity began to seem paltry. Sure, on one of her shows in 2004, each member of the audience had been given, abracadabra, the keys to a new Pontiac G-Six, but in California a wholly owned subsidiary of Washington Mutual supplied a farm worker earning 14,000 dollars per year with all the credit he needed to buy—*do you believe in miracles?*—a 720,000 dollar house.[16] Meanwhile, members of the polo pony set were pulling every silken string they could to be accepted into Bernie Madoff's highly exclusive investment club, which in forty-five years—*have you heard the good news, Brother?*—had never suffered a loss.

For those who cared enough to look, going "all in" had its impact on the books. Even as credit card companies acquired the right to charge usurious interest rates, revolving debt in private households rose precipitously, and the national savings rate, which had averaged a respectable 8–10 percent from 1950 into the 1980s, plummeted to near zero in the same year, 2005,[17] that the federal budget, decimated by tax cuts and the "war on terror," generated a 427 billion dollar deficit. Under the spell of the new evangelical economics, financial gimmickry and consumption on credit had overtaken manufacturing as the go-to means for boosting profits, even as the usual watchdogs (accounting firms, rating services, market analysts, regulatory agencies) were "defining deviancy downward" by loosening their standards. Grade inflation, it seemed, was not limited to politically correct educators; the most dubious securities were being awarded AAA ratings, and stock analysts emerged from their rococo calculations to soberly advise their fee-paying clients: *buy, buy, buy.*

The leaders and the led, corporations and their supervisory agencies, political consultants and economic experts: most all had adopted the new consensus on the harmlessness of extensive debt in an economy where 71 percent of the Gross Domestic Product was dependent on consumption.[18] By 2005, when the housing market really took off, thrift was a virtue so archaic that most young Americans had never heard of the word, much less witnessed its characteristic habits in action. Credit itself was driving the American credo now, supplying the hot air necessary to keep that market's ever-expanding bubble afloat. It was, after all, still *morning* in a America— prudence could wait until the late afternoon. And why bother to save for a rainy day when, under the reign of scientific capitalism, the problem of rain itself had been solved?

The Emperor's New Clothes

While the underlying psychology of deception that feeds any financial bubble remains largely the same, the mechanics do vary from case to case, and, radically compressed, the narrative of the great crash of 2008 went something like this.

Given the sheer size and past stability of our economy, newly wealthy foreigners and their governments, including a China fat with cash from our trade imbalance, wanted to invest their profits here. At the same time, to prevent an extended recession after the bursting of the Internet bubble, Greenspan's Fed dramatically lowered the prime interest rate, allowing the major banks to borrow large sums at next to no cost. Awash with new capital from both at home and abroad, those same deregulated financial giants then began generating new "investment opportunities" to exploit the demand. That those new opportunities were centered on real estate's tangible assets seemed an encouraging sign to the day's investors—at least when compared to the vaporware promised by all those Internet start-ups in the late nineties. But given the size of the demand, there weren't nearly enough standard mortgages to package for sale, nor could such plain-vanilla instruments promise anything more than a modest return, and so new financial products were created to take advantage of this upswing in housing values.

The subprime market proved especially attractive because brokers could charge more when providing mortgages to those with poor credit ratings, and as a lure to the customer, most of those mortgages were then structured in such a way as to feature initially low interest payments which would later reset at much higher rates. The brokers selling these highly risky ARMs (adjustable rate mortgages) didn't have to worry, however, because home lending, which had once been the province of the local savings bank, had been marketized since the 1980s. The risky loans they made were immediately sold to larger financial institutions, who then packaged them as mortgage-backed securities and resold them as investments around the world.

The irresponsibility exhibited at the lower end by brokers who, in the rush to earn more, were offering loans to potential homeowners with "no income, no job, and no assets" (the so-called Ninjas) was evident at every other level along the way. Huge investment firms like Lehman Brothers and Bear Stearns began to slice and dice the mortgages they bought, intermixing the risky with the safe, and repackaging them as "collateralized debt obligations" (CDOs) to be sold to investors at home and abroad. Created by math whizzes who were aptly dubbed "quants," these new instruments were impenetrable in their complexity to all but the expert few. One might have presumed, and many did, that those few would include the rating services, such as Moody's and Standard & Poor's, who were charged with assessing the CDOs' true value for the investing public. But they, too, saw the pixie-dust data and believed in the magic that, abracadabra, turned a "toxic asset" into a secure investment. BBB loans (the worst of the worst) went into the sausage factory of the CDO and—*do you believe in miracles?*—somehow emerged, according to the rating services, as AAA.

These miraculous makeovers were verified by yet another of those "laws of engineering" brought to us by evangelical economics: a statistical correlation derived from something called the Gaussian copula function, which was discovered in 2000 by David X. Li. Misused by the industry as a means for predicting risk in the marketplace, Li's was a formula that few in the business fully understood but everyone applied, widely praising its "elegance"—an elegance that just so happened, time and again, to ratify the creditworthiness of the new CDOs and CDSs (credit default swaps) that the investment houses were churning out, making mucho money for everyone involved.[19]

If at the time, though, one was more interested in graphing the alignment of the players' motives than in praising the elegance of their math, such a result would have seemed as suspect as it was unsurprising. For aping the model we saw earlier in the pharmaceutical industry, those rating services were being paid by the same investment firms whose products they were "objectively" assessing on behalf of the investing public. Just as the marketizing of pharmaceuticals had led to a medical-industrial complex whose industry-financed testing mills and ghost-written scientific papers torqued the truth about the safety and effectiveness of therapeutic drugs, the marketizing of lending had led to a financial-industrial complex that generated just the sort of evaluations that were needed to keep Wall Street's numbers surging upward. In the marketplace, it is the customer, after all, who is always right, and the paying customers here were not Joe and Joelene but Goldman Sachs and Lehman Brothers.

That is not to say that the rating services indulged in criminal behavior; in many instances, however, there is a very fine line between outright fraud and convenient incompetence. To help illuminate the difference, we need to recall the distinction I drew in *The Politics of Pain Dissuasion* between two kinds of duplicitous leaders: the Machiavellian man and the Disingenue. While Bernie Madoff's fifty-billion-dollar Ponzi scheme was Machiavellian in the extreme—the man was bald-facedly lying to his customers, the rating services, and regulatory agencies from the very start—most of the catastrophically inaccurate analysis and advice that led to the crash was of the disingenuous type. The falsity there was rooted in a "willing suspension of disbelief," a strong inclination toward self-deception when the immediate rewards for "seeing no evil" were so great. After hearing the CEO of Moody's defend his company's rosy subprime ratings, one of the housing market's rare skeptics got to the heart of the problem when he bluntly concluded: "With all due respect, sir, you're delusional."[20]

Given its profitability, however, that delusionary view was contagious. And when the same group of skeptics inquired at Moody's rival, Standard & Poor's, they discovered that the mathematical model their rating system used to evaluate the real estate market was so constructed that it couldn't accept negative numbers: it had no provision at all for home prices declining.[21] Like Ronald Reagan's mind, these elegant instruments for measuring risk were programmed to exclude unhappy news; their science, like Hollywood's films, was rigged to only churn out endings "as we like it."

Of course, if the government had been as closely regulating the financial safety of Wall Street's products as it does, say, the physical safety of Detroit's cars, the complicit incompetence of the rating services would not have proven so consequential. But thanks to an ideological conversion in the nation's capital whose pace and progress had been much enhanced by Wall Street's massive donations to both parties, the political philosophy of privatization had won the day, and where government oversight over financial markets wasn't overtly slashed, the agencies involved proved to be either unwilling or unable to protect the public.

Perhaps the most egregious example was the failure of the Security Exchange Commission (SEC) to uncover Madoff's Ponzi scheme. For nine years, independent accounting analyst Harry Markopolos had been hectoring the agency with detailed statistical analyses of Madoff's operation, including a memo he sent in 2005 entitled "The World's Largest Hedge Fund Is a Fraud"—all to no effect. Whether too dense to comprehend the damning math or too cowardly to take on a figure of Madoff's wealth and social standing, the SEC failed to act, and it was only when the stock market crashed, forcing too many of his over-extended customers to call in their cash, that the epic scam came to light. In the end, in a bitter parody of the Market's supposedly self-regulating morality, Madoff was compelled by events to out himself.[22]

But even given the size, duration, and sheer audacity of Madoff's con—as early as 1989, the man's hedge fund was responsible for 5 percent of all the trading on the New York Stock Exchange—his efforts were dwarfed by the imaginary paradise of prosperity that had been spun out of the dung of the subprime market by the enlightened self-interest of his fellow traders. Deregulated, the big investment firms had allowed their debt-to-equity ratios to soar. Riddled with hidden toxic assets, the CDOs they bought and sold were dangerous enough, but as a form of insurance on those mortgage-backed securities, CDSs could be marketed again and again, creating multiple obligations for the same dubious loans, many of whose creditworthiness had been magically revised from BBB to AAA. Ever more removed from the real-world economy of goods, services, and sustainable properties, the mega banks had generated a Plato's cave of virtual profitability, selling shadows on the wall, and then shadows of the shadows, borrowing more to buy or insure a series of debts which, fed by the feverish dreams and acquisitive schemes of lower-end speculators, were themselves highly leveraged.

In the guise of a financial paradise, our deregulated banking system had created a gargantuan self-destruction machine. As economist Herbert Stein once famously observed, channeling the spirit of Yogi Berra: "That which cannot go on forever *won't*." But for those riding the giddy high of a bubble mentality, such mundane tautologies don't compute. Common sense had said that supply-side policy couldn't work, that it was "voodoo economics," but the Reagan administration's quants insisted that it would—until, that is, it *didn't* and federal deficits exploded. This time the trigger on the bomb would be the reset button built into all those subprime ARMs, for when the teaser rates expired, monthly mortgage payments would shoot up, exposing the under-qualified owners for the credit risks they always were. And once those owners began to default on their loans, faith in the eternal expansion of home equity (the *new* voodoo economics) suddenly dissolved. The housing market flipped from hot to frigid, values deflating as fast as they had risen, and with many of those mortgage-backed securities failing, trillions of dollars of credit default swaps would soon come due.

Although this deflationary process had already begun by the middle of 2006, the Market remained in a state of delusionary denial for more than a year, its numbers still shooting upward until a single analyst, Meredith Whitney, played the role of the child in "The Emperor's New Clothes" by stating that CitiBank had vastly overextended itself. The bubble then burst, but its deflation was relatively slow at first, only accelerating into a general panic in the fall of 2008 when the full extent of our mega banks' indebtedness began to become clear, and their gigantic Ponzi scheme, entirely legal thanks to the chainsaws and tree shears of deregulation, self-destructed in a flash.

The same Lehman Brothers that had given out billions in bonuses less than two years before was toast by the middle of September. Bear Stearns, which had pioneered some of those complex mortgage-backed securities, was sold off at a pittance. Merrill Lynch, whose brand was famously bullish on investment, had been stampeded by its own recklessness and was forced to merge with Bank of America even as Washington Mutual, which had been one of the nation's fastest growing banks, was shut down by regulators and sold off to JP Morgan Chase. Despite the publicity supplied by Oprah's grand surprise, the entire Pontiac line was canceled by General Motors, which was then forced, despite many billions of dollars of federal support, into bankruptcy court.

Nor was the nation's once dominant automaker alone in seeking federal assistance. The financial services industry, that epicenter of libertarian rectitude, pleaded for and received a 700 billion dollar federal bailout. (In the jaded words of one former Wall Street CEO: "It's laissez faire until you get in deep shit.") Nevertheless, true to the narcissistic age they led, the self-esteem of the Street's managerial class didn't seem to suffer. After reflecting deeply on their performance in 2008, a year when they had overseen the worst collapse in investment values since the Great Depression, and while currently on the federal dole, these apostles of the Market's meritocracy awarded themselves more than eighteen billion dollars in bonuses.[23]

Meanwhile, of the original big five investment banks, Goldman Sachs, reborn in a new form due to its own inept investments, appeared to make out the best from the patchwork pattern of federal bailouts and backups—which, of course, had nothing to do with the fact its former CEO, Henry Paulson, was Secretary of the Treasury when the crisis struck. As the mandarins of money always insist: the laws of engineering, and not the lubrications of cronyism, were directing the bailout's "decision-making process."

The Narrative of Stupidity as "Maximum Deniability"

After the collapse, perennial make-nice columnist David Brooks—whose mission it is to soothe the fevered soul of the elite establishment that consented to invite him into their club, and who, like the good middle son, works to mend their feuds and absolve their faults—decided that it was, primarily, the "narrative of stupidity," compounded by "uncertainty," and not the "narrative of greed" that had devastated our economy. It was quite an admission from someone who had touted our system as a true meritocracy, equating awesome SAT scores and Ivy League degrees with managerial competence. But given the fiasco before him, acknowledging an *intellectual* failure was far preferable to admitting an *ethical* one—which, after all, could have far graver legal and political consequences. And as embarrassing as stupidity was, the fig leaf of uncertainty was offered up as a partial excuse. For more than two centuries, disastrous misjudgments on the battlefield had been attributed to the "fog of war," and now, Brooks was hinting, the great crash and credit freeze of 2008 had arisen from an analogous opacity in the human circumstance—the obscure complexities of our newly digitized economy.[24]

Predictably, when called before a congressional committee investigating the collapse, both Christopher Cox, chairman of the SEC, and ex-Fed chief Greenspan agreed with that assessment: like Brooks's banking executives, they in their roles as government regulators couldn't have possibly anticipated the crisis at hand. Never mind the SEC's decision in 2004 to allow the investment firms to triple their debt-to-equity ratio, which they immediately did, greatly increasing the scope of the calamity. Discount as well that, three years prior to the crash, Cox's agency had received that subtly suggestive memo "The World's Largest Hedge Fund Is a Fraud." No, the fog of financial complexity was thickening the air then, and surely it would have taken an interpretive genius to read the danger lurking within signs so obscure.

Our then recently retired Fed chief sadly concurred. Despite his twenty-year reign as the most influential voice on our banking policies; despite his decision in that role to flood the marketplace with the cheap money that had helped to keep the bubble swelling; despite his oft expressed contempt for government regulations, his official endorsement of budget-busting tax cuts and, no doubt, his awesome SAT scores, Greenspan also denied any personal accountability, embracing instead the unaccustomed modesty of an excusable ignorance. Suitably disoriented by this sudden reversal of roles from market sage to average baffled Joe, and having the general appearance of a deer caught in the headlights of a speeding Hummer (another brand that a desperate General Motors planned to sell or drop), our former Oracle of the Numbers admitted to the committee that, yes, he did now spot a flaw in his libertarian ideology.

Nevertheless, he added reflectively, "if you go back and ask yourself how in the early years anybody could realistically make a judgment as to what was ultimately going to happen in subprime, I think you're asking more than anybody is capable of judging." The Fed was "as good an economic organization as exists . . . in the world," and "if all those extraordinarily capable people were unable to foresee" the dangers of the housing bubble, then we had to "ask ourselves why is that?" Having posed such a profound question, he quickly supplied a philosophical answer, and one that would have appalled his mentor Ayn Rand, who had trumpeted the triumph of individual intelligence. "We're not smart enough as people," Greenspan ruefully concluded. "We cannot see events that far in advance."[25]

In the Olympic event of "maximum deniability," as periodically staged in the nation's capital, this was a gold medal performance. Note how, though asked about his own culpability, Greenspan managed to pole-vault away from the pronoun of personal accountability, quickly converting "I" to "you" and then to "anybody," finally placing the burden on "we" as people. Though his thinking had dominated the Fed's decision-making, the failure to predict the subprime fiasco was suddenly now spread to the entire organization. Nor, given its cast of "extraordinarily capable" employees, was the agency as a whole really at fault. The failure, after all, was not simply personal or even institutional. As embraced by the ex-Fed chief, Brooks's alibi for the elite, his narrative of stupidity compounded by uncertainty, was now extended beyond even the transient complexity of our historical moment to the permanence of the human condition. Donning the unaccustomed robes of Socrates, this former meritocrat was endorsing instead the wisdom of humility, confessing to the condition of an existential ignorance shared by you and me. If stupidity was to blame, then the spotlight of shame would have to be shared, apparently, by our entire species.

That's a helluva lot of dunce caps to hand out. But it was a fact inconvenient to Greenspan's theory of universal ignorance (and so egalitarian blame) that *some* members of our species had indeed been "smart enough" to warn us about the approaching catastrophe. These impressively credentialed folks weren't just "anybody" and included Nobel Prize winner Joseph Stiglitz and New York University economist Nouriel Roubini, who had been mocked at the time as "Dr. Doom" for his pessimistic predictions. And, as Michael Lewis reported, there had been credible naysayers inside the industry as well. The skeptics I cited earlier were centered in an investment fund led by Steve Eisman, who made a fortune betting against the housing market, and whose brusque contempt for the idiot optimism fueling the bubble was very publicly expressed.

In 1991, as a neophyte analyst with Oppenheimer Securities, Eisman had been asked to specialize in the subprime market, and he hadn't forgotten either the lamentable quality of that market's products or his own employer's unwillingness to be honest when rating them. The same pattern of disingenuous duplicity for rampant profit-seeking that would finally send the market into a tailspin was fully evident to the young Eisman seventeen years before. "What I learned from that experience," he said, speaking of both the corporate analysts and the subprime market they assessed, was "that these guys lied to infinity" and that "Wall Street didn't give a shit what it sold."[26]

Utterly undermining the benign meritocracy once proselytized by ideologues like Greenspan and blessed by apologists like Brooks, Eisman's insider testimony prompts one to ask whether members of *this* club should ever be licensed to the run the show. This was precisely why defenders of the system found it essential to recast the problem as, primarily, an intellectual one—as a flaw in a theory and not a stain on the character of those mandarins of money and their many allies in the nation's capital. Theoretical flaws, after all, would have theoretical cures. One simply had to send the quants back to work, touching up the numbers, readjusting their algorithmic functions in ways that would keep the money flowing in the same overall direction. A technical fix, wed to a few make-nice reforms like those that had followed the S&L crisis, and not a dismantling of the oligarchic club, was the solution implied by such a diagnosis.

By attributing the industry's misuse of Li's Gaussian copula function to his stupidity narrative, Brooks avoided confronting the possibility that the formula was used precisely because it was stupid in an immediately profitable way, and that if it *hadn't* generated results as they like them on the Street, then the investment firms and rating services, ready to "lie to infinity" to sell their "shit," would have found another version of Melville's bogus Counterfeit Detector to certify as bona fide their actually toxic investment opportunities. That most of those same firms eventually got burned by their own products is a true index of their ultimate stupidity, but that narrative of stupidity was always subsidiary to the narrative of greed—to the thoroughly Mammonite motive of *more* that was driving the entire show from the start.

And where *more* reigns supreme, the eventual consequences are bound to be grim. Just as the idiot optimism directing the invasion of Iraq resulted in a mayhem that killed far more civilians than actual combatants, the giddy expectations of a riskless prosperity triggered an economic tsunami that crushed the innocent along with the guilty. It was hard to feel sorry for the many speculators who were wiped out when the real estate bubble burst, but given the deliberate mixing of toxic and healthy assets and the magical elevation of BBB loans to AAA status, many investors had no idea that they were, in fact, speculating. Even expert money managers hired by philanthropies, universities, public employee trust funds, and dutifully diversified retirement plans were stunned to find that, beneath the masquerade of scientific certainty staged by Wall Street, their conservative investment strategies had actually been reckless.

Likewise, anyone who had bought a house during the bubble years, even those with real incomes and reasonable loans, had been taken to the cleaners, the price they paid artificially elevated by the speculative fever. As house values continued to plummet in 2009, some 22 percent of homeowners suddenly owed more on their houses than they were worth.[27] And due to the credit freeze and general panic that followed the market's meltdown, many businesses failed or drastically cut back their payrolls, nearly doubling the nation's unemployment rate and sending previously creditworthy citizens into financial distress, including the threat of defaulting on their once secure mortgages.

The damage spread quickly. Just eight months after the crash, a majority of the homes facing foreclosure were no longer ones saddled with subprime loans, and a radical decline in income and sales tax receipts led to busted budgets in the public sphere: teachers laid off, parks closed, prisoners released early, health care for the poor suspended. Nor could many private charities step in to make a difference, for due to drastic reductions in both endowment income and donations, they were also forced to cut back their services. As a consequence of this vast episode of national delirium, lives would be lost, families splintered, careers ruined, and businesses far removed from real estate investment destroyed forever as the economy spiraled downward into what soon came to be known as the Great Recession.

The Narrative of Greed as the American Dream

As the hidden facts emerged in the near aftermath of the collapse, a complex lineage of fault began to become clear. On the political side, the privatization movement was deeply implicated, for once set free of regulatory oversight and provided with the alibi that, disciplined by the Market alone, unchecked self-interest would become "enlightened," the wizards of Oz behind the curtain immediately began to game the system. The libertarian version of our Fable of Innocence was mustered to justify the motive of greed, which then generated the narrative of stupidity that I have detailed here: the housing bubble's version of voodoo economics.

When their bottom lines were bulging, investment CEOs like Richard Fuld were all for their pay reflecting their so-called merit—the shameless credit they took for highly profitable (but actually toxic) financial products that they only dimly understood. So it would only seem fair to apply the same logic when apportioning blame and, borrowing that ratio in pay discrepancies generated during the boom years, insist that these top executives were 360 times more at fault than the average American employee. Of course when the bottom fell out, we didn't hear such mea culpas from the mandarins of money, for the masquerade of their meritocracy, with its radically unequal rewards, always ceases to apply on the subject of fault when they "get in deep shit."

Still, we don't need to endorse the moral socialism of egalitarian blame, as ridiculously proposed by Alan Greenspan, to recognize that this crisis was caused by fundamental flaws in our shared moral field. Thanks to their political enablers, Wall Streets' leaders did lead us over the precipice, but in doing so they were expressing—within their separate spheres of enormous and so potentially catastrophic influence—the reckless moods, values, and attitudes that had been infecting the nation's conventional thinking for many years. At the lower end of the subprime scheme, some mortgage brokers allowed would-be borrowers to fill in imaginary incomes on their loan applications with the tacit promise, a wink and a nod, that the truth of those numbers would never be investigated. These aptly nicknamed "liar loans" were representative of the willing collaboration of deceit and self-deception, all the winking and nodding, that was inflating the bubble at nearly every level of financial exchange.

In the immediate aftermath of the crash, the nation's economists, most of whom had failed to predict the crisis, were belatedly recalling that the word *credit* had evolved from *credo*, whose Latin roots meant *I believe.* They were reminding themselves, while informing the public they had long misled, that the smooth running of our economy was dependent, in the end, less on "laws of engineering" than on the tacit covenants of faith and trust. And because the focus then, in the midst of the panic, was on quickly finding the means for restoring that faith, less energy was expended on exploring the deeper origins of the crisis—which were, in fact, rooted in the dubious quality of our now default beliefs. The unpleasant truth was this: the narrative of greed driving the credit crisis was supplying us then with the most vivid sign yet of a profound revision in the nation's actual credo. It marked the triumph of a magical worldview that, scripting the roles of Quack and Dupe, was now affecting the judgment of every social class and niche.

We saw evidence of that triumph in the many wealthy investors who had simply presumed that they ought to receive, without fail or variation, the 18 percent annual return promised to them by Madoff's agents.[28] We saw it in the middle-class homeowners who, simply presuming that real estate values would rise forever, borrowed on their houses as if they were the fabled golden goose; and we witnessed it, too, in those farm workers, nannies, and street musicians who thought it made sense, who simply presumed, that one could own a king's castle on a servant's wages. When facing the subsequent wreckage of their economic lives and asked how they could have believed in such dubious schemes, so many of them answered with seeming sincerity that they thought they were "living the American Dream."

But whose version of that dream did they imagine they were living? Whose climate of expectations was inhabiting their hearts and haunting their heads? It certainly wasn't the foundational one espoused by Adams or Jefferson, nor the one reformed and revived by Lincoln or King. No, the now commonly held dream of the republic had been fully freed from the communal obligations and personal sacrifices required to sustain any healthy social compact. Neither spiritual nor political, the new covenant of hope and trust was magical in its makeup, composed from the dust of cinematic pixies and evoked by the superstitious ritual of wishing upon a star.

Even history's rudest interruptions couldn't break that spell. When, a mere ten days after the 9/11 attacks, the president encouraged us to take our families to Disney World "to enjoy life the way we want it to be enjoyed," he was not only attempting to reboot the nation's tourist industry, which was threatened then by a collective grief that shunned any indulgence in life's lighter pleasures as unseemly; he was also revealing something profound about "the way we wanted [life] to be" at the start of the twenty-first century.[29] For however traditionally virtuous our communal grief might have been then, it clearly was not good for *business*, and in a society where money had replaced meaning in the hierarchy of values, the obligation to enjoy life, as exemplified by a theme park visit, was now greater than the obligation to honor the dead by sacrificing all those mundane pleasures that they, by dint of their ultimate sacrifice, would never enjoy again. Because Mammon was the one now leading us on, mourning must give way to family fun—fun, that is, as processed for a fee by airlines, restaurants, souvenir shops, and amusement parks.

This exhortation to stay "in character" despite the occasion—the worst attack on the nation since Pearl Harbor—came just one day after the president had proclaimed our "war on terror," and that surreal prescription of righteous rage overseas and frivolity at home defined in miniature both the official policies pursued and the collective attitude assumed for the next seven years. With the exception of the families whose sons and daughters did the fighting, the terrible reality of Iraq and Afghanistan was cushioned from the consciousness of the domestic populace. Despite an exhaustion of manpower, a military draft was not revived; despite the enormous cost of conducting two wars at once, taxes were never raised, nor war bonds pitched, nor rationing introduced. In an act of pain-dissuading censorship, even our military dead were hidden from view, photographs of their flag-draped coffins officially banned.

And while the few died (or lost their limbs or their minds) in the toxic fog of war, the many played. The mega lottery, online poker, dancing with the stars, crowning the next seasonal idol, flocking to casinos, resorts, and those ever pricier arenas extorted from local governments by the pashas of pro sports: with "support for the war" confined to placing a yellow ribbon on the car, we were enjoying life then "the way we want it to be enjoyed." We were pursuing the American Dream as preached by the civic religion of Disneyism, its holy principles revived by a family pilgrimage to its pristine shrines in Orlando and Anaheim, whose combined attendance rose to over thirty million in 2005.[30]

While heroin production soared in Afghanistan and our under-armored Humvees were being destroyed in Iraq by roadside bombs, while our combat units were required to return for their second or third tours and some prisoners of war were being tortured to preserve our way of life, Americans on the home front were buying more, eating more, both the government and its people indulging in an orgy of consumption fueled by credit, running up record federal deficits and personal indebtedness: fun, fun, fun until reality in the form of the repo man, court order in hand, took the T'bird, the house, the summer boat, and the time-share all away.

Surely an honest outside observer, if asked to assess our national character during this period, would have delivered the same summary judgment that was given to (and ignored by) that "conscience" of Wall Street, Moody's perpetually upbeat boss.

"With all due respect, sir, you're delusional."

The calamitous invasion of Iraq and the crash that led to the Great Recession—serial fiascoes in our national story whose full ethical, financial, and geopolitical dimensions have yet to be plumbed—were no accidents but the all too plausible consequences of the decades of reality dissuasion that I have been analyzing here. They emerged, in William Stafford's words, from "many a small betrayal in the mind." When a community begins to prefer feeling good about itself over knowing itself, and when the bitter herb of the moral life is replaced by the saccharine dessert of the disingenuous mind, a demise of virtue relentlessly ensues. When adults choose to cling to pixie-dust dreams even as they assume the potent offices of authority, "the fragile sequence" that sustains the civilized life will eventually break, "sending with shouts the errors of childhood / storming out to play through the broken dyke."

And that actual play, unlike so many of the virtual ones whose sound tracks we hum and false memories obey, will not work out as we like it.

Exit: The Reprise of American Virtue

All things fall and are built again.[1]

—W. B. Yeats

As we have seen in the preceding nine chapters, the moral masquerade of a utopian materialism has now invaded nearly every domain of our daily lives, a list that would include, but is not limited to, the following disturbing trends and events.

— A democratic government, whose origins were rooted in a principled revolt against imperial rule, pursued and proselytized its own imperial ambitions.

— A right-wing alliance, proudly touting its conservative principles, practiced instead a spendthrift economy, endorsing the golden goose of a taxless prosperity, creating enormous deficits and exhausting natural resources.

— A left-wing cause that laid claim to the moral authority of the civil rights and free speech movements nevertheless aimed to limit rights and censor "incorrect" speech in its own domains.

— An intensely cynical entertainment industry imagineered a "mythic America" oozing with sentimentality, its highly rationalized engines of narrative production formulaically projecting the romantic fantasies of feel-good triumph.

— A Protestantism once rooted in a sober recognition of sinfulness, and whose savior threw the money-lenders out of the temple, began to sell instead the promissory notes of a prosperity theology: spiritual deal-making for material and psychological profit-taking in the here-and-now.

— A whole host of cultural liberators proclaimed their righteous freedom from this or that oppressive system only to commit to alternative regimens that proved more punitive than the ones they rejected: from a heady pursuit of bacchanalian bliss or therapeutic mood enhancement into the deadening trap of chemical dependency; from a giddy promotion of "consumer choice" into the grim schedules of compulsive shopping and credit-card indebtedness; from a libertarian rejection of governmental regulation into the draconian regimes of corporate efficiency and the rigged markets of global monopolies and Ponzi schemes; from a celebration of the "sovereign self" into a passive submission to the robotic schedules of self-esteem and self-help.

An anti-imperial imperialism, a conservative avidity, a multicultural illiberalism, a cynical sentimentality, a spiritual materialism, a liberating bondage: together these conceptual, ethical, and emotional nullities have been skewing the compass of our collective judgment. Their internal incoherencies have animated a Virtual America, within whose baffling spaces traditional symbols, beliefs, and rituals have been thinned to masks that conceal, in fact, an accelerating allegiance to their near opposites. When the cultural common sense gravitates toward the nonsensical, we need to start mapping the values prescribed inside the social spaces that we now call home.

This wide-ranging book has attempted just such a mapping by highlighting the discrepancies between those virtues espoused by our nation's foundational ethical traditions (both the republican and the Judeo-Christian) and those virtues actively induced inside Virtual America's characteristic domains. Through a relentless campaign of architectural enclosure and psychological saturation over the last sixty years, our consumer economy has managed to gain effective control over both our physical and virtual homes. By directing the regimens of work and the rituals of play through its privatization of most civic spaces, and by sponsoring the daily flow of electronic information, that economy has succeeded in rescripting the nation's conscience after its own image. By touting the "good news" of its utopian solutions to our perennial problems and mustering a masquerade of pseudo-conservative values to conceal the changes actually underway, this economic system (America's applied version of rational materialism) has converted us to the core Mammonite belief that *more must equal better:* more efficiency in the workplace and more consumption in the marketplace to produce more and more profits. Under the reductive regime of its bottom-line thinking, all professions of meaning are being made to submit to the measures of money.

Such a crude calculation of human value could only prevail within a closed social sphere where, to cite Beckett again, the natural order is no longer "in the vicinity" to guide our thinking; for in Nature 1, from we which come and whose laws our culture's Nature 2.0 can only flout at its own peril, *more* of the tonic necessities of life (more salt, more water, more food, more stimulation) only proves *better* up to a point, after which it quickly turns toxic. That underlying physiological irony predicates a perennial moral one. When too narrowly defined and avidly pursued, the *more* of any cultural or personal good (aesthetic refinement, technological advancement, economic productivity) will soon prove destructive, collaterally razing those hard-won social and psychological equilibriums—between duty and desire, between tradition and innovation, between social classes, political factions, and the generations—that both energize and stabilize the body politic. The part, over-valued and so over-extended, will carelessly shred the delicate web of restraints and obligations that have civilized the social whole.

It is in the very nature of the masquerade underway—its seductive flattery of our personal autonomy, its sly endorsement of our pseudo-rebellious ways—that we should presume ourselves individually immune to the many baneful changes depicted here. Oh, the average Joe or Joelene might be susceptible to the "reality dissuasion" perpetually pitched on our video screens; our enemies in the culture wars might have fallen for the folly of one of our economy's evangelizing schemes, whether a genialized tax policy, a cosmeceutical makeover, or the science that supplies "happiness in a pill." But you and I, our friends and families, we are too smart or sophisticated, too hip or high-church to be duped in such ways. We hew only to the hive of our own clear intentions, feeding on the honey of our unadulterated will. In the words of Wendell Berry, "the issue of obedience is obsolete in the modern mind."[2] Which really means, however, that our era's investment in self-esteem has rendered us insensible to all the many ways we are being herded and swayed in our everyday lives..

The existential uniqueness of persons and the cultural diversity of our pluralistic society haven't been eradicated by this Evangelical Mammonism. But the biases of its now ubiquitous moral field *have* been drawing all our many vivid differences in the same general direction, so that any presumption of an automatic personal, professional, or parochial immunity to its influence—the transposition of American exceptionalism into the moral domain—is delusionary.   In *Paradise Lost*, Milton's Mammon argues that, rather than trying to break out, the newly fallen angels should *stay* in Hell. He predicts that, over time, their terrible torments there will become their native elements, and that the punishing pain of Hell's "piercing fires" will eventually seem "as soft as now severe." That optimistic premise of Satan's lieutenant—the acclimatization that makes the hellish seem normal, seem native—ironically defines the urgency that has been driving these pages. If we choose to stay inside Virtual America's enclosed spaces, which have been designed, after all, to Mammon's own specifications, his prediction is bound to come true: "our temper" will be "changed into their temper."[3] And I do mean *our* temper.

I. Visualizing the Demise of American Virtue

To further specify these changes, I have drawn a series of linear directionals $(a \rightarrow b)$ on page 219 to visualize the demise of virtue as I have defined it here: that is, the "transfer of sovereignty" between contesting sets of ethical ideals. The chart provided sketches a point-to-point picture of this widespread shift in the character of the virtues we now frequently prefer, if not always openly profess. Four qualifications, however, do apply.

First, in noting this turn from a "virtuous" toward a "virtual" America, I don't mean to suggest that there ever existed an ethical Eden here. I am charting an active transformation in our conventional ideals, not just a collective failure to meet self-professed standards, which I presume to be a common occurrence in human affairs and from which Virtuous America has been no exception—witness the nation's long-term hypocrisy on the issue of racial equality. Second, for the sake of visual simplicity, the chart avoids depicting the self-contradictory duality of traits (Dr. Jekyll at work, Mr. Hyde at home) that our economy requires. The chart's assertion that self-discipline has been devolving into self-indulgence, for example, favors the ethos of marketing over that of management, which, for the sake of efficiency, demands instead a strict obedience to its rationalized schemes. A more complete picture of the conversion underway, and a model for how some of the others might be framed, would divide the demise of self-discipline into two separate spheres: self-indulgence in the marketplace and submissiveness in the workplace.

Third, not all of the qualities associated with Virtual America are harmful in and of themselves; often the danger emerges instead from the extremity of the allegiance they have now acquired, especially from the frequent extension of material means into moral ends. Up to a point, after all, an increase in productivity can enhance generosity by multiplying the resources available to give, and in a different cultural environment—the old Plymouth Plantation, say, or tribal Pakistan today—a little self-esteem might prove to be a welcome corrective to an otherwise grim and guilt-ridden character.

Finally, the changes traced here are not as complete or uncontested as their simple visualization implies. Long embedded in our customs, covenants, and institutional structures, the traditional virtues do retain an appeal in our public and private deliberations, which is why their symbols are so often hijacked to mask their own decline. I'm charting a demise by degrees here, not an instant or automatic conversion.

Nevertheless, and over time, the co-opting of those virtues has become a real phenomenon. Humility and honesty haven't disappeared inside Virtual America, but they do tend to get "edited out" by an economy that adamantly esteems the counter values of self-promotion and salesmanship. And when taken together, these "virtual" values do form a mutually reinforcing moral field: one whose current saturation of our civic spaces and electronic communications has been, to use one of Tom Peters's favorite terms, cannibalizing both our republican and Judeo-Christian traditions of virtue.

II. Imagining the Reprise of American Virtue

He preferred to be, rather than to seem, good.[4]

—Sallust

It was the early Greek philosopher Heraclitus who observed that a man's character drives his fate (*ethos anthropos daimon*), and although exaggerated to fit the aphoristic form, that relative truth also applies to the character of whole communities. To the extent that a people *is* allowed to shape their own future, the quality of their life to come will depend not just on their capacity to enforce their will on a recalcitrant world but also on the quality of the thinking directing that will, and a nation led by Mammon has no plausible chance to cultivate a better life for itself. Unable to think holistically, it will continue to generate those radical imbalances that, misconceived as progress, are inimical to good governance, fomenting instead institutional instability and rank injustice.

Of this I am now convinced: our current condition, as driven in large part by our own actions and inventions, demands a reconfiguration of the moral imagination on an order last seen during that critical pivot between the medieval and the modern mindsets. Given the size, novelty, and sheer complexity of the task, defining in detail what that reconfiguration might entail lies beyond the reach of this already extensive book, whose primary purpose, after all, has been to convince my readers that such an epochal reformation is now urgently necessary. "All things fall," that is the one incontestable truth, but I am also proceeding on the hopeful belief, as voiced by Yeats, that a new graceful version of the American mind and the American place can be "built again." As much a preface to the sequel I hope to write as

TABLE 3: Character Edit under Evangelical Mammonism

Virtuous America		Virtual America
HONESTY (actuality (plain speaking	⟶	SALESMANSHIP plausibility) jargon / hype / spin)
HUMILITY (fallibility accepted (parable of the Fall (minding one's place	⟶	VANITY / NARCISSISM sovereignty proclaimed) Fable of Innocence) "mind is its own place")
GENEROSITY (circulation of gifts	⟶	PRODUCTIVITY / EFFICIENCY multiplication of commodities)
GRATITUDE (thank-you note)	⟶	RESENTMENT / ENTITLEMENT gossip column / law suit)
SELF-DISCIPLINE (thrift / abstinence (cultivation of reticence	⟶	SELF-INDULGENCE consumption / addiction) culture of complaint)
SELF-AWARENESS (know thyself (discover one's destiny (self-correction	⟶	SELF-ESTEEM / SELF-GENESIS feel good about yourself) fashion one's image) self-promotion)
SELF-RELIANCE (stoic initiative	⟶	SELF-HELP commodified dependence)
PRAGMATISM ("there's no free lunch"	⟶	MAGICAL THINKING "dreams come true out of the blue")
PIETY (ethical reform (spiritual harmony	⟶	PROGRESS technical fix) material accumulation)
MATURITY (internalizing reality's truths (providing for one's children	⟶	ARRESTED ADOLESCENCE chasing Fountain of Youth) pampering one's "inner child")
FRIENDSHIP (getting along	⟶	NETWORKING getting ahead)
MENTORSHIP (passing on one's wisdom	⟶	COMMERCIAL SPONSORSHIP renting out one's reputation)
HEROISM (admiration earned (quality of actions	⟶	CELEBRITY publicity gained) quantity of attention)

a climax to the book now nearing completion, here is a tentative list for how such a reprise of virtue might be pursued.

⮎

Know Thyself. Every successful reformation, personal or communal, is rooted in self-knowledge, and so, stepping outside our convention hall, we need to acknowledge some painful truths about ourselves and the places we now inhabit, starting with these five.

1. A nation cannot license a set of inherently amoral money machines to run its work spaces, public gathering places, and primary media for telecommunications and then expect the behavior of its people to remain morally sound. The core social contention of the privatization movement—that ethical behavior is a kind of epiphenomenon of rationalized greed; that inside a fully marketized society, self-interest will, routinely, become enlightened—is a disingenuous delusion. It is a con game that we have played on ourselves, the particular way that American "reason panders will."

2. An economic system that mechanizes production is always in danger of mechanizing the minds of its employees, managers and underlings alike, and that conversion will then persist beyond the factory and the office to affect the quality of the choices that are made inside the family home and civic square.

3. In an electronic age, when messages invade every social niche and private space, a telecommunications system whose underlying intention is to promote acquisition will eventually produce an overly acquisitive population.

4. When the bottom line prevails, when more matters most, extreme efficiency at work and consumption at home (Mechanism and Mammonism in Carlyle's old terms) will be pursued without consideration of the collateral social, psychological, and political damages that may result, for such damages no longer readily "compute."

5. Insomuch as human beings are not machines, nor merely the sum of their physical appetites, the pursuit of efficiency and avidity on behalf of more money is not a ruling purpose worthy of our obedience, nor one conducive to cultural or psychological coherence, and no society (democratic or otherwise) can long survive the conversion of its logos, mythos, ethos, and polis to the service of such dehumanizing lies.

⊹

Refuse Rational Materialism as a Ruling Worldview. As the thinking species, we construct our societies from sets of ruling ideas, and the current poor design of ours is directly linked to a philosophical error that has been characteristic of the modern era. Both scientific socialism (aka communism) and scientific capitalism (the purely privatized political economy touted by the libertarian right) are applied expressions of rational materialism, and although very differently configured, their separate failures do supply a cautionary tale whose underlying lesson we now must heed.

As a methodological tool, that philosophical approach is narrowly astute and can be highly effectual, but as a teleological compass, it is actually incompetent and, therefore, dangerous. To submit fully to any instituted form of rational materialism is to be ruled by an idiot savant whose narrow pursuit of the one segment of human life it knows and overvalues—whether political control, economic profit, or technological progress—shall soon wreak havoc on the harmony of both the cultural and the psychological whole. A potentially fatal infatuation with deterministic schemes, an ever emergent belief in the infallibility of its own machines and techniques, haunts the core of this philosophy's expectations. Like T. S. Eliot's wayward parishioners, its various adherents are trying to escape the human condition "by dreaming of systems so perfect that no one will need to be good."[5] But to believe in that dream and pursue the construction of those utopian schemes is to promote—collaterally at least and sometimes directly—the demise of virtue.

The importance of cultivating character, in the dual form of communal covenants and private conscience, gives way to a faith-based obsession with engineering progress. Why bother training one's self or one's children in the difficult art of "preferring not to" when all one has to do instead is tweak the economy's delivery system or change the dose on one's latest prescription? Studies have been done, and the numbers have proven the plausibility of becoming richer than rich, better than well. And yet "the man that is will shadow / the man that pretends to be."[6] As will the actual society behind Virtual America's "reality TV."

⊹

Recognize the Dangers of Technological Progress. Endowed now with our new digital machines, we do have at our disposal extraordinary means to map and enact whichever changes we might choose to make. But as history has amply demonstrated, rapid material and mental advances are also likely to prove morally dangerous. In a collective version of classical tragedy, the hubris engendered by technological progress is a common source for social regress. So it was that Darwin's brilliant theory was quickly hijacked by racist politicians and industrial tyrants to justify their vicious schemes. So it was, too, that the same miraculous system of broadcast sound that brought Mozart to the masses and the beauty of black music to millions of whites also supplied an exponentially empowered megaphone for the radioed rantings of Hitler and Mussolini.

Knowledge *is* power, but more power is rarely better at first. As in the fairy tales of old, the earliest avatar of the new saving prince is a frightening monster, and one whose evolution into heroic status, properly understood, is not the work of an instantaneous magic but an arduous moral and psychological passage: an achieved self-mastery over those monstrous strengths and their reapplication to virtuous ends. Although it won't be "ever after"—no achievement is—*that* is the happier ending we now must work toward. *Ethos anthropos daimon:* our fate as a nation will only change for the better if our character evolves in ways that can successfully civilize our now crudely applied technological advances.

Reject the Allure of Edenic Nostalgia. Although we will need to borrow from our collective past to map that happier ending, we can never simply "get back" to where we once belonged. A culture is not a car that can be thrown into reverse, with the expectation of a safe return to some hallowed point of origin. Like the utopian's faith in a perfectible future, the reactionary's infatuation with an Edenic past is an exercise in self-delusion: another SDI concocted by the mind to protect itself from the uncertainties attendant to the moral life.

Cultural nostalgia in America today comes in two distinct accents: cold rationalist and cute romantic. Our national past is either treated as a fundamentalist tract to be read through "strict construction," or as a sentimentalist's dream to be restaged in the fantasylands of our amusement parks and evoked through the rousing rhetoric of political campaigns. Either way, these supposed preservations bear the stamp of idolatrous thinking. They exude the sickly scent of an ancestor worship, and one whose presumption that the history of virtue triumphantly ended with the Constitutional Convention of 1787—or in the Living's Towns of the 1950s or, contrarily, on the rockin' fields of Woodstock in 1969—can only further the demise of our national character.

There are no fixed and final solutions to the problems of human governance, and to presume so is to embrace the vanity that precedes calamities of the self-induced sort. Our collective past can supply inspirational guidance but no fail-safe guarantees. It bequeaths us cultural instruments (myths, histories, civic traditions) through which we might strive to make sense of our predicaments—but not the site-specific interpretation that each new predicament requires. As was the case for Washington and Lincoln in the midst of the crises that proved their worth, a mere memorization of past instructions is insufficient by itself to the challenges inherent to the moral life.

↔

Review Other Eras for Relevant Clues. Although the condition of human freedom does challenge the moral imagination in all times and places, there *are* some "times that try men's souls" more than others.[7] As even Descartes recognized, there can be a telling difference in certain eras between what a people *think* they believe and what they actually believe—that is, the values encoded in the changing pattern of their everyday actions.[8] Such discrepancies are a defining characteristic of transitional times, and what was true in 1620, when the late medieval mind was being confounded by the collateral effects of modernity's new tools (its telescope, microscope, and printing press), applies as well today when our all too amazing *post*modern technologies are challenging the covenants that once successfully domesticated the modernizing mind and place.

Of special interest then was the emergence of an initially disruptive individualism, a newly private sense of self and of personal ambition that, empowered by the spread of literacy, threatened the stability of the old feudal order. Before that individualism could be licensed economically and politically, leading to the free-market democracies of the modern West, it had to be ethically domesticated. Potentially sociopathic, the new "monstrous" mental powers of the Machiavellian man—his combined capacities for acute rational analysis, self-centered calculation, and emotional detachment—had to be tamed in ways that were conducive to the common good. The deliberations of his secret self needed to be infused with an active sense of right and wrong, forging an acutely anxious inner voice of conscience: a civilizing psychological process whose drama was recorded in the spiritual diaries and dramatic soliloquies unique to the age.

Those then new literary forms supply us with archeological evidence of the West's moral imagination hard at work, struggling to domesticate the new mental empowerments generated by technological progress—the same scary mission, that of psychological rebirth and cultural reinvention, that we now face.

↢⊖

Review the Conditions that Spawned Our Traditional Virtues. What we are witnessing in those early diaries and soliloquies is the creation of what I have been calling the Protestant self, a term I chose because the long transition into a civilized modernity was first fully engaged in the religious sphere. Its political completion, however, didn't really occur until our Revolution, which is the other transitional period most obviously relevant to the crisis at hand. Any plausible plan for a reprise of virtue here will have to be rooted in a profound understanding of those conditions that helped to generate the traditional American ethos in the first place.

Textbook accounts of the Revolution tend to stress the provocation of the British crown's attempt to reassert its authority after the French and Indian Wars. Although the initiating events did center on issues like "taxation without representation," the ensuing crisis was psychological as well as political and economic. It exposed an internal incoherence within the colonists themselves, and how what they *thought* they believed was undermined by what they *actually* believed—by those values revealed in their increasingly rebellious political actions.

To cite McLuhan again: "Everyone experiences far more than he understands. Yet it is experience, rather than understanding, that influences behavior." In 1770, most Americans still *understood* themselves to be subjects of the crown, with all the emotional affiliations and social duties that implied. But their everyday *experiences* as settlers of a rural outpost a wide ocean away from the imperial court were very differently configured. The practical independence of both their material lives as independent farmers or craftsmen and their mental lives as the world's most literate population at the time encouraged a set of values—initiative and innovation over obedience and tradition, egalitarian merit over inherited status—incompatible with the character of an imperial subject. Many of the colonists had been living proto-democratic lives, and the political crisis of the early 1770s brought to the threshold of consciousness a long-simmering inner conflict between their de facto and de jure cultural identities.

The period we celebrate as foundational to the American identity is that relatively brief phase when the "common sense" of our democratic nature was self-consciously formulated for the first time. But when reviewing this period in hopes of penetrating the fog of our own era, we mustn't forget that its underlying moral logic was powerfully prefigured by many years of site-specific colonial experience. America's founders were self-consciously minding how that colonial experience had already changed their deepest presumptions as to what was true and good about human life, and they were articulating what those changes implied about the best possible form of political governance. Those then revolutionary presumptions constitute the now traditional American virtues, whose praises we still sing on the appropriate holidays but whose demise has become the unacknowledged theme of our everyday lives.

Insomuch as they constitute our default understanding of the democratic life, the key values of our traditional ethos are easy to enumerate. They would include: the dignity of the individual and the right to pursue happiness independently, the value of privacy and private property in protecting that dignity and empowering that pursuit, the importance of self-reliance as both a psychological spur for individual achievement and the political guarantor of democratic freedom, and the virtue of plain speaking to promote an atmosphere of trust in a political economy of private deal-making.

Behind this familiar array of virtue claims lay a deeply engrained philosophical presumption. Democracy was finally "declared" because its form of governance best fit the underlying facts of the human condition as the revolutionaries, strongly influenced by the nature of their everyday experience, now understood those facts. Democracy was declared because, in their view, human beings were—natively, naturally—free.

Test the Old Ethos within the New American Place. Using our foundational history as guide, we can begin by noting one crucial similarity between revolutionary and postmodern times: we, too, are suffering an internal conflict between our traditional instruments of moral understanding and the actual moral logic driving our everyday actions—only now the traditions being undercut are precisely those revolutionary ones first articulated by our democracy's founders. To state the obvious, we no longer live in a rural colony of economic freemen whose intellects have been shaped by print literacy alone, and beneath the blame-game of our culture wars has been percolating a not unjustifiable fear that our foundational values can no longer make sense of the *post*modern place within whose spaces we now think, work, love, and play.

What, after all, does self-reliance really mean in a corporate economy where only a small percentage of the workforce remains self-employed?

What do private property rights mean in a time when science keeps discovering new ways in which our private acts can transgress our deeded boundaries to harm or help our neighbors?

What do ownership, authorship, originality mean in an age whose technologies (with their linking and webbing and real-time interactions) both expose and enhance the collaborative nature of human creativity?

What does freedom of choice really mean when living inside architectural and virtual spaces whose perceptual fields have been designed to seduce us—venues whose moral fields have been reduced to servicing commercial intentions?

And how profound is our allegiance to an existential freedom, whether endowed by a Creator or by the forces of Nature, when we subscribe to a rational-materialist agenda of progress deeply configured by its own belief in deterministic schemes?

Can plain speaking survive as a value in a society whose ruling intention has become closing the sale? Can it even be recognized in a time when (in another reincarnation of the confidence-man's Counterfeit Detector) sincerity itself is routinely faked—when it has become the default mode for damage control in a handbook written by the campaign consultants and celebrity hand-holders at Jargonese & Jade?

What inherent value does the dignity of the individual retain in a digital and televisual culture where the commercially sponsored spectacle is replacing the civic and the spiritual ritual; where gossip is subsuming news; and where, as the "reality TV" craze has repeatedly shown, many Americans now prefer a shameful or even sham notoriety to a life of anonymity, however admirable in the traditional sense?

And this demise of dignity as an active value poses questions about the privacy once mustered to protect it. In an age when the government feels free to eavesdrop on millions of its citizens' phone calls and emails; when our hard drives are implanted with corporate cookies that report our every digital transaction; when our children are rushing en masse to post their most intimate facts and photos on Facebook and Instagram; when the once secret diary has been megaphonically "outed" into the blog, and webcams now stream closeted poses to a global audience of wired voyeurs—in an age of both idealized and vulgarized transparency, can privacy retain anything more than a vestigial value?

Probing the painful divide between our traditional and actual moral identities, these are not trivial questions, and although posing them helps to map the coordinates of our current confusion, the predicament they sketch will not readily submit to a merely technical fix. Like Descartes and Shakespeare, like John Adams and Thomas Paine, we live in times "that try men's souls," and so are obliged to self-consciously examine and artfully revise the values that are now misdirecting our lives.

↤

Identify the Key Premises for a Cultural Continuity. Which are the elements of the ethos now passing that must be preserved or revived to assure a continuity of values—a reprise of virtue in a truly American key? I see three features of our traditional credo as still indispensable: one an existential presumption, the next an ethical standard, the last a principle of design that is applicable in all places and times. There may well be more, but we can start with these.

First, in the spirit of our founders' initial declaration, we should continue to believe that we are endowed with both the rights and the responsibilities of the natively free, and that, as a consequence, *some* form of democratic governance best expresses and fulfills our basic nature.

Second, as is exemplified in most mythic renderings of the American hero, we should continue to believe in the indispensable value of plain speaking in all our dealings. The quality of the freedom that is ours to fulfill is inextricably linked to our willingness to think clearly and speak truly to ourselves and others.

Finally, as is exemplified in the documents that founded our republic, we should continue to believe in the enduring wisdom of "checks and balances." Although the exact ratios will have to shift to fit our current circumstances, a mutually enforced moderation of parts (and their special interests) on behalf of the whole remains an essential principle of graceful design—and one that applies to both the constitution of national governments and the internal organization of individual minds.

↤

Identify the Forces Now Threatening Those Key Premises. Yet, as we have seen in detail here, due to significant revisions in our myths, laws and standard jobs, in the spaces where we gather and the information we receive, each of those key premises for an effective democracy has now become an endangered species. Beneath the surface diversity of postmodern life, Evangelical Mammonism has been drawing our behavior in the same overall direction

227

by creating a moral field that reduces the joys and obligations of democratic freedom to the robotic schedules of production and consumption.

Cultural conservatives, beginning with Burke, were the first to recognize the dangers inherent in rational materialism's utopian project. Repulsed by the violence of the French Revolution, they saw how this philosophy's so-called science lacked a civilizing empathy, and how, when taken together, its contempt for the past and its confidence in a perfectible future would free its adherents from all moral restraints, leading to that distinctly modern abomination: the rationalized extermination campaign. As a result, they were not fooled by the pretty promises made by the communist regimes; recalling the Reign of Terror, they anticipated the new show trials, gulags, and killing fields that would soon be plotted by the self-excusing logic of utopian thought.

But reading history all too literally, most American conservatives failed to recognize that, contrary to the clichéd advice of *real politik*, the enemy of their enemy might also be their enemy. Unaware of the secret similarities beneath the obvious differences, they allied themselves politically with a homegrown version of rational materialism (scientific capitalism) whose own assault on the old virtues and civic associations that conservatives most cherished would prove far more effective than the clumsy attempts of its Cold War rival. In America, with its Protestant and entrepreneurial roots, its looser class structure, and its foundational antipathy to tyrannical government, Marxism's "dictatorship of the proletariat" had little lasting appeal. True to our national character and its inherited weaknesses, economic greed would be the id monster released by *our* over-investment in rational materialist expectations. The magical mechanism of the marketplace, and not the marvelous machine of a utopian politics, would supply us with a "system so perfect that no one would need to be good."

Rather than the warning it should have supplied, communism's spectacular self-destruction only served to intensify our faith in the imminent perfection of the marketized society. Drunk on the notion of our new hyperpower status, we hastened the demise of virtue already underway, doubling down on a Mammonite ethos whose decadence, inseparable in the end from gross incompetence, ironically led to the Market's own collapse. Although it didn't have to happen, arising instead from choices that we made, this particular route to a communal fall from grace was, like slavery, a danger deeply encoded in our civic origins. When designing the first formal democracy since classical times, our founders focused on prohibiting the two institutional enemies of freedom that they knew best, a centralized church and a monarchical state, while never grasping how a threat to democracy might emerge from the same desanctified and deroyalized economy they preferred. Although uncommonly prudent for revolutionary thinkers, they never fully imagined, and so didn't "check and balance," that hallmark creation of scientific capitalism: the modern corporation.

As was quickly demonstrated, these highly specialized institutional "bodies" could produce economic goods in astonishing quantities, and thus potentially provide a liberation from poverty: a goal seemingly at one with our democratic values and even with our Judeo-Christian ones. Yet the nature of those bodies' internal governance—strictly rationalized methods serving narrowly materialistic ends—was neither Judeo-Christian nor Jeffersonian. In the modern corporation, the rational-materialist mind had recast the economy's institutions after the image of a machine, and machines are, by definition, neither existentially free nor inclined to be their brother's keeper. In the scale of preferences that calibrated the internal moral field of the modern corporation, efficiency trumped liberty and profitability replaced compassion.

Consequently, the primary moral drama of American society since the end of slavery has been whether the undeniable productivity of these essentially amoral money machines—unimagined and so unrestrained by our Constitution—could be yoked to serve the same democratic purposes and Judeo-Christian values that they internally refused. Could the narrow "savvy" of their instrumentality be licensed without granting them the moral and teleological authority that they were bound to perform "idiotically"? Not just the so-called reforms that led to the mortgage mess but the broader monetizing of our artistic, scientific, and religious practices highlight our failure to pass that test.

✧

Marry the New Monster. In Shakespeare's time, it was the rise of an intellectually empowered, but also estranged and amoral, individualism that threatened the moral coherence of the day. In *that* era, for *that* crisis of cultural identity, as induced by *that* specific technological shift in the texture of everyday experience, preaching to the individual in ways that emphasized the dangers of his or her self-centered isolation was an effective strategy for restoring order. By taming the Machiavellian monster, the evolution of this Protestant self proved to be a necessary psychological precedent for establishing both a stable economy of individual opportunity and a workable democracy

That approach, however, cannot redress the imbalances of an age in which the poles of peril have been reversed. Today, the threat of the amoral individualist has been replaced by that of the sociopathic organization. An appeal to the private conscience does not resonate with the same authority inside a culture where, thanks to our digital media, extraversion has been replacing introspection as the primary "place" for moral deliberation. Nor is it likely to change our communal behavior when the prevailing patterns and purposes of everyday life are strongly determined by the decision-making of enormous social organizations. Although heirs to a democracy first designed for the literate thinker and economic freeman in a rural setting demanding self-reliance, we now live inside a paved and digitized social sphere where most working adults are wage employees. The old ethos of self-reliant individualism can no longer, on its own, civilize this new American mind and place.

But although we can't simply return to our traditional ethos, the Evangelical Mammonism that has been co-opting its authority is neither a desirable nor a sustainable alternative. As our mythic imagination once understood, any "body" that combines extraordinary power with an unchecked appetite (the ogre by the bridge, the giant atop the beanstalk) can ravage the human enterprise. Rather than doubling our faith in the marketplace following the Soviet collapse, we should have reread and believed "The Three Little Pigs." For the real ravenous wolf knocking on the door has been our own worst self: that collective beast unleashed by privatization whose deadly combination of gargantuan size, enhanced techniques, and unbridled appetite—whose highly efficient rage for *more*—is threatening to blow our whole house down.

Born into one of those transitional eras when material progress tends to induce moral regress, we need to muster the means to tame this new monster. That project will have to begin by reining in the sociopathic behavior of the postmodern corporation, which, like the Machiavellian plotter of old, has been usurping the authority of public governance while shirking the responsibilities attendant to it. Just as the successful emergence of the modern democracies required the moralization of an initially brute individualism, so will a reprise of virtue in the postmodern era require morally refining these crude money machines, along with the many social spaces they now command. We will need to imagine a public and extraverted equivalent to the private and introspective voice of conscience that once converted the rogue individualist into the Protestant self, preparing the way for democracy.

To that end, and because only the truth can make us free, we will need to cultivate new or renewed gathering places, physical and virtual, where plain speaking can prevail again—that is, where most of the information that we seek and give is not being "brought to us by" either the soft duplicities of salesmanship or the cold efficiencies bent solely on boosting commercial production. Out of those plain conversations, we will need to co-create a more complete and conscientious conventional intelligence: one as heart-rich as it is head-smart, one committed to enhancing the good of the whole and not just advancing a favored part.

Whatever form this conscientious thinking finally takes, it will have to master the site-specific meaning of our postmodern place, and so be capable of both accurately describing and morally refining the impact of all those new machines, from smart phones to search engines, that are rapidly revising the underlying tenor of our everyday lives. Marrying the old to the new, this conscientious thinking will also have to include some perennial truths, starting with the recognition that *more* is not necessarily better, and that any successful pursuit of happiness requires an astute moderation of both our physical appetites and the expectations of our favorite mental schemes.

As such, our taming of the monster will mark the end of our submission to Evangelical Mammonism. Supplanting its utopian schemes with plausible goals, this more complete and conscientious conventional intelligence will remind us that our best chances for improvement paradoxically depend on a rejection of perfection as a possible ending to the human story. Reinfusing our ambition with a humility once preached by the Jews and the Greeks, *this* enlightenment will "know itself" and so admit its own limits. It will remind us that our powers, while real, are never so hyper that they aren't imperiled by the insufficiency of our knowledge and the fallibility of our character. Reprising virtue in an American key, it will restore the realization that to fulfill the rights of those born free is to live in a moral world, not a magical or merely mechanical one, and that, vigilance the cost of consciousness, there is no spell we can cast, no pill prescribe, or system install that can relieve us of the need "to be," rather than merely to seem, "good."

Notes

Entrance: Virtual America's Convention Hall

1. After the fall of the Berlin Wall, the American political scientist Francis Fukuyama argued that, with the triumph of the free-market democracies over Communism, the perennial problem of political governance had been solved, and that we had reached the "end of history." See Francis Fukuyama, *The End of History and the Last Man* (New York: Free Press, 1992), xi.

2. T. S. Eliot, "Choruses from 'The Rock,'" *Collected Poems*, 1909–1962 (New York: Harcourt, Brace & World, 1963), 160.

3. Emily Dickinson, "There's a certain Slant of light," #258. (Dickinson's poems are untitled, and so they are typically identified today by the first line and an assigned number.)

Chapter 1: Mutiny of the Scrivener

1. Jeremy Bentham, *An Introduction to Principles of Morals and Legislation*, Chapter X ("Of Motives"), Article X: "Now, pleasure is in *itself* a good: nay, even setting aside immunity from pain, the only good: pain is in itself an evil, and, indeed, without exception, the only evil."

2. An interview with Anne Sexton, *The Paris Review* 13, number 52, 1971.

3. G. K. Chesterton, *Orthodoxy: The Romance of Faith*, (New York: Doubleday, 1990), 79.

4. Samuel Beckett, *Endgame* (New York: Grove Press, 1958), 11.

5. The two quoted phrases are from a highly successful ad campaign conducted by the Coca-Cola Company to market its products in the 1970s.

6. Richard Saltus, "Order out of Odor: It All Makes Scents, Cents, Sense," *Boston Globe*, 29 December 1992.

Chapter 2: In the Mall of Virtual America's Mind

1. Music by Cole Porter, lyrics by Cole Porter and Robert Fletcher, "Don't Fence Me In," 1934.

2. Thomas Carlyle, *Past and Present* (Boston: Houghton Mifflin, 1965), 30–31.

3. Fukuyama, xi.

4. Marshall McLuhan, *Understanding Media: The Extensions of Man* (New York: New American Library, 1964), 277.

5. On limiting free speech in malls see the chapter "The Politics of No Politics," James J. Farrell, *One Nation Under Goods* (Washington: Smithsonian Institution, 2003), 215–32.

6. David Guterson, "Enclosed. Encyclopedic. Endured. One Week at the Mall of America," *Harper's*, August 1993.

7. Guterson.

8. Roland Barthes, "That Old Thing, Art," *The Responsibility of Forms: Critical Essays on Music, Art, and Representation,* tr. Richard Howard, (Berkeley, CA: University of California Press, 1991), 206.

9. On the percentage of households that owned a TV see Robert J. Samuelson, "The Internet and Gutenberg," *Newsweek,* 24 January 2000.

10. On the average American's TV viewing see Tony Schwartz, *The Responsive Chord,* (Garden City: Anchor/Doubleday, 1973), 52.

11. On the average viewing time for all media in 2010 see: http://www.newmedia-trendwatch.com/markets–by–country/17–usa/123–demographics.

Chapter 3: In the Shrine of Virtual America's Soul

1. George Gerbner, "TV or Not TV?" *Bill Moyer's Journal,* 29 April 1979.

2. William Irwin Thompson, *The American Replacement of Nature: The Everyday Acts and Outrageous Evolution of Economic Life* (New York: Doubleday, 1991), 32. See his entire chapter on Disney: 17–68.

3. Refrain from the show tune, "Overture" (lyrics by Lee Adams, music by Carl Strouse), *Bye, Bye Birdie,* 1960.

4. Bruno Bettleheim, *The Uses of Enchantment: The Meaning and Importance of Fairy Tales,* (New York: Knopf, 1976), 7.

5. J. O. Halliwell-Phillipps, *The Nursery Rhymes of England* (London: Percy Society, 1842).

6. Andrew Lang, *Green Fairy Book,* edited by Brian Alderson, (New York: Viking, 1978), 393–97. For a psychiatric interpretation of the original see: Bettleheim, 41–45.

7. Helen Cresswell and the Golden Books staff, *Classic Fairy Tales* (Western Publishing Co., 1994).

8. For an overview of Disney's career see Richard Schickel, *The Disney Version* (New York: Simon and Schuster, 1968). On the origins of Mickey Mouse: 115–36.

9. Carlo Collodi, *The Adventures of Pinocchio,* translated with an introduction and notes by Nicolas J. Perella (Berkeley, CA: University of California Press, 1986).

10. Glauco Cambon, "*Pinocchio* and the Problem of Children's Literature," *Children's Literature 2* (1973), 50–60.

11. "When You Wish Upon a Star," music by Leigh Harline, lyrics by Ned Washington, performed by Jiminy Cricket (Cliff Edwards) in: Walt Disney Productions, *Pinocchio* (Burbank: Walt Disney Home Video, 1993): videorecording of the 1940 animated film.

12. Jackson Lears, *Fables of Abundance: A Cultural History of Advertising in America* (New York: Basic Books, 1994), 49.

13. Schickel, 364.

14. Henry A. Giroux, *The Mouse that Roared: Disney and the End of Innocence* (Lanham, MD: Rowman & Littlefield, 1999), 35.

15. Richard E. Foglesong, *Married to the Mouse: Walt Disney World and Orlando*

(New Haven, CT: Yale University Press, 2001), 5.

16. All citations from Disney's video promotion for the Orlando project: Andrew Ross, *The Celebration Chronicles: Life, Liberty, and the Pursuit of Property Value in Disney's New Town* (New York: Ballantine, 1999), 54. For further history on the origins of Epcot see Foglesong: xi, xii, 58–62, 66–7.

17. Foglesong: 6–8, 58–70, 100–107.

Chapter 4: *The Pharmacy of Pain Dissuasion*

Much of the technical and historical information in this chapter comes from the following four books: Carl Elliott and Tom Chambers, editors, *Prozac as a Way of Life* (University of North Carolina Press, 2004); Joseph Glenmullen, M.D., *Prozac Backlash: Overcoming the Dangers of Prozac, Zoloft, Paxil, and Other Antidepressants with Safe, Effective Alternatives* (New York: Simon & Schuster, 2000); David Healy, *Let Them Eat Prozac: The Unhealthy Relationship between the Pharmaceutical Industry and Depression* (New York : New York University Press, 2004); Edward Shorter, *A History of Psychiatry* (New York: John Wiley & Sons, 1997).

1. Herman Melville, *The Confidence-Man: His Masquerade* (New York: Grove Press, 1955), 106–7.

2. For tripling the prescriptions of painkillers see: http://oxywatchdog.com/2012/05/drug–poisoning–huge–factor–in–u–s–deaths–report/.

3. For the increase in antidepressant prescriptions see: http://healthland.time.com/2011/10/20/what–does–a–400–increase–in–antidepressant–prescribing–really–mean/#ixzz28Sy0ANMz.

4. Shorter, 315–19.

5. Peter D. Kramer, *Listening to Prozac* (New York: Viking, 1993), 300.

6. Kramer, 15.

7. Kramer, xvi–xix.

8. Sharon Begley, "Beyond Prozac: How Science Will Let You Change Your Personality with a Pill," *Newsweek*, 7 February 1994, 36–43. Also J. Solomon, "Breaking the Silence from Congress to Hollywood: Prominent Americans are Trying to Erase the Lingering Shame of Mental Illness" *Newsweek*, 20 May 1994, 20–21.

9. Sherwin Nuland, "Pill of Pills?" *New York Review of Books*, 9 June, 1994: 4–8.

10. Breggin was one of Kramer's earliest and most dogged critics, both in print and on television; see Peter R. Breggin and Ginger Breggin, *Talking Back to Prozac: What Doctors Aren't Telling You about Today's Most Controversial Drug* (New York: St. Martin's Press, 1994).

11. See Thomas J. Moore, "No Prescription for Happiness," *Boston Globe*, 17 October 1999.

12. Glenmullen, 8.

13. See Kirsch et. al., "Initial Severity and Antidepressant Benefits: A Meta-Analysis of Data Submitted to the FDA," *PLos Medicine, 2008. PubMed #18303940.*

14. "Romanticizing melancholy" is not Kramer's actual phrase, but it does reflects his belief that the attacks on the SSRIs are often rooted in a cultural bias (especially prominent in intellectual and artistic circles) that actively prefers the melancholic view of life and that is suspicious, therefore, of any therapeutic treatment that threatens that view by eliminating the mood that drives it. See Peter D. Kramer, "The Valorization of Sadness: Alienation and the Melancholic Temper" in Elliott and Chambers: 48–58.

15. Robert Burton, from "The Author's Abstract of Melancholy" in *The Anatomy of*

Melancholy, in three volumes (New York: Dutton, 1932), 20.

16. Sigmund Freud, "Mourning and Melancholia," *Collected Papers* (volume 4), tr. Joan Riviere (New York: Basic Books, 1959), 153–55.

17. See, for example, Hans Moravec, *Mind Children: The Future of Robot and Human Intelligence* (Cambridge MA: Harvard University Press, 1988) 1, 4, 109, 117.

18. William Cowper, "Charity," I. 59.

19. Chesterton, 159.

20. David Healy, "Good Science or Good Business?" in *Prozac as a Way of Life*, 73–74.

21. Maureen Dowd, "Liberties; She's Not Really Ill…", *New York Times*, 10 June 2001.

22. W.B. Yeats, "Lapis Lazuli," *Selected Poems and Two Plays of William Butler Yeats* (New York: Collier Books, 1962), 159–60.

23. Healy, 30–33. Breggin and Breggin, 36–58.

24. Thomas Bodenheimer, "Uneasy Alliance: Clinical Investigators and the Pharmaceutical Industry," *New England Journal of Medicine (NEJM)* 18 May 2000.

25. Glenmullen, 208.

26. Marcia Angell, "Is Medicine for Sale?" *NEJM*, 18 May 2000.

27. See Terence Monmaney, "Medical Journal May Have Flouted Own Standards 8 Times," *Los Angeles Times*, 21 October 1999.

28. Pharmaceutical companies can spend more money marketing their drugs than testing them. See Elliott and Chambers, 5.

29. Healy, 215–16.

30. Jeffrey M. Drazen and Gregory D. Curfman, editorial, "Financial Associations of Authors," *NEJM*, 13 June 2002.

31. Melville, 210.

32. Melville, 294.

33. Huey Long: "If fascism comes to America, it will come in the guise of anti-Fascism." There are numerous versions of this quotation attributed to Long; it has clearly entered the echo chamber of common usage, with all the distortions that implies. I originally ran across this particular version in R. W. B. Lewis's afterword to Melville's *The Confidence-Man: His Masquerade* (New York: New American Library, 1964), 263.

Chapter 5: The Politics of Pain Dissuasion

For most of the biographical facts about Ronald Reagan and the behind-the-scenes narrative of his candidacies and presidency I drew on two exhaustive accounts by his primary chronicler, Lou Cannon: *Reagan* (New York: Putnam, 1983) and *President Reagan: The Role of a Lifetime* (New York: Simon and Schuster, 1991), henceforth referred to as *ROL*. For Reagan's entertainment career and his intimate relation with the larger themes and narratives of American culture, I have drawn on Gary Wills's insightful study: *Reagan's America* (New York: Penguin, 1988).

1. Melville, *The Confidence-Man* (Grove Press), 208–9.

2. Melville, 210.

3. For a first-person account of Bush's mockery of the condemned prisoner Karla Faye Tucker, see Tucker Carlson, "Devil May Care," *Talk Magazine* (September 1999), 106.

4. Melville, "Benito Cereno," *Great Short Works of Herman Melville* (New York: Harper & Row, 1969), 27.

5. On Reagan's failure to connect emotionally with family, friends, and political

colleagues, note the following quotations taken from an article by his official biographer, Edmund Morris in "The Unknowable: Ronald Reagan's Amazing, Mysterious Life," *New Yorker*, 28 June 2004, 40–51. "Yet for all their emotional awkwardness, one cannot imagine [Jimmy Carter or George H.W. Bush] ignoring their first grandchild, as Reagan did for two years, or walking away from the brain-damaged James Brady with nothing more than a cheerful 'Hi, Jim'" (44). And "Reagan's scrupulously kept Presidential diary is remarkable for a near-total lack of interest in people as individuals. In all its half-million or so words, I did not find any affectionate remark about his children" (47).

6. Delmore Schwartz, "The True-Blue American," *Summer Knowledge: New and Selected Poems, 1938–1958* (Garden City: Doubleday, 1959), 163.

7. Delmore Schwartz, "Metro-Goldwyn-Mayer," *Last and Lost Poems of Delmore Schwartz* (New York: New Directions, 1989), 22.

8. Wills, 219.

9. Wills, 181.

10. Cannon, *Reagan*, 65; Wills, 189–191.

11. Wills, 170–71; Cannon, *ROL*, 51.

12. Shelley Winters, *Shelley* (New York: Morrow, 1980), 286–87.

13. Cannon, *Reagan*, 294–98.

14. Cannon, *ROL*, 133.

15. Cannon, *ROL*, 520.

16. Cannon, *ROL*, 401–2.

17. Cannon, *ROL*, 180–81.

18. Morris: 44, 47; Cannon, *ROL*: 174–78, 228–29.

19. Cannon, *ROL*, 143–49.

20. Cannon, *ROL*, 132–140.

21. Cannon, *ROL*, 56–57.

22. Cannon, *ROL*, 55.

23. For an insider's view of the budget fiasco see David A. Stockman, *The Triumph of Politics: How the Reagan Revolution Failed* (New York: Harper & Row, 1986). Stockman's account, an extended mea culpa by one of the primary ideologues of supply-side theory and the person in the administration most responsible for its practical implementation, is devastating. His pithy conclusion: "The Reagan Revolution was radical, imprudent, and arrogant" (395).

24. During the first term, family income for the middle class rose only 1 percent and actually fell nearly 8 percent for the poorest one-fifth of American families; meanwhile, the most affluent one-fifth gained nearly 9 percent. See Cannon, citing an Urban Institute study, *ROL*, 516.

25. That Reagan, and not a Democratic Congress, was the primary author of the nation's steep descent into indebtedness was recognized by conservative columnist George F. Will: "The middle six budgets tell Reagan's story. Those budgets produced deficits totaling 1.1 trillion. The budgets Reagan sent to Congress proposed 13/14ths of that total. Congress added a piddling 90 billion, just 15 billion a year." See Will, "How Reagan Changed America," *Newsweek*, 9 January 1987.

26. Cannon, *ROL*: 320, 326; Wills, 465.

27. Cannon, *ROL*: 326, 329–33.

28. Cannon, *ROL*, 761.

Chapter 6: The Masquerade of Faux Rebellion

1. As cited in Robert I. Fitzhenry, editor, *The Harper Book of Quotations*, third

edition (New York: HarperPerennial, 1993), 387.

2. Emily Dickinson, "Tell all the Truth but tell it slant —," poem #1129.

3. Ezra Pound borrowed the phrase "make it new" from Confucius, and it was the title of one of his essay collections. See *Make It New: Essays by Ezra Pound* (London: Faber, 1934). Also note his allied assertion: "Literature is news that STAYS news," in *ABC of Reading* (New York: New Directions, 1960), 29.

4. "A willful suspension of disbelief" was a concept introduced by Samuel Coleridge. See Chapter XIV, *Biographia Literaria*, 1817.

5. On "balancing 'decency' with 'diversity'": The decency requirement was challenged legally and, after a long process, upheld by the Supreme Court. See *National Endowment for the Arts v. Finley*, 524 U.S. 569 (1998).

6. This figure, 341 billion, was the estimate of the General Accounting Office as stated in "Resolution Trust Corporation's 1995 and 1994 Financial Statements," 2 July 1996, and as cited at: http://www.citizen.org/documents/corporateabusetax.pdf. For an extended account of the scandal, see Stephen Pizzo, Mary Fricker, and Paul Muolo, *Inside Job* (New York: McGraw-Hill, 1989) 1–2. There, President Reagan, at his Sunny Jim best when at the signing ceremony, called the bill that licensed one of the largest financial scandals in American history "the most important legislation for financial institutions in 50 years." He added then, "All in all, I think we've hit the jackpot."

7. Neil Bush, a son of the then sitting vice president, was on the board of the Silverado Savings and Loan whose collapse cost the taxpayers one billion dollars. For a brief account of Bush's controversial life see: Peter Carlson, "The Relatively Charmed Life of Neil Bush," *Washington Post*, 28 December 2003.

8. See "Censorship and the Arts," *The A.W.P. Chronicle*, May 1990: "As we went to press, congressional aides estimated that letters and calls to the White House and to Congress were running at least 20 to 1 *against* the NEA."

9. Kim Masters, "Arts Groups Agree to NEA Plan," *Washington Post*, 26 May 1990.

10. Bruce Barcott, "The Sexual Evolution," *Seattle Weekly*, 5 September 1990.

11. As paraphrased by Barcott.

12. Televangelist Jim Bakker was sentenced to forty-five years and fined half a million dollars for fraud in 1989. See: Peter Applebome, "Bakker Sentenced to 45 Years For Fraud in His TV Ministry," *New York Times*, 25 October 1989. A year earlier, Jimmy Swaggart was defrocked by the Executive Presbytery of the Pentecostal denomination after "reports linked him to lewd acts with a prostitute." See: "Church Defrocks Swaggart for Rejecting Its Punishment," *New York Times*, 9 April 1988.

13. "Mr. Counterculture Meets Corporate Culture in an Ad for Nike," *Lawrence Journal-World*, 9 July 1994.

14. Brett Pulley, "How a Nice Girl Evolved into a Gangster Rapper," *Wall Street Journal*, 2 February 1994.

15. Thomas Frank, *One Market under God: Extreme Capitalism, Market Populism, and the End of Economic Democracy* (New York: Doubleday, 2000).

16. "They . . . think they know": Tom Peters, citing Peter Littman, former CEO of Hugo Boss, in *The Circle of Innovation* (New York: Knopf, 1997), 119.

17. "DECONSTRUCTION IS COOL!": Frank, 245.

18. "Cannibalize Yourself": Frank, (citing *Fortune*, August 1999), 244.

19. Tom Peters, *Thriving on Chaos: Handbook for a Management Revolution* (New York: Knopf, 1987). And *Liberation Management: Necessary Disorganization for the Nanosecond Nineties* (New York: Knopf, 1992), henceforth *LM*.

20. Peters, *LM, 15–18*.

21. Peters, *LM, 15–18*.

22. For an account of changes in the fashion industry see Thomas Frank, *The*

Conquest of Cool: Business Culture, Counterculture, and the Rise of Hip Consumerism (Chicago: University of Chicago Press, 1997).

Chapter 7: The Iron Cage of Age Dissuasion

1. William Stafford, "A Ritual to Read to Each Other," *The Way It Is: New & Selected Poems* (Greywolf Press, 1998).

2. "'In two hundred years doctors will rule the world. . . . Mankind wants to live—to live.'" Josef Conrad, *The Secret Agent* (New York: Anchor Books, 1953), 277.

3. As calculated by a private watchdog site, the national debt as of November 2007, a year before the stock market imploded, was over 9 trillion dollars. More than 22 percent of that debt was owed to foreign governments or international investors. See: http://www.brillig.com/debt_clock/.

4. At the height of the housing bubble in 2004, the Bureau of Labor statistics calculated that the median hourly wage for child care workers was $7.34, less than half of the $15.60 earned by automotive technicians and mechanics. See http://www.bls.gov/oco/cg/cgs032.htm and http://www.bls.gov/oco/ocos181.htm#.

5. W. H. Auden, "In Memory of W. B. Yeats," *Selected Poetry of W. H. Auden* (New York: Modern Library, 1958), 52–54.

6. Tracy Shryer and Shawn Hubler, "Parents Leave, Girls Cope in Real-Life 'Home Alone' Family: Daughters, 4 and 9, Fended for Themselves. Mother, Father Jailed on Return from Acapulco Vacation," *Los Angeles Times*, 30 December 1992.

7. Miles Corwin, "Tumor Victim Loses Bid to Freeze Head before Death," *Los Angeles Times*, 15 September 1990.

8. Ezra Pound cites this example as a kind of pedagogical parable at the start of his poetic primer *ABC of Reading* (New York: New Directions), 17–18.

9. Danny Hillis, one of the inventors of parallel computing, had this to say about the possibilities of downloading one's "self" into a software program to escape the trials of mortality: "I think I'm not going to get to be immortal, but maybe my children will." See Stewart Brand, *The Media Lab: Inventing the Future at M.I.T.* (New York: Pantheon, 1987), 200.

10. *Ecclesiastes* 9:11.

11. Max Weber, *The Protestant Ethic and the Spirit of Capitalism* (New York: Scribner, 1958), 182.

Chapter 8: Auguries of Decadence

1. T. S. Eliot, "Burnt Norton," 176.

2. On the Bush administration's claim that Saddam Hussein was on the verge of acquiring nuclear weapons, see Tim Russert's interview with Vice President Dick Cheney on NBC's *Meet the Press*, 16 March 2003: "We know [Saddam Hussein is] out trying once again to produce nuclear weapons and we know that he has a long-standing relationship with various terrorist groups, including the al-Qaeda organization." Both assertions proved false.

3. Cheney, in the same *Meet the Press* interview, on the reception he expected our troops to receive from the Iraqi people: ". . . my belief is we will, in fact, be greeted as liberators."

4. An interview with Monty Hall, timed to the revival of his show, in *ohio.com*, 4 March 2003.

5. On "defining deviancy downward": the phrase was coined by Sen. Daniel Patrick Moynihan to describe the slow demise of social and ethical standards among the lower classes. See his essay "Defining Deviancy Downward," *American Scholar* (Winter 1993).

6. The full quotation: "Be true! Be true! Be true! Show freely to the world, if not your worst, yet some trait whereby the worst may be inferred!" Nathaniel Hawthorne, *The Scarlett Letter* (New York: New American Library, 1959), 242.

7. The accusation against Rockwell was uncovered by the website *The Smoking Gun.* See: http://www.thesmokinggun.com/millionaire/millionaire.html.

8. Conger's misrepresentation of her military service was uncovered by the celebrity gossip TV show *Inside Edition.* For a brief summary of the charges, see Internet Movie Data Base, 29 February 2000: http://posters.imdb.com/news/sb/2000–02–29#tv2.

9. Bill Carter, "After Wedding Fiasco, Fox TV Vows No More Exploitation Programming," *New York Times*, 25 February 2000.

10. The last half-hour of the show was watched by 22.8 million viewers, reportedly one-third of all females under 35, a highly desirable demographic for marketeers. So many women rushed to sign up for a potential follow-up show that the registration website crashed. See Veena Thompson, *The Tech (Online Edition)*, 22 February 2000: "Hypnotizing Multimillions Sadly, Viewers Captivated By Shallow, Pathetic Marriage Show": http://www–tech.mit.edu/V120/N7/colo7veena.7c.html.

11. See Brill Bundy, "Is 'Joe' Really Faux?" *Zap2it, TV News*, 19 January 2003: http://www.fansofrealitytv.com/forums/joe–millionaire/3857–joe–really–faux.html.

12. Herman Melville, *The Confidence-Man*, Chapter 45: 277–94. For the passages about the Counterfeit Detector see: 288–92.

13. The 850 million dollars in lottery sales is a conservative estimate. The total lottery sales for the 2003 year, according to the American Association of State and Provincial Lotteries, was over 45 billion dollars, an average of almost 869 million weekly. Actual week by week statistics, however, were not supplied. See: www.naspl.org/sales&profits.html.

14. Nicholas D. Kristof, "God, Satan and the Media," *New York Times*, 4 March 2003.

15. Eric Berne, a Canadian-born psychiatrist, created the therapy. See *Transactional Analysis in Psychotherapy: A Systematic Individual and Social Psychiatry* (New York: Grove Press, 1961). He was also the author of the highly popular *Games People Play: The Psychology of Human Relationships* (New York: Grove Press, 1964).

16. William Shakespeare, *Othello, The Moor of Venice*, I.3.

17. Dr. Perricone's website can be found at: http://www.nvperriconemd.com/index.cfm?action=home.topsellers.

18. Dyer's doctorate is in educational counseling. He is the author or co-author of more than 20 self-help books, and sells related CDs, DVDs, workbooks, calendars, and note cards. His first trade publication, *Your Erroneous Zones* (1976), is one of the nation's all-time best-sellers.

19. Benny Hinn speaking as a guest on *Praise the Lord*, 10 September 1999.

20. Steve McGonigle, "What's Happened to Hinn's Promised Healing Center?" *Dallas Morning News*, 23 June 2002.

21. For a brief biography of Benny Hinn see: http://www.samaw.com/infohub/benny_hinn.htm.

22. Paul and Jan Crouch co-founded TBN in 1973 with Jim and Tammy Faye Bakker. After a falling-out, the Bakkers later left to form their own broadcasting empire, which then collapsed when Jim Bakker was accused of sexual misconduct by an employee and convicted of fraud in federal court. The Crouches were among the most prominent advocates of prosperity theology during this period, and they certainly prospered themselves from their faith-based message. The network was collecting more than $120

million a year from its viewers then. That income supported the substantial salaries of the founders—in 2004, Paul was paid a $403,700 annual salary; Jan, $361,000—along with some 30 separate homes, including two mansions in Newport Beach and a Texas ranch. See William Lobdell, "The Prosperity Gospel, TBN's Promise: Send Money and See Riches." *Los Angeles Times*, 22 September 2004.

23. References to this show (19 October, 1999) are virtually omnipresent online, a favorite instance of heresy cited by Benny Hinn and Paul Crouch's many evangelical critics. For a longer excerpt from the broadcast's transcript, see: www.raptureready.com/rapture/ssbh.html.

24. In early July of 2003, when the rosy prediction that American forces in Iraq would be greeted as liberators was being challenged by the facts on the ground, President Bush held a press conference during which, in a moment that echoed the cinematic bravado favored by Ronald Reagan, he stated: "There are some who feel like that the conditions are such that they can attack us there. My answer is bring 'em on. We've got the force necessary to deal with the security situation." See Sean Loughlin, "Bush Warns Militants Who Attack U.S. Troops in Iraq," *CNN.com*, 3 July 2003.

Chapter 9: *Truth or Consequences*

1. Simone Weil, *Gravity and Grace* (Lincoln, NE: University of Nebraska Press, 1997), 101.

2. In 1974 just 3 percent of retiring senators became lobbyists. By 2012, 50 percent of retiring senators and 42 percent of retiring congressmen were doing so. As cited in Christopher Buckley's review of *This Town* by Mark Leibovitch, "A Town of Lunches," *New York Times Book Review*, 25 July 2013.

3. Max Boot, "The Case for American Empire: The Most Realistic Response to Terrorism Is for America to Embrace its Imperial Role," *Weekly Standard*, 15 October 2001.

4. Yeats, "The Second Coming," 91.

5. "In a scene reminiscent of Somalia, frenzied crowds dragged the burned, mutilated bodies of four American contractors through the streets of a town west of Baghdad on Wednesday and strung two of them up from a bridge after rebels ambushed their SUVs." See "Violence Strikes Sunni Triangle," *Associated Press*, 31 March 2004.

6. Waterboarding (covering the face of a prisoner with a water-soaked cloth) simulates drowning and is considered torture by most interpreters of the Geneva Conventions. After World War II, the United States military imposed a 15 year prison sentence on a Japanese soldier who waterboarded a captured American citizen. After his capture by U.S. forces, Khalid Sheikh Mohammed was reportedly waterboarded 183 times.

7. The slaughter of surrendering soldiers on the battlefield did occur on both sides during the Revolutionary struggle; as a matter of policy, however, Washington rejected the practice as unworthy of the ideals that the revolutionaries were fighting to secure. In a letter to one of his officers regarding British prisoners, he wrote: "Treat them with humanity, and Let them have no reason to Complain of our Copying the brutal example of the British army in their Treatment of our unfortunate brethren." See David Hackett Fischer, *Washington's Crossing* (New York: Oxford University Press, 2004), 377–79.

8. The now widespread practice of governmental employees taking jobs in corporations or starting private companies that specialize in the fields they once supervised also tainted the procurement process for the Iraq war. Vice President Cheney, one of the primary advocates for and administrators of the invasion and occupation, formerly headed Halliburton, the largest corporate recipient of no-bid federal contracts. Neil Livingstone, a former Senate aide and Pentagon adviser, who publicly called for the

overthrow of Saddam's regime, subsequently led Global Options, Inc., a corporation that provided contacts and consulting services to companies doing business in Iraq. Joe M. Allbaugh, who managed George W. Bush's 2000 campaign, helped set up New Bridge Strategies and Diligence, LLC, to promote business in postwar Iraq. See Walter F Roche and Ken Silverstein, "Advocates of War Now Profit from Iraq's Reconstruction," *Los Angeles Times*, 14 July 2004.

9. Calculations as of July 2007 determined that there were more private contractors and subcontractors being paid by U.S. funds than troops stationed there. See T. Christian Miller, "Contractors Outnumber Troops in Iraq," *Los Angeles Times*, 4 July 2007.

10. John Gutfreund, former CEO of Salomon Brothers, in conversation with Michael Lewis, as reported by Lewis, "The End," *Portfolio*, December 2008.

11. The full quote by Robert E. Lucas in his 2003 keynote address to the American Association of Economists: "The central problem of depression-prevention has been solved, for all practical purposes and has in fact been solved for many decades." See Joseph Epstein, "Past Their Prime (Rate)" *Newsweek*, 16 March 2009.

12. Larry Summers, speaking in 1991, as cited by Naomi Klein, "Why We Should Banish Larry Summers from Public Life," *washingtonpost.com*, 19 April 2009.

13. Paul Krugman, "Blindly Into the Bubble," *New York Times*, 21 December 2007.

14. Dick Meyer, "A Puritan View of the Crash," *NPR*, 12 February 2009.

15. For a more detailed list of the grossly inflated salaries, bonuses, and "golden parachutes" given to Wall Street executives in the years just before, during, and after the crash, see: http://whatilearnd.com/post/52449126/golden–parachutes.

16. The heavily mortgaged home was in Bakersfield, CA. See Lewis.

17. Not only did the savings rate dive to nearly zero in 2005; revolving consumer debt level did the opposite, moving from near zero in 1980 to over $8000 per year in 2008. See Richard Thaler, "It Doesn't Have to Hurt," *Newsweek*, 20 April 2009.

18. See Nouriel Roubini, "Twenty Reasons Why We're Not Consuming" *Fortune*, 20 November 2008.

19. For an extended analysis of the impact of the misapplication of Li's Gaussian copula function, see Felix Salmon, "Recipe for Disaster: The Formula That Killed Wall Street," *Wired Magazine*, 23 February 2009.

20. The quotation is by Vincent Daniel, an associate of Steve Eisman, whose company made a fortune betting against the housing market. See Lewis, "The End."

21. Lewis.

22. Michael Lewis and David Einhorn, "The End of the Financial World as We Know It," *New York Times*, 4 January 2009.

23. Ben White, "What Red Ink? Wall Street Paid Hefty Bonuses," *New York Times*, 29 January 2009. For a further breakdown of bonuses bank by bank, see Eric Dash, "Big Banks Paid Billions in Bonuses Amid Wall St. Crisis," *New York Times*, 31 July 2009.

24. David Brooks, "Greed and Stupidity," *New York Times*, 3 April 2009.

25. All of Greenspan's quotations have been taken from a transcript of the congressional hearings found at: http://www.pbs.org/newshour/bb/business/july–dec08/crisis-hearing_10-23.html.

26. Lewis, "The End."

27. As reported by Zillow, the online real estate firm. See Susan R. Miller, "More Homeowners Drowning in Mortgage Debt," *Orlando Business Journal*, 7 May 2009.

28. Asked how much he was promising his prospective clients, Michael Bienes, who ran one of Madoff's feeder funds at Avellino and Bienes, replied: "All depends. Big amounts—18 percent. Smaller amounts—17, 16, even as low as 15." See a transcript of his interview, "The Madoff Affair," *Frontline*, 13 May 2009: http://www.pbs.org/wgbh/pages/frontline/madoff/interviews/bienes.html#sullivan.

29. President George W. Bush, speaking to airline employees: ". . . one of the great goals of this nation's war [on terror] is to restore public confidence in the airline industry. It's to tell the traveling public: Get on board. Do your business around the country. Fly and enjoy America's great destination spots. Get down to Disney World in Florida. Take your families and enjoy life, the way we want it to be enjoyed." See, "At O'Hare, President Says "'Get On Board'":
http://georgewbush–whitehouse.archives.gov/news/releases/2001/09/20010927–1.html.

30. See Robert Niles, "Disney Slams Universal in 2005 Theme Park Attendance," *Theme Park Insider,* http://www.themeparkinsider.com/flume/200512/2/.

Exit: The Reprise of American Virtue

1. Yeats, "Lapis Lazuli," 160.

2. Berry, 85.

3. "Our torments also may in length of time / Become our Elements, these piercing Fires / As soft as now severe, our temper chang'd / Into their temper . . . ," *Paradise Lost,* 2: 274–77.

4. The Roman historian Sallust (*Gaius Sallustius Crispin*), praising Cato in *The Conspiracy of Catiline.* See *The Cambridge History of Classical Literature,* ed. P. E. Easterling and E. J. Kenney (Cambridge: Cambridge University Press, 1982), 274–75.

5. Eliot, "Choruses from *The Rock,*" 160.

6. Eliot, 160.

7. Thomas Paine, "The American Crisis." This pamphlet, written in late December 1776, a year after "Common Sense" and when the war against Britain was going poorly, served to rally the soldiers and the populace.

8. See René Descartes, "Discourse on Method," *Descartes—Philosophical Writings,* ed. Elizabeth Anscombe and Peter Thomas Geach (Indianapolis: Bobbs-Merrill, 1971), 24–25. "In order to have real knowledge of [my countrymen's] opinions, I thought I must attend to what they practiced rather than what they preached; not only because, in the corruption of our manners, few will say what they really believe, but also because . . . the mental act of believing a thing is different from the act of knowing that one believes it; and the one act often occurs without the other."